ON INTERSUBJECTIVITY AND CULTURAL CREATIVITY

THE HERITAGE OF SOCIOLOGY

A Series Edited by Donald N. Levine

Morris Janowitz, *Founding Editor*

MARTIN BUBER

ON INTERSUBJECTIVITY AND CULTURAL CREATIVITY

Edited and with an Introduction by
S. N. Eisenstadt

THE UNIVERSITY OF CHICAGO PRESS
Chicago and London

The University of Chicago Press, Chicago 60637
The University of Chicago Press, Ltd., London
© 1992 by The University of Chicago
All rights reserved. Published 1992
Printed in the United States of America

01 00 99 98 97 96 95 94 93 92   5 4 3 2 1

ISBN (cloth): 0-226-07805-1
ISBN (paper): 0-226-07807-8

Library of Congress Cataloging-in-Publication Data

Buber, Martin, 1878–1965.
    On intersubjectivity and cultural creativity / Martin Buber :
edited and with an introduction by S. N. Eisenstadt.
        p.   cm. — (The Heritage of sociology)
        1. Sociology—Philosophy. 2. Culture. 3. Man. 4. Community.
I. Eisenstadt, S. N. (Shmuel Noah), 1923–   . II. Title.
III. Series.
HM24.B76   1992
301′.01—dc20   91-47187
                                                                    CIP

Contents

     CULTURAL RENOVATION

     7 Religious Renovation 167
          The Teaching of the Tao 167

     8 Pioneering—"Halutziuth" 190
          An Experiment That Did Not Fail 190

IV   THE DYNAMICS OF SOCIAL RETROGRESSION

     9 The Interrelations between the Social and the
        Political Dimensions of Human Existence 205
          Society and the State 205
          The Demand of the Spirit and Historical Reality 217
          *The Validity and Limitation of the Political
          Principle* 229
          Lenin and the Renewal of Society 238

Acknowledgments

The idea of presenting Buber's approach to sociological analysis in the Heritage of Sociology series was first broached in conversations I had about twenty years ago with the late Morris Janowitz, the founder of the series. For a variety of reasons, the implementation of the idea was postponed till now. I would like to thank Don Levine, the present editor of the series, and Doug Mitchell of the University of Chicago Press for their interest and help. I would especially like to thank Paul Mendes-Flohr for his extremely valuable advice and help in substantive and organizational matters alike; and to thank Rachel Shacko, Debby Maza, Alberto Gluzman in Jerusalem and Debra Romanick in Chicago for their assistance.

The late Raphael Buber showed great interest in the preparation of this volume of his father's writings and gave me great encouragement throughout the years.

S. N. Eisenstadt
Jerusalem, August 1991

Introduction

Intersubjectivity, Dialogue, Discourse, and Cultural Creativity in the Work of Martin Buber

1

One may be rather surprised to find Martin Buber—the philosopher, the religious figure, the author of the *Tales of the Hasidim*—in the Heritage of Sociology series. Was not Buber's connection with sociology very tenuous, possibly related to his emphasis on the dialogue, or to his interest in utopian communities, but not going beyond it? Was Buber "really" interested in sociological analysis, or was this interest in a way imposed on him by his teaching obligations in Jerusalem? There is indeed the biographical fact that from 1938, when he came to Palestine, until his retirement in 1950, he was professor of Social Philosophy at the Hebrew University of Jerusalem, where he was in charge of teaching "Cultural Sociology"—this was the name of the discipline which in the curricular scheme was only a "minor subject"; one could not graduate from it. From 1947 until his retirement he was the first chairman of the newly established Department of Sociology and of the Committee on Social Sciences (the future Faculty of Social Sciences).

But even these biographical events may seem to be accidental, possibly owing to the fact that, according to the accepted academic wisdom in Jerusalem, this appointment was due to academic politics, as he was not given either the Chair of Philosophy or that of Bible, to which he aspired.

These facts do attest, of course, to his central role in the development of sociology in Israel, and they provide the background to my being one of the fortunate ones to have studied with him; and enable me to write this introduction and to present this selection from his writings. But this biographical information in itself does not answer the question whether he was really in any way interested in sociology—and even more important, whether he contributed anything significant to sociological analysis, through his teaching or his writings?

2

Let's start with a few general biographical details about Martin Buber and follow with some more specific ones that are especially pertinent for an understanding of his relation to sociology.

Martin Buber (1878–1965) was primarily a religious and social philosopher and Zionist leader. He was raised between the ages of three and fourteen in his paternal grandparents' house.[1] His grandfather Shlomo Buber was a renowned Talmudic scholar, schooled in the traditional ways but already employing in his work some aspects of modern scholarship. His grandmother was a highly educated woman who introduced him to language, culture, and literature, with an emphasis on German studies. He studied in a general Polish gymnasium in Lemberg (Levov), while at the same time he became well acquainted with the life of traditional, especially Hasidic, Jewish communities.

The environment in which he grew up was a typical one of Jewish Enlightenment (Haskala), in which multilingualism was natural. In this period of the Austro-Hungarian Empire, he encountered also the problem of nationalities.

From the late eighteen-nineties he became closely involved in the Zionist movement, participating in Zionist congresses and being very active in various Zionist circles. He was one of the founders of the "Democratic Faction," which was established by Chaim Weizman and others in opposition to Herzel. However from 1904 he withdrew from active participation in Zionist politics. He published with Chaim Weizman and Berthold Feiwel a pamphlet about the necessity to establish a specifically Jewish institute of higher learning—a manifest which was to lead to the establishment of the Hebrew University.

He lived in Berlin from 1906 until 1916, and worked as an editor in a publishing house, Rütten and Loening, while at the same time being engaged in far-ranging free-lance writing.

From 1916 until 1938, when he came to Palestine, he lived in the small town of Heppenheim near Frankfurt am Main. In 1923 he became a lecturer in the Study of Jewish Religion and Ethics at the University of Frankfurt, and in 1930 an adjunct professor of general religious studies. Up to 1938 he was director of the Center for Jewish Adult Education in Nazi Germany. From 1938 to his death in 1965, Buber lived in Jerusalem, where he held the post as professor of sociology of culture (social philosophy) and was later the first chairman of sociology at the Hebrew University of Jerusalem. He taught such subjects as the sociology of religion and ethics, social philosophy, and the history of sociology. He was the first president of the Israel National Academy of Sciences and Humanities.

His literary and public activities moved continuously between two poles—that of Jewish lore, religion, and culture and that of general, especially German, philosophy, with an emphasis on philosophy of religion. His literary activities were oriented to bridging these two worlds and to transcending them by emphasizing the common human elements.

He was continuously engaged in public affairs, particularly in Jewish and Zionist affairs, where he espoused a humanitarian vision of Zionism, with a strong emphasis on cooperation with the Arabs—and with his move to Palestine he engaged intensively in activities in this direction.

Buber's studies ranged over a great many fields, beginning with his work on the Hasidic communities and traditions (*The Origin and Meaning of Hasidism* 1921; translated into English in 1954), which brought this central stream of Jewish sectarianism and mysticism to the attention of a wide Western public. In his works on educational and religious philosophy (for instance, *Eclipse of God: Studies in the Relations between Religion and Philosophy* 1952a; *Daniel: Dialogues on Realization* 1913; *For the Sake of Heaven* 1943–44; "Rede über das Erzieherische" 1926; "Urdistanz und Beziehung" 1951; "Das Problem des Menschen" 1948; and most explicitly in his book *I and Thou* [1923]), he developed the principle of the "dialogue." He studied biblical thought, especially the conception of kingship and polity in biblical times (*The Prophetic Faith* 1942) and, mainly through his translation (with Franz Rosenzweig) of the Bible into German, he became involved in biblical exegesis. His publications in social philosophy centered on utopian social thought and the experiments in collective life in Palestine and Israel (*Paths in Utopia* 1947) and on Judaism and Zionism (*At the Turning: Three Addresses on Judaism* 1952b; *Israel and the World: Essays in a Time of Crisis* 1921–43). He was editor of the series Die Gesellschaft, which published books by leading German sociologists and literary and journalistic figures.

Buber's methodological and analytical approach combined influences from many sources. In his philosophical emphasis he was close to the traditions of social philosophy associated with Georg Simmel, Max Scheler, and Martin Heidegger, and to those of religious existentialism identified with Paul Tillich, Reinhold Niebuhr, and Jacques Maritain. He was also close to that tradition of German sociologists, represented by Lorenz von Stein, who following Hegel, but changing the major thrust of Hegel's analysis, first asserted that the "social" is independent of the "political"; and to such utopian and religious thinkers as Saint-Simon, Proudhon, Gustav Landauer, and Eduard Heimann, who looked for regenerative forces in modern and contemporary bureaucratic mass society.

Within this general biographical framework, it might be worthwhile to mention some earlier facts about Buber which are certainly not accidental and which explain his very deep interest in sociology and his close connection with it. The first such fact was Buber's personal and intellectual proximity to the European sociologists, especially the German ones, beginning from the early years of the twentieth century, when as a young man he was editor of the Gesellschaft series. His close personal relationship with these and other scholars, and especially with Georg Simmel, with whom he studied in Berlin, was indeed of crucial importance for the development of his own thinking. These friendships were not only personal—some of them deeply affected Buber's work. Indeed, as Paul Mendes-Flohr has recently shown, the central concept of Buber's dialogical philosophy, *das Zwischenmenschliche* (the interhuman), first expounded in the short statement with which Buber introduced the Gesellschaft series in 1906, and the language of that statement, about social forms, objective structure (*Gebilde*), association (*Vergesellschaftung*), and interaction (*Wechselwirkung*), are very close to Simmel's sociological framework.[2]

His basic conception of the nature of the interpersonal, of the core of social relations, also provided the guideline for the collections in Die Gesellschaft, which he edited in the first decade of this century and which he initially wanted to be edited by Simmel. It is the editing of Die Gesellschaft that constitutes the second important biographical fact about his own sociological discussions. This paperback collection comprised more than forty volumes. It contained not only highly theoretical works—some of them classics like G. Simmel's *Die Religion*, F. Tönnies's *Die Sitte* (Custom), W. Sombart's *Das Proletariat*, G. Landauer's *Die Revolution*, and F. Oppenheimer's *Der Staat*. It contained also many volumes on very concrete aspects of modern life, such as, for instance, on *Das Warenhaus* (the department store), *Der Arzt* (the physician), *Die Börse* (the stock exchange), or a volume on sport, and the like—in many ways reminiscent of the later monographs of the Chicago school, although the books published in this series were not usually based on systematic fieldwork. They were, however, very much oriented toward an understanding of the concrete aspects of modern social life and of the significance of those aspects for living in modern conditions.

This combination of the concrete and the analytical was not specific to Buber; it was a basic characteristic of German sociology in the last part of the nineteenth and the first two decades of the twentieth century. It was characteristic of the publications of the Verein für Sozialpolitik; of the contents of the major German sociological journal—the famous *Archiv fuer Sozialwissenschaft und Sozialpolitik,* the very title of which attests to this combination—and of the numerous discussions at the yearly meetings of the German Sociological Association.

This combination was also characteristic of the work of the major figures of German sociology in this period: be it Max Weber, with his analysis of the conditions of agricultural workers of East Prussia or of the "Psychophysik" of industrial work or of the stock market; Ferdinand Tönnies, who side by side with the famous *Gemeinschaft und Gesellschaft* published also a major analysis of public opinion and numerous articles on current events; or, of course, Simmel, whose entire opus combined theoretical analytical essays with minute analysis of concrete situations.

The common denominator of all these attempts to combine the analytical and the concrete was the search for an understanding of the specific problematics and predicaments of modern society.[3] It was this search that also constituted the starting point of Buber's directions for the various volumes of Die Gesellschaft. But from the very beginning his special emphasis was to look for (as he indicated in a letter to Mr. Stehr, whom he invited to prepare a volume for the series) "concrete psychological realities which are borne from human beings working together —above all those psychological realities which are created through the mutual interaction between many individuals—and which are beyond the capacity of any single individual."[4]

This combination of theoretical approaches and concrete subjects published in Die Gesellschaft is of very great importance for the understanding of Buber's approach to sociology—namely, the continuous emphasis on the combination of the theoretical, the analytical, and the concrete. We, his students in Jerusalem, witnessed this combination when he greatly encouraged the pursuit of empirical sociological work.

Indeed, already in 1945 in his opening speech in a symposium[5] on the Jewish village in Israel, he proclaimed that this symposium signaled the intention to focus the sociological endeavor at the Hebrew University on the study of the Yishuv (the Jewish community in Palestine). At the same time he encouraged my late colleague Yonina Talmon and me to do a field study of the cooperative settlements (the Moshavim), which was finished in 1947 and was not published because of the difficulties in the period of the War of Independence. He then established in 1946–47 a seminar on the empirical study of the social structure of the Yishuv, under the auspices of which I published the first research report on the

"Oriental Jews" in Jerusalem. With the establishment of the Department of Sociology in 1947 and its further development after the War of Independence he continuously encouraged the undertaking of different empirical research projects which has become a basic and natural component of the Department of Sociology at the Hebrew University. It was this combined emphasis on the analytical and the concrete that he continuously emphasized in his lectures and seminars.

3

What did we learn in these lessons, what have we learned from these seminars and lectures—the lectures on the sociology of culture, the sociology of religion and morality, and later, with the establishment of the Sociology Department, on general sociology? Although, with a few exceptions, the lectures he delivered were not prepared by him in a final form for publication, yet they remained deeply imprinted in the memory of those students who were privileged to listen to them and to participate in his classes and seminars.

In these lectures and seminars, we were introduced to the major classics of sociology, such as Marx, Durkheim, Tönnies, Simmel, Max and Alfred Weber, and to such writers as Lorenz von Stein, Vico, and Sorel; as well as, as indicated above, to the various utopists and to analysis of the classical texts of the great civilizations—the Greek, the Chinese, and of course the Jewish. Thus for instance, the Tao Te Ching was the first text that those who enrolled in his classes in 1940 encountered —and this reading, as many others, emphasized the distinct approach of such thinkers to the understanding of the moral and intersubjective nature of social life and to the importance of intersubjectivity for the understanding of the problematics of social life and cultural life.

In more private conversations—in what could be called tutorials— he introduced those who were interested to classical and modern anthropology, from Tyler, Fraser, Jane Harrison to Franz Boas, A. Kroeber, Margaret Mead, Malinowski and his school—and to American sociology, from Lester Ward and Giddens to George Herbert Mead up to the early Talcott Parsons.

Thus in these lectures, seminars, and private meetings, we were confronted with the gamut of sociological, anthropological, and social philosophical literature in all languages published in Europe and in the United States. His willingness to give counsel and assistance to whoever would request it, from permission to use his extremely well-stocked library to extremely judicious and selective advice on how to use this library, and his encouragement to read even what was not worth reading in order to become able to discern what was not important were crucial parts of the experience of studying under Buber.

These various modes of instruction never served as introductory or monographic courses in the accepted meaning of the term. Their aim was not to survey the literature or the research carried out in those fields, even if in fact they served this purpose as well. They always presented and analyzed the literature in a selective manner, stressing those problems of their fields which were conceived as central by Buber. Moreover, in all these encounters we were confronted with a very broad comparative perspective, a broad civilizational approach, and with a view of sociology as part of the tradition of intellectual reflexivity of the Great Civilizations, especially of the Western one.

These lectures and seminars not only enabled us to come face to face with Buber's own philosophy—in itself no small matter—but introduced us to some of the main problems and problematics of sociological analysis, throwing a very illuminating light on its classical problems in a very special way. As Buber's students, we had a feeling that we were privileged to be exposed to a vision that was unique yet closely attuned to central problems of sociological analysis. This feeling was bound up not only in the power of his charismatic personality working within the framework of the university, but in the fact that his power was directed to a large extent to the elucidation of questions and problems which were, and still are, the focal point of the central problematics of modern social thought in analysis.

4

His basic attitude to sociology, to sociological analysis, was in principle similar to his attitude toward other scholarly disciplines—and yet with a certain difference. He mastered the formal—the conceptual, methodological, and technical—tools of the various disciplines he dealt with: philosophy, *Religionswissenschaft,* biblical scholarship, study of Hasidism, and the like. But his involvement in these disciplines and the use of their basic tools, concepts, and methods did not constitute for him an end in themselves, nor did he accept the framework and the *Problemstellung* of the respective traditions of each discipline as determinative. He did not permit them to put fetters upon his own work. He always endeavored to master these theoretical and analytical tools in order to direct them toward the specific points which were central to his own philosophical concerns. Just because of this he often succeeded in casting new light upon the dominant problems of a variety of scientific and philosophical areas. There were those who took issue with him because of this. The most famous of such criticisms was Gershom Sholem's of Buber's analysis of the Hasidic tales, to which we shall return later on.[6] Such criticisms were justified to some extent from their point of view—for at times he ignored the internal problems or particular aspect of these fields as they developed in their respective scholarly traditions.

But we shall see later on that most of these criticisms missed the point, because they misunderstood Buber's basic approach.

5

In principle one could find in Buber's work a similar attitude with respect to social philosophy and sociology, but here an additional element has to be taken into account. This additional element was the fact that some of the central problems of sociology were very closely related to Buber's own central concerns—as was the case with respect to religious philosophy. What was then Buber's basic "Stellung" to sociology and the basic sociological question or problem with which he was mostly concerned?

His basic sociological problem was closely related to his concern with the human situation, with *man's* nature, with his place in the cosmos and with the human predicament—a predicament most fully manifest in the problem of the nature, limits, and problematics of human creativity in general, of cultural creativity in particular. The dominant focus of Buber's sociological concern was the search for the understanding of the relation between the social and interhuman contacts, intersubjectivity on the one hand and the process of human creativity, cultural creativity, on the other. His sociological analysis can only be understood through this connection to the analysis of the creative processes of the human spirit.

The exploration of the nature of intersubjectivity in the human experience, and of its relation to cultural creativity, became one of the pillars of his teachings, one central to most of his fields of endeavor. Buber's specific sociological or social philosophical concern was to define the nature and conditions of social and cultural creativity, the conditions of the development of authentic intersubjective social relations as opposed to those of stagnation or of the demise of societies and cultures. He sought to identify the situations where creativity really can occur, and he believed that these situations exist to some extent in all cultures but that their fullest development occurs only rarely.

6

Before examining the social aspects of this creative process, or the role of human interaction and intersubjectivity in it, it might be worthwhile to take a look at the nature of the process of human, especially cultural, creativity and its problem as conceived by Buber. The most succinct formulation of the problematics of human creativity in general, and cultural creativity in particular, can be found in Buber's ideas on the essence of culture, which he taught in one of the seminars he gave at the Hebrew University, and which he later published in a book of his essays. From the onset he conceived of culture not as an ideological system, but as a life-style, a mode of life existing in the mundane world. According to him, this life-style was constructed around several poles, around several contradictions. In his scathing pronouncements against the simplistic distinction between culture and civilization which was quite widespread in the sociological and historical discourse in Europe in the last part of the nineteenth century and the first three decades of the twentieth, he singled out four basic components of duality or polarity in culture:

a) . . . There are two aspects of culture: creativity and tradition. On the one hand, all cultural life is based on personal creative production. Culture derives its vitality from the plethora of creativity, and when in any culture the flow of innovation ceases, its power is annulled, since that culture lacks any power if it does not have the power of innovation, the power of constant renewal: or self-renewal. But on the other hand, none of these productions succeeds in developing a social character; that is to say, does not become an integral part of that culture, unless it enters into the process of give and take; if it does not become material which can conveniently be passed on and be joined to all productions created throughout the generations to become something paradoxical: a form of generality. There are two sides to culture: revolution and conservatism, i.e., initiative and routine existence. Each one alone has great historical value, but only the two together have cultural value.

b) Cultural activity is characterized by a basic duality. First of all it gives to life itself form and permanence, restriction, and elaboration, molds people's behavior, raises the standard of their association and develops social relationships through selection and concentration. Secondly, it creates over and above life, or at least beyond it, a world of matter in the same way as nature is a world of matter, a world of beings independent of each other, like creatures of nature which are bound to each other by invisible bonds: this is the second world, the unique world of mankind . . .

Cultural life which does not conceive of a world of beings and does not receive from it new conceptions is subject to the danger of the apathy of accepted routine behavior, and a world of creativity which does not need to count the passing hours is doomed to the danger of spiritual isolation. The linkage of the two activities, crucial linkage, can be brought about through education.

c) There are two basic elements related to the crystallization of culture: the development of form and the development of awareness. Both of them, form and awareness, exist within man's experience as a matter of potential. Form grows, as it were, of its own volition . . . but awareness can also grow, as it were, within us on its own, but it remains within us and does not wish to leave us. I believe that it is able to grow because there are different types of awareness. There is total, sort of physical, awareness, awareness of our entire being, which spreads through out all our organs, reaching our hand which when touching a sculptured form does not have to send messages to the brain to ask whether the form is beautiful and if it is permitted to derive joy from it, but rather the hand itself has awareness which suffices with touch and the joy derived from it. There is also the awareness of the secluded brain, the brain which can be seen not as another organ of the living being, but as a sort of parasite which is stronger than itself, which derives strength from the entire being within man and uses it for his own unique purposes.

d) Every culture that is in a state of full development tends to produce a number of cultural types and areas which are totally independent, each of which has its own domain and immutable laws, that is, it has a tendency to pluralism of spiritual spheres. Despite the fact that the unity of systems of life, or at least styles of life, continues, the boundaries between such different spheres tend to be stressed more and more, until culture reaches a state at which although there is still a link between each area and the vital or varied core, the link between the areas themselves has weakened. For example, in a newly fledged developing culture, there is often a strong link between ethics and music, there is a strong link between cosmology, the theory of the universe, and architecture, but in a mature culture each area constructs its own independent world, and what is created in one world no longer comes within the realm of the other. This situation heralds the disintegration of culture. With the progression of this disintegration the tendency towards the re-establishment of the original unity commences. (*The Face of Man*, pp. 383–86; in Hebrew)

7

The foregoing passages point to the fact that Buber does not conceive of cultural creativity as being either a static, one-time situation or a situation without conflict. On the contrary, he depicts it as a state of continuous interaction between the various potentially opposing elements or components of culture that come into contact with each other through constant reciprocity and tension.

The possibilities of cultural creativity and social regeneration appeared to Buber to be greatest in those situations where the opposites exist in a state of tension that preserves the autonomy of each component. The domination of any one element over the others, and the potential annihilation of any such element by others, may produce just routine organizational or structural change, or it may lead to the stagnation, or even to the demise, of a society or culture. Buber was especially concerned, as we shall see in greater detail later on, with the possibility rooted in the European experience, especially in the thirties, that the state might dominate the more generative forces of social and cultural spontaneity. He thought that such a possibility was inherent in all political systems, but that it became especially dangerous in modern totalitarian societies.

8

It was thus natural that Buber's central sociological concern was to identify those situations in which cultural creativity can be developed, fostered, promoted; those forces and social conditions which create the possibilities for the crystalization of human creativity in its various multiple expressions. In other words, he searched for the conditions of cultural creativity and of social authenticity which may possibly lead to great social transformation, but which even in more routine situations may serve as crucial antidotes to stagnation.

What are then the major characteristics of the situations in which such authentic creativity may develop?

The central characteristic of such situations conducive to creativity is the existence of dialogue, of communicative openness—a dialogue between man and man and a dialogue between man and God. Such communicative openness is maximized in situations which have certain structural attributes. The most important such attribute is that the participants have a strong commitment both to direct interpersonal relations, transcending and cutting across more institutionalized and formalized frameworks, and to direct relations to the realm of the sacred, the transcendental, to the sphere of ultimate values.

It is the combination of open intersubjective dialogue with a dialogue between man and God, between man and the sacred or the transcendental, that gives rise in different sectors of society to the development or crystalization of a common discourse, and it is such common discourse that is essential for holding a society together, for meeting conditions conducive to cultural creativity and for counteracting the possible stagnative or destructive forces that are endemic in any society.

The emphasis on such communicative situations seems close to the more recent formulations by Jurgen Habermas.[7] There is, however, a very important difference between Buber and Habermas—namely that for Buber such creative communication can be achieved only when open interpersonal relations are connected with a strong orientation to the sacred, with a search for ultimate values. It is in the situation in which these two types of dialogue develop that the gates of creativity are thrown open; cultural content is changed; and organizational and institutional forms changed, new ones crystalized; and new levels of human experience are attained.

9

Buber's emphasis on the crucial importance of community and education in the fabric of social relations developed in the context of this approach. This emphasis is to be found above all in his analysis of Hasidic communities, his analysis of the kibbutz, and his analysis of some specific educational encounters—as well as in his more practical educational endeavors, such as the Jewish "house of study" (*Lehrhaus*) founded by Franz Rosenzweig in Frankfurt in the twenties, which Buber reestablished during the period of Nazi oppression, and the seminars for teachers of adult education which he established in Jerusalem in the early fifties to cope with the problem of the atomization of the new immigrants. In many ways he assumed that a fully fruitful dialogue, a framework of common discourse, can develop only in such a community, which, as Paul Mendes-Flohr has shown, is oriented to a center beyond itself.[8]

It is only through the development and maintenance of such a center and of the concomitant common discourse that communities—primordial, religious, or cooperative—are kept from stagnation. Such common discourse can be rooted in various givens, above all in primordial attachments to a land or a nation. But even such primordial attachment has to be continuously reflected upon in a continuous discourse which reaches beyond the primordial givens of the community—and the same is true of the political religious communities or of different cooperative ventures.

10

The crucial importance to cultural creativity of such openness to intersubjective social relations and to dialogue with the sacred is rooted in the fact that it is only in situations in which such openness develops that the tension between the various elements of cultural creativity can be maintained in a constructive way.

It is this combination between the intersubjective dialogue and the orientation to the transcendental that may, but only may, assure the very tenuous balance between the various components of cultural creativity. In the absence of such conditions, any one particular area can easily dominate and stifle all other areas.

Such a balance of cultural creativity in any process is a quite precarious one. It is precarious because of the tensions inherent in the very acts of such creativity; it is almost like walking a tightrope. Such tension exists first of all between the interpersonal dimension—the element of community—and the orientation to the transcendental, to the sacred. Secondly, these tensions or confrontations may develop between the moral or transcendental orientation, on the one hand, and primordial and political reality on the other. Such confrontation may entail a profoundly tragic element, as seen for instance in the case of Antigone, which gives rise to personal crisis, to moral protest, and possibly also to personal and social disintegration.

Another tension inherent in the process of creativity is that between the different elements of social organization, a tension which may give rise to the tendency of one such element to dominate all the others. Of all the various possibilities of the type of domination of one social element over others, Buber was particularly concerned, as we have indicated above, about the domination of the state over society. The potential of such domination has been present in almost every historical situation, but it has reached its climax in modern society in general, and particularly in totalitarian regimes. This domination leads, in its "simple" forms, to the weakening of the spontaneous basis of social relationships and cultural creativity. In its more severe forms, the domination of state over society can lead, as we have witnessed in the current century, to the disintegration of social life and culture.

However, Buber did not take the simple path followed by the negators of political power and those utopians who attempt, as it were, to flee from it. He feared the domination of the political element over social spontaneity, but saw in the political component of social life an essential and legitimate element of every human and social experience. He refused to denigrate political activity as such; rather, he saw it as a basic, essential, autonomous component of social life, which if kept within proper limits—limits that change according to circumstances— constitutes a positive force in the process of social creativity. Buber was well aware that it is not weak, unstable governments or leadership that can guarantee social freedom, the conditions of creativity—the op-

posite holds true. Weak governments probably increase the likelihood of
the domination of the political element, of creating a situation of "excess
of the political element." Thus Buber never advocated the reduction of
state powers in themselves, but rather their restriction according to a
particular area or period. Nor did he propose simple formulas or pre-
scriptions. As he put it:

> The question to be asked is not whether centralization or decentraliza-
> tion, but rather what are the areas within which are allowed a large propor-
> tion of decentralization of validity determination by the state? And it is not
> necessary to stress that this area must be amended and renewed constantly
> according to the changing conditions. (*Face of Man* [Hebrew], p. 412)

For Buber was aware that without such amendment and renewal according to changing conditions the transformative component of any
society can be lost.

Such consideration applies, according to him, not only to the political arena, but also to that of primordial relations, to various mundane activities be they economic or colonizatory, and even to religious
ones.

11

Buber was interested in the situations of great historical-civilizational
creativity, although he fully recognized that such situations of fully
fledged charismatic creativity are rare in the history of mankind. He saw
the ultimate apexes of such cultural creativity in the crystalization of the
great classical civilizations—in the Kingdom of God of the Israelite
commonwealth; in the civilizations of China and Greece, during their
periods of transition from tribalism to universalism; and also in the culture of the Renaissance period, in which he saw the embodiment of the
fruitful meeting between those contrasting elements which constitute
human creativity.

In his analysis of the history of Israel, of the "Kingdom of God," in his
work on the Prophets, in his analysis of Hasidic communities, and in his
lectures on different civilizations, he attempted to analyze in a comparative phenomenological way the specific characteristics of each of such
modes of cultural creativity. He was not interested in the *history* of these
communities or civilizations as such, but in their distinct phenomenol-
ogy in terms of the combination of the basic elements or components
of cultural creativity. Hence Gershom Sholem's famous criticism of
Buber's work on Hasidism, to which we have referred above, was basically misdirected, because it was conducted on a different—historical—

level from that of Buber's own work, which was phenomenological in the sense mentioned above. It was also misdirected because, in line with this phenomenological interest or emphasis of his, Buber employed what in that period was often seen as methodologically questionable approaches such as that of oral history—approaches which lately have been fully validated.

Buber was, as we said, fully aware that such great cultural transformations are not common in the history of mankind. And he was not solely interested in the great moments of such creativity, even though he paid special attention to them. He was also, of course, fully aware that not every process of historico-social or cultural change is a process of such a great transformative nature—perhaps the contrary is true—but it may contain the kernels thereof. Cognizant as he was of the various pitfalls of any such process, and perhaps afraid of too frequent proclamation of such creativity, he sought to identify the situations where genuine creativity can occur beyond the great moments of cultural history. He believed that these situations exist to some extent in all cultures, in all societies, although their fullest development occurs so rarely. He thought the transformative, creative potential may exist in many seemingly routine situations, and he attempted to identify and foster those forces which are able to guarantee a certain prospect of such transformation in seemingly routine situations, so that they will become, as he described the *kvutza* (cooperative village) in Eretz Israel, "an experiment which has not failed."

Thus Buber's approach to the problems of social and cultural creativity and regeneration differed greatly from the usual utopian views, which tended to be static and to emphasize a flight from various constraints of modern society or present an unattainable model of a desirable society—a model which is then tried out in small, isolated communities.

Unlike many of the utopians, Buber attempted to identify situations that permit some creativity or authenticity within the more routinized and formalized conditions generally prevalent in societies, especially in modern ones. This quest for identifying, and if possible creating, such situations and frameworks, whether in Eretz Israel or in other societies, whether in theory or practice, constituted Buber's main concern, and it also guided his approach to sociological analysis. He found these favorable conditions in modern religious and inter-religious dialogue and in educational institutions (particularly those devoted to adult education)—in which frameworks of common discourse can be developed.

He strongly believed that these situations are not tied to any concrete contents: cultural and social regeneration does not come from a social system established according to some formula; rather, it results from a continuous ongoing process.

In his teachings and personal contacts Buber continually stressed the fact that no particular solution, and perhaps no particular problem, constitutes the focal point of this search, but rather that the crucial issues are the continuous quest for such creativity and the readiness to retain an openness toward the variety of ways, methods, and content of the solutions.

It is in this context that it is also possible to understand Buber's strong emphasis on education—above all, on adult education. His basic conception of the constructive potentialities of adult education can perhaps be best illustrated by the explanation he gave me, in the very early fifties, that he had established the center for teachers of adult education in order to address the problems of integration of the new immigrants, who were coming then to Israel especially from Near Eastern ("Oriental") countries. The absorption of these immigrants posed an immense economic and organizational challenge for the new State, and I was a bit skeptical about the priority that should be given to adult education. When I asked him about it he answered me saying, "This is very important in order that we can converse together and dream together." At that time this answer rather puzzled me. Only lately, observing the breakdown of frameworks of common discourses between different sectors of Israeli society, a process which can be found also in many other Western societies, did I fully understand Buber's meaning.[9]

He saw adult education—the development of which he followed in Europe, in Western Europe, and in Scandinavian countries—as being able, if properly constructed, to generate frameworks of common discourse between different, often disparate, sectors of a society. Such possibility could, however, materialize in institutions of adult education only insofar as it was constructed as a situation of open dialogue, intersubjective dialogue and dialogue between man and the sacred, the transcendental. It was in this mold that he hoped to shape the institution he created in Jerusalem.

Buber's approach to social and cultural creativity and regeneration did not differ only from that of the utopians. To no smaller degree, it differed greatly also, as we shall see in greater detail later on, from the basic attitude of some of the major figures of modern, especially German, sociology to the predicaments of modern life—whether from Weber's fear of the *Entzauberung* or from Simmel's aesthetic approach of distancing from many arenas of modern life.

12

Buber's approach is most clear in his attitude to Eretz Israel. His social theories were always organically linked to the Zionist movement and to the social developments in Israel, from both of which he drew inspiration. Buber followed the development of the various forms of cooperative settlement—the Kibbutz and the Moshav—from their beginnings, and always endeavored to comprehend the extent of the validity of the bases of the authentic human relationships that developed within them. At the same time, as can be seen in the lecture he delivered in a symposium on these settlements held at his initiative at the Hebrew University in 1945, he did not ignore the danger that these elements would become distorted, especially through the routinization of the cooperative experience.[10]

After the establishment of the State of Israel, he viewed with trepidation the dangers inherent in the intensification of political power in its midst. But he never advocated the annulment of the political framework or the political symbols. Rather, he sought suitable ways to interweave them into the acts of social renewal and cultural creativity emerging in this process of renaissance, and he sought to identify in this new reality situations and frameworks within which to develop this renewal and creativity.

Even in his political polemics and criticisms, he did not deny the validity of political or even of defense or other military considerations—he was only afraid of their becoming predominant, total. Such predominance would, from his point of view, be counterproductive not only in moral terms but also in those of realpolitik. He saw his political criticisms of Israeli policies with respect to the Arab question, military government and the like, not as utopian dreams, but as very realpolitik attitudes.

13

A closer look at Buber's analysis of the problems of human creativity, especially of cultural creativity, indicates, despite the fact that his vocabulary was rather different, a very close relation to the classical problems of sociological analysis, to the major foci of the sociological tradition as expounded by the founding fathers of sociology—Durkheim, Weber, and to some extent Marx and Simmel—as well as to the central problematics and predicaments of modern society as these were perceived by them.

From the outset of modern social thought the questions of creative transformation vis-à-vis stychic change, of disintegrating anomie vis-à-vis anomic conditions which may give rise to renewed creativity; the question of the destructive force of charisma versus its constructive power, of the relations between primordial relationships and orientations to the transcendental realm; the question of the role of political power as the embodiment of creativity and as its greatest enemy have been among the basic foci of sociological analysis and research and of the attempts to understand the predicaments.

These concerns became incorporated in the sociological tradition through the work of the founding fathers. Not all of them accepted the assumption, implicit in utilitarian ethics and in classical economics, of the predominance and sufficiency of the market as the regulator of social order, as a mechanism which assures the maintenance of the social division of labor. The founding fathers did not deny the importance of the market as such as a mechanism. Indeed, in many ways, they elaborated on the processes of exchange in social life in general and the market in particular. But they all questioned whether such mechanisms were sufficient to explain the very structure, reproduction, and continuity of any concrete social division of labor, of any concrete social order. In different ways they all showed how such mechanisms in general and the market in particular cannot assure such working. They stressed that the very organization of social division of labor, of social exchange in general and of the market in particular, generates in regard to certain aspects of social order several problems which make questionable or uncertain the working of any concrete social division of labor.

The affected aspects of social order have been, first, the construction of trust and solidarity, stressed above all by Durkheim and to some degree by Tönnies; second, the regulation of power and the overcoming of the feelings of exploitation attendant to them, stressed above all by Marx and Max Weber; and third, stressed in different ways by all of them, the provision of meaning and of legitimation to the different social activities in general and to power in particular.

They all emphasized that the very construction of social division of labor generates uncertainties with respect to each of these dimensions of social order, that is, with respect to trust, regulation of power, the construction of meaning and legitimation—but at the same time, and because of these very uncertainties, no concrete social division of labor, no concrete social order, can be maintained without these dimensions or problems being taken care of. Therefore they all stressed that the construction of these dimensions of social order is conditioned on the development of some combination between the organizational structure of division of labor with the construction of trust, meaning, and legitimation.

Buber's emphasis on the construction of the social center,[11] his emphasis on the combination of community—*Gemeinde,* solidarity—with the orientation to the transcendental, to God, with the search for meaning, is very much in line with these basic assumptions of sociological tradition, and it indicates that Buber's major concerns were indeed very closely related to these central issues of modern social philosophy, sociological analysis and research.

Hence, like the founding fathers, he never minimized the importance of such components of social life as the social division of labor or, as we have briefly mentioned above, the element of power of the state, of the political dimensions of life. Neither did he belittle the importance of primordial attachments and relations, in the family or in the relation between people and territory. This last was most clearly seen in his analyses of the relations between the Land of Israel and the people of Israel and those between (the charismatic) leader and his followers. Although he never sanctified territory as such, and was afraid of such sanctification, at the same time he was fully aware of the crucial importance of such primordial attachments. He stressed this most forcefully in his exchange of letters with Gandhi in which he explained why Eretz Israel is the only place in which a Jewish national renaissance can take place.

However, important as all these social forces were, they could not, according to Buber, assure continuous social and cultural creativity and regeneration by themselves.

His most original contribution to sociological analysis was the emphasis on the crucial importance of the combination of intersubjectivity as manifest in interpersonal dialogue with a strong orientation to the sacred, to the transcendental, for the continuous reconstruction of social fabric and cultural creativity. Through this emphasis, he went beyond the dichotomy in sociological analysis, that between "contents"—represented by Marx, Durkheim, and Weber, and later by Parsons—and "form," as represented by Simmel, and later by scholars like Vierkandt, T. Geiger, and L. V. Wiese.[12] He recognized the stagnative possibilities of all cultural contents and institutions (especially the political institution), and he claimed that such stagnative potentialities could be overcome only by certain "forms" of social life—the dialogical and communal ones. But these forms of social life could serve as bases of creativity only insofar as they were not enclosed, embedded in themselves, but went beyond themselves, orienting themselves to the sacred or transcendent, to the search for a specific content.

Through his examination of the conditions of cultural creativity,

Buber's analysis also contributes to the understanding of the proper place of charisma in social processes and helps to identify both the creative and destructive possibilities inherent in charismatic orientations. Of crucial importance here is his analysis of the variety of social and cultural forms that permit the creative possibilities of charismatic orientations to find expression. By not limiting the charismatic to any given contents, such as the political or religious, Buber connected it directly with the total process of cultural creativity and social regeneration. This analysis related the authenticity of the charismatic dimensions to the existence of direct, unmediated relations of man to man and man to the sacred. Buber defined the nature and structure of the open situations in which the charismatic quality can become effective in the processes of social and cultural transformation.

In contrast to those views which identify the charismatic dimension of human activity and interaction only with exceptional circumstances and often also with destructive tendencies, Buber searched for the ways in which the charismatic is constitutive of the very construction of the social order and of its routine working—and above all he sought the possibilities of its continuous regeneration in multiple depressed situations.

Such an approach to the charismatic dimensions of the human being was later on independently, systematically elaborated by Edward Shils, especially in his analysis of societal centers.[13] Buber was, however, less interested in the relations between charisma and the center of society than in the possibilities of the dispersion of the charismatic components and their possible contribution to the regeneration of many sectors of social life.

14

Perhaps even more than the conceptual and sociological analysis, Buber shared with the great German sociologists the search for an understanding of the predicament of the modern world, of modern society, and it is with respect to such understanding that his basic approach to the processes of social regeneration stands out.

Weber and Simmel alike perceived the specific modern institutional frameworks—especially those of the market and, above all, those of the different bureaucratic formations—as alienating ones, as devoid of any authentic meaning in terms of either transcendental vision or personal authenticity. Whereas for Weber these institutional frameworks constituted the "iron cage," for Simmel, they represented the major arenas of the fleeting reality of the modern world. Common to them as well as to many others, especially but not only to the German social thinkers of their generation, were two assumptions: namely, first that it is such over-all institutional frameworks, and the centers of society, that provide the natural arenas in which transcendental, charismatic meaning can be implemented, and, second, that modern society's main institutional frameworks and its centers cannot serve as such arenas.

Hence any actual stance in the political arena was very problematic for them. Contrary to many would-be promulgators of charismatic politics to break through the iron cage, Weber opted for "politics of responsibility"—but in many ways these were for him politics of despair. Simmel, however, basically opted *out* of the political arena, while Tönnies and others searched, not very successfully, for some new overall ethical vision which would encompass the totality of modern institutions.[14]

Buber did not, as we have seen above, share either of these suppositions. He believed not only that such arenas of creativity can—and should—be developed and crystalized in the centers of societies, but that they can be identified and generated also in other sectors of society. At the same time he did not shy away from political activity, nor did he conceive of such activity as rooted in some deep despair.

It is therefore not surprising that the importance of Buber's contributions has become even more visible in the so-called "postmodern" era, in which there has taken place far-reaching decharismatization of large social formations like nation, state, and ideological parties—of the centers of society—and of such cultural domains as science. These processes of decharismatization gave rise in large parts of the contemporary discourse to the denial of the search for truth and of the validity of any absolute values.

Buber was also always skeptical about the possibility of imbuing such large social formations in the modern world with the charismatic dimension. He always looked for the manifestation of the charismatic and the utopian in the more dispersed and less central situations. In this sense he seemingly was a "postmodern" fully aware of the multiplicity of the authentic forms of life and of social interaction. But for him such authenticity was tied in with the search, even if an endless search, for the sacred, with a basic orientation to the transcendental, to absolute values.

The quest for solutions to the central problems of the sociological tradition has evolved new conceptual approaches and methods which differ greatly from Buber's specific approach. But all the same his approach was indeed addressed—in his own way—to the central problems of sociological analysis, and it shed a very specific light on them.

—S. N. Eisenstadt

Notes

1. A biography of Buber is to be found in G. Schraeder: "M. Buber—A Biographical Sketch," in N. N. Glazer and P. Mendes-Flohr (eds.), *The Letters of Martin Buber* (Schowen Books, New York, 1992).

2. Paul Mendes-Flohr, *From Mysticism to Dialogue: Martin Buber's Transformation of German Social Thought* (Detroit: Wayne State University Press, 1989); and see the review by Donald N. Levine, in *Contemporary Sociology* 20, no. 5 (September 1991): 807–8.

3. For a good discussion of this period in the development of German sociology, see L. A. Scaff, *Fleeing the Iron Cage—Culture, Politics and Modernity in the Thought of Max Weber* (Berkeley and Los Angeles: University of California Press, 1991).

4. According to the text presented in S. N. Eisenstadt, "The Sociological Teachings of Martin Buber," in *In Memory of Martin Buber Twenty Years after His Death* (Jerusalem: The Israel National Academy of Sciences and Humanities, 1987), pp. 8–10; in Hebrew.

5. See *The Social Contours of the Jewish (Hebrew) Village in Eretz-Israel: A Symposium Organized by the Hebrew University with the Federation of Agricultural Workers, 8–11 August 1945* (Jerusalem: The Hebrew University, 1946), p. 8; in Hebrew.

6. See G. Scholem, "Martin Buber's *Interpretation of Hasidism*," in his *The Messianic Idea of Judaism* (New York: Scheuer Press, 1971), 227–51.

7. See J. Habermas, *The Theory of Communicative Action,* translated by T. McCarthy (Boston: Beacon Press, 1984–86).

8. See P. Mendes-Flohr, "Nationalism in the Heart: Philosophical Dimensions of Buber's Hebrew Humanism," in *In Memory of Martin Buber* (see note 4), pp. 48–50.

9. On these processes in Israeli society, see S. N. Eisenstadt, *The Transformation of Israeli Society* (London: Weidenfeld and Nicholson, 1985), chaps. xvi, xvii.

10. See *The Social Contours of the Jewish (Hebrew) Village* (cited in note 5), p. 6.

11. See P. Mendes-Flohr, "Nationalism in the Heart" (cited in note 8).

12. See D. Levine, "Simmel and Parsons Reconsidered," in *American Journal of Sociology* 96, no. 5 (March, 1991): pp. 1097–1116.

13. E. Shils, "Charisma, Ritual and Consensus," part 2 of his *Center and Periphery, Essays in Macro-Sociology* (Chicago: University of Chicago Press, 1975), pp. 111–238. See also pages 3–17 of his book.

14. See L. A. Scaff, *Fleeing the Iron Cage* (cited in note 3).

Selected Bibliography of Buber's Works

(The initial dates are those of first publication in the languages concerned.)

1913 *Daniel: Dialogues on Realization.* New York: Holt, 1964. First published in German.

1921–43 *Israel and the World: Essays in a Time of Crisis,* 2d ed. New York: Schocken, 1963. Contains essays originally published in German and Hebrew.

1921–54 *The Origin and Meaning of Hasidism.* New York: Horizon, 1960. Contains essays originally published in German and Hebrew.

1926 "Rede über das Erzieherische," vol. 1, pp. 787–809 in Martin Buber, *Werke.* Munich: Kosel, 1962.

1936 *I and Thou,* 2d ed. New York: Scribner, 1958. First published in German.

1942 *The Prophetic Faith.* New York: Macmillan, 1949. First published in Hebrew. A paperback edition was published in 1960 by Harper.

1943–44 *For the Sake of Heaven,* 2d ed. New York: Harper, 1953. First published as *Gog and Magog.*

1947a *Paths in Utopia.* New York: Macmillan, 1950. First published in Hebrew.

1947b *Tales of the Hasidim.* New York, Schocken Books, 1947.

1948 "Das Problem des Menschen," vol. 1, pp. 307–407 in Martin Buber, *Werke.* Munich: Kosel, 1962.

1949 *Between Man and Man.* London, Routledge and Kegan Paul, 1949.

1951 "Urdistanz und Beziehung," vol. 1, pp. 411–23 in Martin Buber, *Werke.* Munich: Kosel, 1962.

1952a *Eclipse of God: Studies in the Relations between Religion and Philosophy.* New York: Harper, 1959.

1952b *At the Turning: Three Addresses on Judaism.* New York: Farrar, 1952.

1957 *Pointing the Way.* New York: Harper & Bros., 1957.

1962– *Werke.* Vols. 1–3. Munich: Kosel, 1962. A projected multivolume work.

The Face of Man, quoted in this Introduction, has not been translated into English and is available only in the Hebrew. Jerusalem: Mossad Bialik Institute, 1962.

For a full bibliography of Buber's writings, see *Martin Buber: A Bibliography of His Writings 1897–1978,* compiled by Margot Cohn and Raphael Buber. Jerusalem: The Magnum Press, The Hebrew University; Munich: K. G. Saur, 1980.

23

I

THE ANTHROPOLOGICAL
PHILOSOPHY OF MAN

The excerpts presented here from Buber's philosophical writings bear on his basic views on the nature of man. In the excerpts gathered in chapter 1, Buber addresses himself to anthropological philosophical questions of the nature of man—and strongly emphasizes that no conception which perceives man as a separate monad is adequate. It is the intersubjective component and the orientation to the transcendental that provide the clue to what is most fundamental to authentic human experience. The basic implications of this approach are more fully elaborated in the excerpts brought under chapter 2. In these excerpts it is the social dimension of human life that is emphasized and analyzed.

This social dimension of intersubjectivity is not to be confused either with the organizational aspects of social reality or with a psychological conception of us which reduces human experience to the emotions or to the purely subjective. Intersubjectivity is rooted in social interaction, in a continuous dialogue; distance and relation between human beings constitute a basic phenomenological component of the human experience which antecedes both the social-organizational as well as the purely psychological dimensions of human nature.

1

The Nature of Man

Ne connaîtrons-nous jamais l'homme?—Rousseau

What Is Man?: Kant's Questions*

1

Rabbi Bunam von Przysucha, one of the last great teachers of Hasidism, is said to have once addressed his pupils thus: "I wanted to write a book called *Adam,* which would be about the whole man. But then I decided not to write it."

In these naive-sounding words of a genuine sage the whole story of human thought about man is expressed. From time immemorial man has known that he is the subject most deserving of his own study, but he has also fought shy of treating this subject as a whole, that is, in accordance with its total character. Sometimes he takes a run at it, but the difficulty of this concern with his own being soon overpowers and exhausts him, and in silent resignation he withdraws—either to consider all things in heaven and earth save man, or to divide man into departments which can be treated singly, in a less problematic, less powerful and less binding way.

The philosopher Malebranche, the most significant of the French philosophers who continued the Cartesian investigations, writes in the foreword to his chief work, *De la recherche de la vérité* (1674): "Of all human knowledge the knowledge of man is the most deserving of his study. Yet this knowledge is not the most cultivated or the most developed which we possess. The generality of men neglect it completely. And even among those who busy themselves with this knowledge there are very few who dedicate themselves to it—and still fewer who successfully dedicate themselves to it." He himself certainly raises in his book such genuinely anthropological questions as how far the life of the nerves which lead to the lungs, the stomach, and the liver influences the origin of errors; but he too established no doctrine of the being of man.

*Reprinted with the permission of Macmillan Publishing Company from *Between Man and Man* by Martin Buber, translated from the German by Ronald Gregor Smith. Copyright © 1965 by Macmillan Publishing Company.

2

The most forcible statement of the task set to philosophical anthropology was made by Kant. In the *Handbook* to his lectures on logic, which
he expressly acknowledged—though he himself did not publish it and
though it does not reproduce his underlying notes authentically—he
distinguishes between a philosophy in the scholastic sense and a philosophy in the universal sense (*in sensu cosmico*). He describes the latter
as "the knowledge of the ultimate aims of human reason" or as the
"knowledge of the highest maxim of the use of our reason." The field of
philosophy in this cosmopolitan significance may, according to Kant, be
marked off into the following questions. "1. What can I know? 2. What
ought I to do? 3. What may I hope? 4. What is man? Metaphysics answers the first question, ethics the second, religion the third and anthropology the fourth." And Kant adds: "Fundamentally all this could
be reckoned as anthropology, since the first three questions are related
to the last." This formulation repeats the three questions of which Kant
says, in the section of his *Critique of Pure Reason* entitled *Of the ideal of
the supreme good,* that every interest of the reason, the speculative as
well as the practical, is united in them. In distinction from the *Critique of
Pure Reason* he here traces these questions back to a fourth question,
that about the being of man, and assigns it to a discipline called anthropology, by which—since he is discussing the fundamental questions
of human philosophizing—only philosophical anthropology can be understood. This, then, would be the fundamental philosophical science.

But it is remarkable that Kant's own anthropology, both what he
himself published and his copious lectures on man, which only appeared long after his death, absolutely fails to achieve what he demands
of a philosophical anthropology. In its express purpose as well as in its
entire content it offers something different—an abundance of valuable
observations for the knowledge of man, for example, on egoism, on
honesty and lies, on fancy, on fortune-telling, on dreams, on mental dis-
eases, on wit, and so on. But the question, what man is, is simply not
raised, and not one of the problems which are implicitly set us at the
same time by this question—such as man's special place in the cosmos,
his connexion with destiny, his relation to the world of things, his understanding of his fellow-men, his existence as a being that knows it must
die, his attitude in all the ordinary and extraordinary encounters with
the mystery with which his life is shot through, and so on—not one of
these problems is seriously touched upon. The *wholeness* of man does
not enter into this anthropology. It is as if Kant in his actual philosophiz-

ing had had qualms about setting the question which he formulated as the fundamental one.

A modern philosopher, Martin Heidegger, who has dealt (in his *Kant and the Problem of Metaphysics*, 1929) with this strange contradiction, explains it by the *indefiniteness* of the question, what man is. The way of asking the question about man, he says, has itself become questionable. In Kant's first three questions it is man's *finitude* which is under discussion: "What *can* I know?" involves an inability, and thus a limitation; "What *ought* I to do?" includes the realization that something has not yet been accomplished, and thus a limitation; and "What *may* I hope?" means that the questioner is given one expectation and denied another, and thus it means a limitation. The fourth question is the question about "finitude in man," and is no longer an anthropological question at all, for it is the question about the essence of existence itself. As the basis of metaphysics anthropology is replaced by "fundamental ontology."

Whatever this finding represents, it is no longer Kant. Heidegger has shifted the emphasis of Kant's three questions. Kant does not ask: "What *can* I know?" but "What *can* I *know*?" The essential point here is not that there is something I can do and thus something else that I cannot do; nor is it that there is something I know and thus something else that I do not know; but it is that I *can know* something, and that I can then ask what that is that I can know. It is not my finitude that is under discussion here, but my real participation in knowing what there is to know. And in the same way "What ought I to do?" means that there *is* something I ought to do, and thus that I am not separated from "right" doing, but precisely by being able to *come to know* my "ought" may find the way to the doing. Finally, "What may I hope?" does not assert, as Heidegger thinks, that a "may" is made questionable here, and that in the expectation a want of what may not be expected is revealed; but it asserts, first, that there is something for me to hope (for obviously Kant does not mean that the answer to the third question is "Nothing"), secondly, that I am permitted to hope it, and thirdly, that precisely because I am permitted I can learn what it is that I may hope. That is what *Kant* says. And thus in Kant the meaning of the fourth question, to which the first three can be reduced is, what sort of a being is it which is able to know, and ought to do, and may hope? And the fact that the first three questions can be reduced to this question means that the knowledge of the essence of this being will make plain to me *what*, as such a being, it can know, *what*, as such a being, it ought to do, and *what*, as such a being, it may hope. This also means that indissolubly connected with the finitude which is given by the ability to know *only* this, there is a participation in infinity, which is given by the ability to know at all. The meaning is therefore that when we recognize man's finitude we must *at the same time* recognize his participation in infinity, not as two juxtaposed qualities but as the twofold nature of the processes in which alone man's existence becomes recognizable. The finite has its effect on him and the infinite has its effect on him; he shares in finitude and he shares in infinity.

Certainly Kant in his anthropology has neither answered nor undertaken to answer the question which he put to anthropology—What is man? He lectured on another anthropology than the one he asked for— I should say, in terms of the history of philosophy, an earlier anthropology, one that was still bound up with the uncritical "science of man" of the 17th and 18th centuries. But in formulating the task which he set to the philosophical anthropology he asked for, he has left a legacy.

3

It is certainly doubtful to me as well whether such a discipline will suffice to provide a foundation for philosophy, or, as Heidegger formulates it, a foundation for metaphysics. For it is true, indeed, that I continually learn what I can know, what I ought to do, and what I may hope. It is further true that philosophy contributes to this learning of mine: to the first question by telling me, in logic and epistemology, what being able to know means, and in cosmology and the philosophy of history and so on, what there is to know; to the second question by telling me, in psychology, how the "ought to do" is carried out psychically, and in ethics, the doctrine of the State, aesthetics and so on, what there is to do; and to the third question by telling me, at least in the philosophy of religion, how the "may hope" is displayed in actual faith and the history of faith—whereas it can certainly not tell me what there is to hope, since religion itself and its conceptual elaboration in theology, whose task this is, do not belong to philosophy. All this is agreed. But philosophy succeeds in rendering me such help in its individual disciplines precisely through each of these disciplines *not* reflecting, and not being able to reflect, on the wholeness of man. Either a philosophical discipline shuts out man in his complex wholeness and considers him only as a bit of nature, as cosmology does; or (as all the other disciplines do) it tears off its own special sphere from the wholeness of man, delimits it from the other spheres, establishes its own basic principles and develops its own methods. In addition it has to remain open and accessible, first to the ideas of metaphysics itself as the doctrine of being, of what is and of existence, secondly to the findings of the philosophical branch disciplines, and thirdly to the discoveries of philosophical anthropology. But least of all may it make itself dependent on the latter; for in every one of those disciplines the possibility of its achieving anything in thought rests precisely on its objectification, on what may be termed its "dehumanization," and even a discipline like the philosophy of history, which is so concerned with the actual man, must, in order to be able to comprehend man *as a historical being,* renounce consideration of the whole man—of which the kind of man who is living outside history in the unchanging rhythm of nature is an essential part. What the philosophical disciplines are able to contribute to answering Kant's first three questions, even if it is only by clarifying them, or teaching me to recognize the problems they contain, they are able to do only by *not* waiting for the answer to the fourth question.

Nor can philosophical anthropology itself set itself the task of establishing a foundation either for metaphysics or for the individual philosophical sciences. If it attempted to answer the question *What is man?* in such a general way that answers to the other questions could be derived from it, it would miss the very reality of its own subject. For it would reach, instead of the subject's genuine wholeness, which can become visible only by the contemplation of all its manifold nature, a false unity which has no reality. A legitimate philosophical anthropology must know that there is not merely a human species but also peoples, not merely a human soul but also types and characters, not merely a human life but also stages in life; only from the systematic comprehension of these and of all other differences, from the recognition of the dynamic that exerts power within every particular reality and between them, and from the constantly new proof of the one in the many, can it come to see the wholeness of man. For that very reason it cannot grasp man in that absoluteness which, though it does not speak out from Kant's fourth question, yet very easily presents itself when an answer is attempted— the answer which Kant, as I have said, avoided giving. Even as it must again and again distinguish within the human race in order to arrive at a solid comprehension, so it must put man in all seriousness into nature, it must compare him with other things, other living creatures, other bearers of consciousness, in order to define his special place reliably for him. Only by this double way of distinction and comparison does it reach the whole, real man who, whatever his people or type or age, knows, what no being on earth but he can know, that he goes the narrow way from birth towards death, tests out what none but he can, a wrestling with destiny, rebellion and reconciliation, and at times even experiences in his own blood, when he is joined by choice to another human being, what goes on secretly in others.

Philosophical anthropology is not intent on reducing philosophical problems to human existence and establishing the philosophical disciplines so to speak from below instead of from above. It is solely intent on knowing man himself. This sets it a task that is absolutely different from all other tasks of thought. For in philosophical anthropology man himself is given to man in the most precise sense as a subject. Here, where the subject is man in his wholeness, the investigator cannot content himself, as in anthropology as an individual science, with considering man as another part of nature and with ignoring the fact that he, the investigator, is himself a man and experiences his humanity in his inner experience in a way that he simply cannot experience any part of nature—not only in a quite different perspective but also in a quite different dimension of being, in a dimension in which he experiences only this one part of all the parts of nature. Philosophical knowledge of man is essentially man's self-reflection (*Selbstbesinnung*), and man can reflect about himself only when the cognizing person, that is, the philosopher pursuing anthropology, first of all reflects about himself as a person. The principle of individuation, the fundamental fact of the infinite variety of human persons, of whom this one is only one person, of this constitution and no other, does not relativize anthropological knowledge; on the contrary, it gives it its kernel and its skeleton. In order to become genuine philosophical anthropology, everything that is discovered about historical and modern man, about men and women, Indians and Chinese, tramps and emperors, the weak-minded and the genius, must be built up and crystallized round what the philosopher discovers by reflecting about himself. That is a quite different matter from what, say, the psychologist undertakes when he completes and clarifies by reference to his own self in self-observation, self-analysis and experiment, what he knows from literature and observation. For with him it is a matter of individual, objectivized processes and phenomena, of something that is separated from connexion with the whole real person. But the philosophical anthropologist must stake nothing less than his real wholeness, his concrete self. And more; it is not enough for him to stake his self as an *object* of knowledge. He can know the *wholeness* of the person and through it the wholeness of *man* only when he does not leave his *subjectivity* out and does not remain an untouched observer. He must enter, completely and in reality, into the act of self-reflection, in order to become aware of human wholeness. In other words, he must carry out this act of entry into that unique dimension as an act of his *life,* without any prepared philosophical security; that is, he must expose himself to all that can meet you when you are really living. Here you do not attain to knowledge by remaining on the shore and watching the foaming waves, you must make the venture and cast yourself in, you must swim, alert and with all your force, even if a moment comes when you think you are losing consciousness: in this way, and in no other, do you reach anthropological insight. So long as you "have" yourself, have yourself as an object, your experience of man is only as of a thing among things, the wholeness which is to be grasped is not yet "there"; only when you *are*, and nothing else but that, is the wholeness there, and able to be grasped. You perceive only as much as the reality of the "being there" incidentally yields to you; but you do perceive that, and the nucleus of the crystallization develops itself.

An example may clarify more precisely the relation between the psychologist and the anthropologist. If both of them investigate, say, the phenomenon of anger, the psychologist will try to grasp what the angry man feels, what his motives and the impulses of his will are, but the anthropologist will also try to grasp what he is doing. In respect of this phenomenon self-observation, being by nature disposed to weaken the spontaneity and unruliness of anger, will be especially difficult for both of them. The psychologist will try to meet this difficulty by a specific division of consciousness, which enables him to remain outside with the observing part of his being and yet let his passion run its course as undisturbed as possible. Of course this passion can then not avoid becoming similar to that of the actor, that is, though it can still be heightened in comparison with an unobserved passion, its course will be different: there will be a release which is willed and which takes the place of the elemental outbreak, there will be a vehemence which will be more emphasized, more deliberate, more dramatic. The anthropologist can have nothing to do with a division of consciousness, since he has to do with the unbroken wholeness of events, and especially with the unbroken natural connexion between feelings and actions; and this connexion is most powerfully influenced in self-observation, since the pure spontaneity of the action is bound to suffer essentially. It remains for the anthropologist only to resign any attempt to stay outside his observing self, and thus when he is overcome by anger not to disturb it in its course by becoming a spectator of it, but to let it rage to its conclusion without trying to gain a perspective. He will be able to register in the act of recollection what he felt and did then; for him memory takes the place of psychological self-experience. But as great writers in their dealings with other men do not deliberately register their peculiarities and, so to speak, make invisible notes, but deal with them in a natural and uninhibited way, and leave the harvest to the hour of harvest, so it is the memory of the competent anthropologist which has, with reference to himself as to others, the concentrating power which preserves what is essential. In the moment of life he has nothing else in his mind but just to live what is to be lived, he is there with his whole being, undivided, and for that very reason there grows in his thought and recollection the knowledge of human wholeness.

Prospect*

We have seen that an individualistic anthropology, an anthropology which is substantially concerned only with the relation of the human person to himself, with the relation within this person between the spirit and its instincts, and so on, cannot lead to a knowledge of man's being. Kant's question *What is man?* whose history and effects I have discussed . . . , can never be answered on the basis of a consideration of the human person as such, but (so far as an answer is possible at all) only on the basis of a consideration of it in the wholeness of its essential relations to what is. Only the man who realizes in his whole life with his whole being the relations possible to him helps us to know man truly. And since, as we have seen, the depths of the question about man's being are revealed only to the man who has become solitary, the way to the answer lies through the man who overcomes his solitude without forfeiting its questioning power. This means that a *new* task in life is set to human thought here, a task that is new in its context of *life*. For it means that the man who wants to grasp what he himself is salvages the tension of solitude and its burning problematic for a life with his world, a life that is renewed in spite of all, and out of this new situation proceeds with his thinking. Of course this presupposes the beginning of a new process of overcoming the solitude—despite all the vast difficulties—by reference to which that special task of thought can be perceived and expressed. It is obvious that at the present stage reached by mankind such a process cannot be effected by the spirit alone; but to a certain extent knowledge will also be able to further it. It is incumbent on us to clarify this in outline.

Criticism of the individualistic method starts usually from the standpoint of the collectivist tendency. But if individualism understands only a part of man, collectivism understands man only as a part: neither advances to the wholeness of man, to man as a whole. Individualism sees man only in relation to himself, but collectivism does not see *man* at all, it sees only "society." With the former man's face is distorted, with the latter it is masked.

Both views of life—modern individualism and modern collectivism—however different their causes may be, are essentially the conclusion or expression of the same human condition, only at different stages. This condition is characterized by the union of cosmic and social homelessness, dread of the universe and dread of life, resulting in an existential constitution of solitude such as has probably never existed before to the same extent. The human person feels himself to be a man exposed by nature—as an unwanted child is exposed—and at the same time a person isolated in the midst of the tumultuous human world. The first reaction of the spirit to the awareness of this new and uncanny position is modern individualism, the second is modern collectivism.

In individualism the human being ventures to affirm this position, to plunge it into an affirmative reflexion, a universal *amor fati;* he wants to build the citadel of a life-system in which the idea asserts that it wills reality as it is. Just because man is exposed by nature, he is an individual in this specially radical way in which no other being in the world is an individual; and he accepts his exposure because it means that he is an individual. In the same way he accepts his isolation as a person, for only a monad which is not bound to others can know and glorify itself as an individual to the utmost. To save himself from the despair with which his solitary state threatens him, man resorts to the expedient of glorifying it. Modern individualism has essentially an imaginary basis. It founders on this character, for imagination is not capable of actually conquering the given situation.

The second reaction, collectivism, essentially follows upon the foundering of the first. Here the human being tries to escape his destiny of solitude by becoming completely embedded in one of the massive modern group formations. The more massive, unbroken and powerful in its achievements this is, the more the man is able to feel that he is saved from both forms of homelessness, the social and the cosmic. There is obviously no further reason for dread of life, since one needs only to fit oneself into the "general will" and let one's own responsibility for an existence which has become all too complicated be absorbed in collective responsibility, which proves itself able to meet all complications. Likewise, there is obviously no further reason for dread of the universe, since technicized nature—with which society as such manages well, or seems to—takes the place of the universe, which has become uncanny and with which, so to speak, no further agreement can be reached. The collective pledges itself to provide total security. There is nothing imaginary here, a dense reality rules, and the "general" itself appears to have become real; but modern collectivism is essentially illusory. The person is joined to the reliably functioning "whole," which embraces the masses of men; but it is not a joining of man to man. Man in a collective is not man with man. Here the person is not freed from his isolation, by communing with living beings, which thenceforth live with him; the "whole," with its claim on the wholeness of every man, aims logically and successfully at reducing, neutralizing, devaluating, and desecrating every bond with living beings. That tender surface of personal life which longs for contact with other life is progressively deadened or desensitized. Man's isolation is not overcome here, but overpowered and numbed. Knowledge of it is suppressed, but the actual condition of solitude has its insuperable effect in the depths, and rises secretly to a cruelty which will become manifest with the scattering of the illusion. Modern collectivism is the last barrier raised by man against a meeting with himself.

When imaginings and illusions are over, the possible and inevitable meeting of man with himself is able to take place only as the meeting of the individual with his fellow-man—and this is how it must take place. Only when the individual knows the other in all his otherness as himself, as man, and from there breaks through to the other, has he broken through his solitude in a strict and transforming meeting.

It is obvious that such an event can only take place if the person is stirred up as a person. In individualism the person, in consequence of his merely imaginary mastery of his basic situation, is attacked by the ravages of the fictitious, however much he thinks, or strives to think, that he is asserting himself as a person in being. In collectivism the person surrenders himself when he renounces the directness of personal decision and responsibility. In both cases the person is incapable of breaking through to the other: there is genuine relation only between genuine persons.

In spite of all attempts at revival the time of individualism is over. Collectivism, on the other hand, is at the height of its development, although here and there appear single signs of slackening. Here the only way that is left is the rebellion of the person for the sake of setting free the relations with others. On the horizon I see moving up, with the slowness of all events of true human history, a great dissatisfaction which is unlike all previous dissatisfactions. Men will no longer rise in rebellion —as they have done till now—merely against some dominating tendency in the name of other tendencies, but against the false realization of a great effort, the effort towards community, in the name of the genuine realization. Men will fight against the distortion for the pure form, the vision of the believing and hoping generations of mankind.

I am speaking of living actions; but it is vital knowledge alone which incites them. Its first step must be to smash the false alternative with which the thought of our epoch is shot through—that of "individualism or collectivism." Its first question must be about a genuine third alternative—by "genuine" being understood a point of view which cannot be reduced to one of the first two, and does not represent a mere compromise between them.

Life and thought are here placed in the same problematic situation. As life erroneously supposes that it has to choose between individualism and collectivism, so thought erroneously supposes that it has to choose between an individualistic anthropology and a collectivist sociology. The genuine third alternative, when it is found, will point the way here too.

The fundamental fact of human existence is neither the individual as such nor the aggregate as such. Each, considered by itself, is a mighty abstraction. The individual is a fact of existence in so far as he steps into a living relation with other individuals. The aggregate is a fact of existence in so far as it is built up of living units of relation. The fundamental fact of human existence is man with man. What is peculiarly characteristic of the human world is above all that something takes place between one being and another the like of which can be found nowhere in nature. Language is only a sign and a means for it, all achievement of the spirit has been incited by it. Man is made man by it; but on its way it does not merely unfold, it also decays and withers away. It is rooted in one being turning to another as another, as this particular other being, in order to communicate with it in a sphere which is common to them but which reaches out beyond the special sphere of each. I call this sphere, which is established with the existence of man as man but which is conceptually still uncomprehended, the sphere of "between." Though being realized in very different degrees, it is a primal category of human reality. This is where the genuine third alternative must begin.

The view which establishes the concept of "between" is to be acquired by no longer localizing the relation between human beings, as is customary, either within individual souls or in a general world which embraces and determines them, but in actual fact *between* them.

"Between" is not an auxiliary construction, but the real place and bearer of what happens between men; it has received no specific attention because, in distinction from the individual soul and its context, it does not exhibit a smooth continuity, but is ever and again reconstituted in accordance with men's meetings with one another; hence what is experience has been annexed naturally to the continuous elements, the soul and its world.

In a real conversation (that is, not one whose individual parts have been preconcerted, but one which is completely spontaneous, in which

each speaks directly to his partner and calls forth his unpredictable reply), a real lesson (that is, neither a routine repetition nor a lesson whose
findings the teacher knows before he starts, but one which develops in
mutual surprises), a real embrace and not one of mere habit, a real duel
and not a mere game—in all these what is essential does not take place
in each of the participants or in a neutral world which includes the two
and all other things; but it takes place between them in the most precise
sense, as it were in a dimension which is accessible only to them both.
Something happens to me—that is a fact which can be exactly distributed between the world and the soul, between an "outer" event and
an "inner" impression. But if I and another come up against one another, "happen" to one another (to use a forcible expression which can,
however, scarcely be paraphrased), the sum does not exactly divide,
there is a remainder, somewhere, where the souls end and the world
has not yet begun, and this remainder is what is essential. This fact can
be found even in the tiniest and most transient events which scarcely
enter the consciousness. In the deadly crush of an air-raid shelter the
glances of two strangers suddenly meet for a second in astonishing
and unrelated mutuality; when the All Clear sounds it is forgotten; and
yet it did happen, in a realm which existed only for that moment. In the
darkened opera-house there can be established between two of the au-
dience, who do not know one another, and who are listening in the same
purity and with the same intensity to the music of Mozart, a relation which is scarcely perceptible and yet is one of elemental dialogue,
and which has long vanished when the lights blaze up again. In the
understanding of such fleeting and yet consistent happenings one must
guard against introducing motives of feeling: what happens here cannot be reached by psychological concepts, it is something ontic. From
the least of events, such as these, which disappear in the moment of
their appearance, to the pathos of pure indissoluble tragedy, where two
men, opposed to one another in their very nature, entangled in the
same living situation, reveal to one another in mute clarity an irreconcil-
able opposition of being, the dialogical situation can be adequately
grasped only in an ontological way. But it is not to be grasped on the
basis of the ontic of personal existence, or of that of two personal exis-
tences, but of that which has its being between them, and transcends
both. In the most powerful moments of dialogic, where in truth "deep
calls unto deep," it becomes unmistakably clear that it is not the wand of
the individual or of the social, but of a third which draws the circle
round the happening. On the far side of the subjective, on this side of the
objective, on the narrow ridge, where *I* and *Thou* meet, there is the
realm of "between."

This reality, whose disclosure has begun in our time, shows the way, leading beyond individualism and collectivism, for the life decision of future generations. Here the genuine third alternative is indicated, the knowledge of which will help to bring about the genuine person again and to establish genuine community.

This reality provides the starting-point for the philosophical science of man; and from this point an advance may be made on the one hand to a transformed understanding of the person and on the other to a transformed understanding of community. The central subject of this science is neither the individual nor the collective but man with man. That essence of man which is special to him can be directly known only in a living relation. The gorilla, too, is an individual; a termitary, too, is a collective; but *I* and *Thou* exist only in our world, because man exists, and the *I*, moreover, exists only through the relation to the *Thou*. The philosophical science of man, which includes anthropology and sociology, must take as its starting-point the consideration of this subject, "man with man." If you consider the individual by himself, then you see of man just as much as you see of the moon; only man with man provides a full image. If you consider the aggregate by itself, then you see of man just as much as we see of the Milky Way; only man with man is a completely outlined form. Consider man with man, and you see human life, dynamic, twofold, the giver and the receiver, he who does and he who endures, the attacking force and the defending force, the nature which investigates and the nature which supplies information, the request begged and granted—and always both together, completing one another in mutual contribution, together showing forth man. Now you can turn to the individual and you recognize him as man according to the possibility of relation which he shows; you can turn to the aggregate and you recognize it as man according to the fulness of relation which he shows. We may come nearer the answer to the question what man is when we come to see him as the eternal meeting of the One with the Other.

Dialogue*

Original Remembrance

Through all sorts of changes the same dream, sometimes after an interval of several years, recurs to me. I name it the dream of the double cry.

*Reprinted with the permission of Macmillan Publishing Company from *Between Man and Man* by Martin Buber, translated from the German by Ronald Gregor Smith. Copyright © 1965 by Macmillan Publishing Company.

Its context is always much the same, a "primitive" world meagrely equipped. I find myself in a vast cave, like the Latomias of Syracuse, or in a mud building that reminds me when I awake of the villages of the *fellahin*, or on the fringe of a gigantic forest whose like I cannot remember having seen.

The dream begins in very different ways, but always with something extraordinary happening to me, for instance, with a small animal resembling a lion-cub (whose name I know in the dream but not when I awake) tearing the flesh from my arm and being forced only with an effort to loose its hold. The strange thing is that this first part of the dream story, which in the duration as well as the outer meaning of the incidents is easily the most important, always unrolls at a furious pace as though it did not matter. Then suddenly the pace abates: I stand there and cry out. In the view of the events which my waking consciousness has I should have to suppose that the cry I utter varies in accordance with what preceded it, and is sometimes joyous, sometimes fearful, sometimes even filled both with pain and with triumph. But in my morning recollection it is neither so expressive nor so various. Each time it is the same cry, inarticulate but in strict rhythm, rising and falling, swelling to a fulness which my throat could not endure were I awake, long and slow, quiet, quite slow and very long, a cry that is a song. When it ends my heart stops beating. But then, somewhere, far away, another cry moves towards me, another which is the same, the same cry uttered or sung by another voice. Yet it is not the same cry, certainly no "echo" of my cry but rather its true rejoinder, tone for tone not repeating mine, not even in a weakened form, but corresponding to mine, answering its tones—so much so, that mine, which at first had to my own ear no sound of questioning at all, now appear as questions, as a long series of questions, which now all receive a response. The response is no more capable of interpretation than the question. And yet the cries that meet the one cry that is the same do not seem to be the same as one another. Each time the voice is new. But now, as the reply ends, in the first moment after its dying fall, a certitude, true dream certitude comes to me that *now it has happened*. Nothing more. Just this, and in this way— *now it has happened*. If I should try to explain it, it means that that happening which gave rise to my cry has only now, with the rejoinder, really and undoubtedly happened.

After this manner the dream has recurred each time—till once, the last time, now two years ago. At first it was as usual (it was the dream with the animal), my cry died away, again my heart stood still. But then there was quiet. There came no answering call. I listened, I heard no sound. For I *awaited* the response for the first time; hitherto it had always surprised me, as though I had never heard it before. Awaited, it failed to come. But now something happened with me. As though I had till now had no other access from the world to sensation save that of the ear and now discovered myself as a being simply equipped with senses, both those clothed in the bodily organs and the naked senses, so I exposed myself to the distance, open to all sensation and perception. And then, not from a distance but from the air round about me, noiselessly, came the answer. Really it did not come; it was there. It had been there—so I may explain it—even before my cry: there it was, and now, when I laid myself open to it, it let itself be received by me. I received it as completely into my perception as ever I received the rejoinder in one of the earlier dreams. If I were to report with what I heard it I should have to say "with every pore of my body." As ever the rejoinder came in one of the earlier dreams this corresponded to and answered my cry. It exceeded the earlier rejoinder in an unknown perfection which is hard to define, for it resides in the fact that it was already there.

When I had reached an end of receiving it, I felt again that certainty, pealing out more than ever, that *now it has happened.*

Silence Which Is Communication

Just as the most eager speaking at one another does not make a conversation (this is most clearly shown in that curious sport, aptly termed discussion, that is, "breaking apart," which is indulged in by men who are to some extent gifted with the ability to think), so for a conversation no sound is necessary, not even a gesture. Speech can renounce all the media of sense, and it is still speech.

Of course I am not thinking of lovers' tender silence, resting in one another, the expression and discernment of which can be satisfied by a glance, indeed by the mere sharing of a gaze which is rich in inward relations. Nor am I thinking of the mystical shared silence, such as is reported of the Franciscan Aegidius and Louis of France (or, almost identically, of two rabbis of the Hasidim), who, meeting once, did not utter a word, but "taking their stand in the reflection of the divine Face" experienced one another. For here too there is still the expression of a gesture, of the physical attitude of the one to the other.

What I am thinking of I will make clear by an example.

Imagine two men sitting beside one another in any kind of solitude of the world. They do not speak with one another, they do not look at one another, not once have they turned to one another. They are not in one another's confidence, the one knows nothing of the other's career, early that morning they got to know one another in the course of their travels. In this moment neither is thinking of the other; we do not need to know what their thoughts are. The one is sitting on the common seat obviously after his usual manner, calm, hospitably disposed to everything that may come. His being seems to say it is too little to be ready, one must also be really *there*. The other, whose attitude does not betray him, is a man who holds himself in reserve, withholds himself. But if we know about him we know that a childhood's spell is laid on him, that his withholding of himself is something other than an attitude, behind all attitude is entrenched the impenetrable inability to communicate himself. And now—let us imagine that this is one of the hours which succeed in bursting asunder the seven iron bands about our heart—imperceptibly the spell is lifted. But even now the man does not speak a word, does not stir a finger. Yet he does something. The lifting of the spell has happened to him—no matter from where—without his doing. But this is what he does now: he releases in himself a reserve over which only he himself has power. Unreservedly communication streams from him, and the silence bears it to his neighbour. Indeed it was intended for him, and he receives it unreservedly as he receives all genuine destiny that meets him. He will be able to tell no one, not even himself, what he has experienced. What does he now "know" of the other? No more knowing is needed. For where unreserve has ruled, even wordlessly, between men, the word of dialogue has happened sacramentally.

Opinions and the Factual

Human dialogue, therefore, although it has its distinctive life in the sign, that is in sound and gesture (the letters of language have their place in this only in special instances, as when, between friends in a meeting, notes describing the atmosphere skim back and forth across the table), can exist without the sign, but admittedly not in an objectively comprehensible form. On the other hand an element of communication, however inward, seems to belong to its essence. But in its highest moments dialogue reaches out even beyond these boundaries. It is completed outside contents, even the most personal, which are or can be communicated. Moreover it is completed not in some "mystical" event, but in one that is in the precise sense factual, thoroughly dovetailed into the common human world and the concrete time-sequence.

One might indeed be inclined to concede this as valid for the special realm of the erotic. But I do not intend to bring even this in here as an explanation. For Eros is in reality much more strangely composed than in Plato's genealogical myth, and the erotic is in no way, as might be supposed, purely a compressing and unfolding of dialogue. Rather do I know no other realm where, as in this one (to be spoken of later), dialogue and monologue are so mingled and opposed. Many celebrated ecstasies of love are nothing but the lover's delight in the possibilities of his own person which are actualized in unexpected fulness.

I would rather think of something unpretentious yet significant—of the glances which strangers exchange in a busy street as they pass one another with unchanging pace. Some of these glances, though not charged with destiny, nevertheless reveal to one another two dialogical natures.

But I can really show what I have in mind only by events which open into a genuine change from communication to communion, that is, in an embodiment of the word of dialogue.

What I am here concerned with cannot be conveyed in ideas to a reader. But we may represent it by examples—provided that, where the matter is important, we do not eschew taking examples from the inmost recesses of the personal life. For where else should the like be found?

My friendship with one now dead arose in an incident that may be described, if you will, as a broken-off conversation. The date is Easter 1914. Some men from different European peoples had met in an undefined presentiment of the catastrophe, in order to make preparations for an attempt to establish a supra-national authority. The conversations were marked by that unreserve, whose substance and fruitfulness I have scarcely ever experienced so strongly. It had such an effect on all who took part that the fictitious fell away and every word was an actuality. Then as we discussed the composition of the larger circle from which public initiative should proceed (it was decided that it should meet in August of the same year) one of us, a man of passionate concentration and judicial power of love, raised the consideration that too many Jews had been nominated, so that several countries would be represented in unseemly proportion by their Jews. Though similar reflections were not foreign to my own mind, since I hold that Jewry can gain an effective and more than merely stimulating share in the building of a steadfast world of peace only in its own community and not in scattered members, they seemed to me, expressed in this way, to be tainted in their justice. Obstinate Jew that I am, I protested against the protest. I no longer know how from that I came to speak of Jesus and to say that we Jews knew him from within, in the impulses and stirrings of his Jewish being, in a way that remains inaccessible to the peoples submissive to him. "In a way that remains inaccessible to you"—so I directly addressed the former clergyman. He stood up, I too stood, we looked into the heart of one another's eyes. "It is gone," he said, and before everyone we gave one another the kiss of brotherhood.

The discussion of the situation between Jews and Christians had been transformed into a bond between the Christian and the Jew. In this transformation dialogue was fulfilled. Opinions were gone, in a bodily way the factual took place.

Disputations in Religion

Here I expect two objections, one weighty and one powerful.

One argument against me takes this form. When it is a question of essential views, of views concerning *Weltanschauung,* the conversation *must* not be broken off in such a way. Each must expose himself wholly, in a real way, in his humanly unavoidable partiality, and thereby experience himself in a real way as limited by the other, so that the two suffer together the destiny of our conditioned nature and meet one another in it.

To this I answer that the experience of being limited is included in what I refer to; but so too is the experience of overcoming it together. This cannot be completed on the level of *Weltanschauung,* but on that of reality. Neither needs to give up his point of view; only, in that unexpectedly they do something and unexpectedly something happens to them which is called a covenant, they enter a realm where the law of the point of view no longer holds. They too suffer the destiny of our conditioned nature, but they honour it most highly when, as is permitted to us, they let themselves run free of it for an immortal moment. They had already met one another when each in his soul so turned to the other that from then on, making him present, he spoke really to and towards him.

The other objection, which comes from a quite different, in fact from the opposite, side is to the effect that this may be true so far as the province of the point of view reaches, but it ceases to be true for a confession of faith. Two believers in conflict about their doctrines are concerned with the execution of the divine will, not with a fleeting personal agreement. For the man who is so related to his faith that he is able to die or to slay for it there can be no realm where the law of the faith ceases to hold. It is laid on him to help truth to victory, he does not let himself be misled by sentiments. The man holding a different, that is a false, belief must be converted, or at least instructed; direct contact with him can be achieved only outside the advocacy of the faith, it cannot proceed from it. The thesis of religious disputation cannot be allowed to "go."

This objection derives its power from its indifference to the non-binding character of the relativized spirit—a character which is accepted as a matter of course. I can answer it adequately only by a confession.

I have not the possibility of judging Luther, who refused fellowship with Zwingli in Marburg, or Calvin who furthered the death of Servetus. For Luther and Calvin believe that the Word of God has so descended among men that it can be clearly known and must therefore be exclusively advocated. I do not believe that; the Word of God crosses my vision like a falling star to whose fire the meteorite will bear witness without making it light up for me, and I myself can only bear witness to the light but not produce the stone and say "This is it." But this difference of faith is by no means to be understood merely as a subjective one. It is not based on the fact that we who live to-day are weak in faith, and it will remain even if our faith is ever so much strengthened. The situation of the world itself, in the most serious sense, more precisely the relation between God and man, has changed. And this change is certainly not comprehended in its essence by our thinking only of the darkening, so familiar to us, of the supreme light, only of the night of our being, empty of revelation. It is the night of an expectation—not of a vague hope, but of an expectation. We expect a theophany of which we know nothing but the place, and the place is called community. In the public catacombs of this expectation there is no single God's Word which can be clearly known and advocated, but the words delivered are clarified for us in our human situation of being turned to one another. There is no obedience to the coming one without loyalty to his creature. To have experienced this is our way.

A time of genuine religious conversations is beginning—not those so-called but fictitious conversations where none regarded and addressed his partner in reality, but genuine dialogues, speech from certainty to certainty, but also from one open-hearted person to another open-hearted person. Only then will genuine common life appear, not that of an identical content of faith which is alleged to be found in all religions, but that of the situation, of anguish and of expectation.

Setting of the Question

The life of dialogue is not limited to men's traffic with one another; it is, it has shown itself to be, a relation of men to one another that is only represented in their traffic.

Accordingly, even if speech and communication may be dispensed with, the life of dialogue seems, from what we may perceive, to have inextricably joined to it as its minimum constitution one thing, the mutuality of the inner action. Two men bound together in dialogue must obviously be turned to one another, they must therefore—no matter with what measure of activity or indeed of consciousness of activity—have turned to one another.

It is good to put this forward so crudely and formally. For behind the formulating question about the limits of a category under discussion is hidden a question which bursts all formulas asunder.

Observing, Looking On, Becoming Aware

We may distinguish three ways in which we are able to perceive a man who is living before our eyes. (I am not thinking of an object of scientific knowledge, of which I do not speak here.) The object of our perception does not need to know of us, of our being there. It does not matter at this point whether he stands in a relation or has a standpoint towards the perceiver.

The *observer* is wholly intent on fixing the observed man in his mind, on "noting" him. He probes him and writes him up. That is, he is diligent to write up as many "traits" as possible. He lies in wait for them, that none may escape him. The object consists of traits, and it is known what lies behind each of them. Knowledge of the human system of expression constantly incorporates in the instant the newly appearing individual variations, and remains applicable. A face is nothing but physiognomy, movements nothing but gestures of expression.

The *onlooker* is not at all intent. He takes up the position which lets him see the object freely, and undisturbed awaits what will be presented to him. Only at the beginning may he be ruled by purpose, everything beyond that is involuntary. He does not go around taking notes indiscriminately, he lets himself go, he is not in the least afraid of forgetting something ("Forgetting is good," he says). He gives his memory no tasks, he trusts its organic work which preserves what is worth preserving. He does not lead in the grass as green fodder, as the observer does; he turns it and lets the sun shine on it. He pays no attention to traits ("Traits lead astray," he says). What stands out for him from the object is what is not "character" and not "expression" ("The interesting is not important," he says). All great artists have been onlookers.

But there is a perception of a decisively different kind.

The onlooker and the observer are similarly orientated, in that they have a position, namely, the very desire to perceive the man who is living before our eyes. Moreover, this man is for them an object separated from themselves and their personal life, who can in fact for this sole reason be "properly" perceived. Consequently what they experience in this way, whether it is, as with the observer, a sum of traits, or, as with the onlooker, an existence, neither demands action from them nor inflicts destiny on them. But rather the whole is given over to the aloof fields of aesthesis.

It is a different matter when in a receptive hour of my personal life a man meets me about whom there is something, which I cannot grasp in any objective way at all, that "says something" to me. That does not mean, says to me what manner of man this is, what is going on in him, and the like. But it means, says something *to me*, addresses something to me, speaks something that enters my own life. It can be something about this man, for instance that he needs me. But it can also be something about myself. The man himself in his relation to me has nothing to do with what is said. He has no relation to me, he has indeed not noticed me at all. It is not he who says it to me, as that solitary man silently confessed his secret to his neighbour on the seat; but *it* says it.

To understand "say" as a metaphor is not to understand. The phrase "that doesn't say a thing to me" is an outworn metaphor; but the saying I am referring to is real speech. In the house of speech are many mansions, and this is one of the inner.

The effect of having this said to me is completely different from that of looking on and observing. I cannot depict or denote or describe the man in whom, through whom, something has been said to me. Were I to attempt it, that would be the end of saying. This man is not my object; I have got to do with him. Perhaps I have to accomplish something about him; but perhaps I have only to learn something, and it is only a matter of my "accepting." It may be that I have to answer at once, to this very man before me; it may be that the saying has a long and manifold transmission before it, and that I am to answer some other person at some other time and place, in who knows what kind of speech, and that it is now only a matter of taking the answering on myself. But in each instance a word demanding an answer has happened to me.

We may term this way of perception *becoming aware*.

It by no means needs to be a man of whom I become aware. It can be an animal, a plant, a stone. No kind of appearance or event is fundamentally excluded from the series of the things through which from time to time something is said to me. Nothing can refuse to be the vessel for the Word. The limits of the possibility of dialogue are the limits of awareness.

The Signs

Each of us is encased in an armour whose task is to ward off signs. Signs happen to us without respite, living means being addressed, we would need only to present ourselves and to perceive. But the risk is too dangerous for us, the soundless thunderings seem to threaten us with annihilation, and from generation to generation we perfect the defence apparatus. All our knowledge assures us, "Be calm, everything happens as it must happen, but nothing is directed at you, you are not meant; it is just 'the world,' you can experience it as you like, but whatever you make of it in yourself proceeds from you alone, nothing is required of you, you are not addressed, all is quiet."

Each of us is encased in an armour which we soon, out of familiarity, no longer notice. There are only moments which penetrate it and stir the soul to sensibility. And when such a moment has imposed itself on us and we then take notice and ask ourselves, "Has anything particular taken place? Was it not of the kind I meet every day?" then we may reply to ourselves, "Nothing particular, indeed, it is like this every day, only we are not there every day."

The signs of address are not something extraordinary, something that steps out of the order of things, they are just what goes on time and again, just what goes on in any case, nothing is added by the address. The waves of the aether roar on always, but for most of the time we have turned off our receivers.

What occurs to me addresses me. In what occurs to me the world-happening addresses me. Only by sterilizing it, removing the seed of address from it, can I take what occurs to me as a part of the world-happening which does not refer to me. The interlocking sterilized system into which all this only needs to be dovetailed is man's titanic work. Mankind has pressed speech too into the service of this work.

From out of this tower of the ages the objection will be levelled against me, if some of its doorkeepers should pay any attention to such trains of thought, that it is nothing but a variety of primitive superstition to hold that cosmic and telluric happenings have for the life of the human person a direct meaning that can be grasped. For instead of understanding an event physically, biologically, sociologically (for which I, inclined as I always have been to admire genuine acts of research, think a great deal, when those who carry them out only know what they are doing and do not lose sight of the limits of the realm in which they are moving), these keepers say, an attempt is being made to get behind the event's alleged significance, and for this there is no place in a reasonable world continuum of space and time.

Thus, then, unexpectedly I seem to have fallen into the company of the augurs, of whom, as is well-known, there are remarkable modern varieties.

But whether they haruspicate or cast a horoscope their signs have this peculiarity that they are in a dictionary, even if not necessarily a written one. It does not matter how esoteric the information that is handed down: he who searches out the signs is *well up in* what life's juncture this or that sign means. Nor does it matter that special difficulties of separation and combination are created by the meeting of several signs of different kinds. For you can "look it up in the dictionary." The common signature of all this business is that it is for all time: things remain the same, they are discovered once for all, rules, laws, and analogical conclusions may be employed throughout. What is commonly termed superstition, that is, perverse faith, appears to me rather as perverse knowledge.[1] From "superstition" about the number 13 an unbroken ladder leads into the dizziest heights of gnosis. This is not even the aping of a real faith.

Real faith—if I may so term presenting ourselves and perceiving—begins when the dictionary is put down, when you are done with it. What occurs to me says something to me, but what it says to me cannot be revealed by any esoteric information; for it has never been said before nor is it composed of sounds that have ever been said. It can neither be interpreted nor translated, I can have it neither explained nor displayed; it is not a *what* at all, it is said into my very life; it is no experience that can be remembered independently of the situation, it remains the address of that moment and cannot be isolated, it remains the question of a questioner and will have its answer.

(It remains the question. For that is the other great contrast between all the business of interpreting signs and the speech of signs which I mean here: this speech never gives information or appeasement.)

Faith stands in the stream of "happening but once" which is spanned by knowledge. All the emergency structures of analogy and typology are indispensable for the work of the human spirit, but to step on them when the question of the questioner steps up to you, to me, would be running away. Lived life is tested and fulfilled in the stream alone.

With all deference to the world continuum of space and time I know as a living truth only concrete world reality which is constantly, in every moment, reached out to me. I can separate it into its component parts, I can compare them and distribute them into groups of similar phenomena, I can derive them from earlier and reduce them to simpler phenomena; and when I have done all this I have not touched my concrete world reality. Inseparable, incomparable, irreducible, now, happening once only, it gazes upon me with a horrifying look. So in Stravinsky's ballet the director of the wandering marionette show wants to point out to the people at the annual fair that a pierrot who terrified them is nothing but a wisp of straw in clothes: he tears it asunder—and collapses, gibbering, for on the roof of the booth the *living* Petrouchka sits and laughs at him.

The true name of concrete reality is the creation which is entrusted to me and to every man. In it the signs of address are given to us.

A Conversion

In my earlier years the "religious" was for me the exception. There were hours that were taken out of the course of things. From somewhere or other the firm crust of everyday was pierced. Then the reliable perma-

nence of appearances broke down; the attack which took place burst its
law asunder. "Religious experience" was the experience of an otherness
which did not fit into the context of life. It could begin with something
customary, with consideration of some familiar object, but which then
became unexpectedly mysterious and uncanny, finally lighting a way
into the lightning-pierced darkness of the mystery itself. But also, without any intermediate stage, time could be torn apart—first the firm
world's structure then the still firmer self-assurance flew apart and you
were delivered to fulness. The "religious" lifted you out. Over there now
lay the accustomed existence with its affairs, but here illumination and
ecstasy and rapture held without time or sequence. Thus your own
being encompassed a life here and a life beyond, and there was no bond
but the actual moment of the transition.

The illegitimacy of such a division of the temporal life, which is
streaming to death and eternity and which only in fulfilling its tem-
porality can be fulfilled in face of these, was brought home to me by an
everyday event, an event of judgment, judging with that sentence from
closed lips and an unmoved glance such as the ongoing course of things
loves to pronounce.

What happened was no more than that one forenoon, after a morning of "religious" enthusiasm, I had a visit from an unknown young
man, without being there in spirit. I certainly did not fail to let the meeting be friendly, I did not treat him any more remissly than all his contemporaries who were in the habit of seeking me out about this time of day
as an oracle that is ready to listen to reason. I conversed attentively and
openly with him—only I omitted to guess the questions which he did
not put. Later, not long after, I learned from one of his friends—he himself was no longer alive—the essential content of these questions; I
learned that he had come to me not casually, but borne by destiny, not
for a chat but for a decision. He had come to me, he had come in this
hour. What do we expect when we are in despair and yet go to a man?
Surely a presence by means of which we are told that nevertheless there
is meaning.

Since then I have given up the "religious" which is nothing but the
exception, extraction, exaltation, ecstasy; or it has given me up. I possess
nothing but the everyday out of which I am never taken. The mystery is
no longer disclosed, it has escaped or it has made its dwelling here where
everything happens as it happens. I know no fulness but each mortal
hour's fulness of claim and responsibility. Though far from being equal
to it, yet I know that in the claim I am claimed and may respond in responsibility, and know who speaks and demands a response.

I do not know much more. If that is religion then it is just *everything,* simply all that is lived in its possibility of dialogue. Here is space also for religion's highest forms. As when you pray you do not thereby remove yourself from this life of yours but in your praying refer your thought to it, even though it may be in order to yield it; so too in the unprecedented and surprising, when you are called upon from above, required, chosen, empowered, sent, you with this your mortal bit of life are referred to, this moment is not extracted from it, it rests on what has been and beckons to the remainder which has still to be lived, you are not swallowed up in a fulness without obligation, you are willed for the life of communion.

Who Speaks?

In the signs of life which happens to us we are addressed. Who speaks?

It would not avail us to give for reply the word "God," if we do not give it out of that decisive hour of personal existence when we had to forget everything we imagined we knew of God, when we dared to keep nothing handed down or learned or self-contrived, no shred of knowledge, and were plunged into the night.

When we rise out of it into the new life and there begin to receive the signs, what can we know of that which—of him who gives them to us? Only what we experience from time to time from the signs themselves. If we name the speaker of this speech God, then it is always the God of a moment, a moment God.

I will now use a *gauche* comparison, since I know no right one.

When we really understand a poem, all we know of the poet is what we learn of him in the poem—no biographical wisdom is of value for the pure understanding of what is to be understood: the *I* which approaches us is the subject of this single poem. But when we read other poems by the poet in the same true way their subjects combine in all their multiplicity, completing and confirming one another, to form the one polyphony of the person's existence.

In such a way, out of the givers of the signs, the speakers of the words in lived life, out of the moment Gods there arises for us with a single identity the Lord of the voice, the One.

Above and Below

Above and below are bound to one another. The word of him who wishes to speak with men without speaking with God is not fulfilled; but the word of him who wishes to speak with God without speaking with men goes astray.

There is a tale that a man inspired by God once went out from the creaturely realms into the vast waste. There he wandered till he came to the gates of the mystery. He knocked. From within came the cry: "What do you want here?" He said, "I have proclaimed your praise in the ears of mortals, but they were deaf to me. So I come to you that you yourself may hear me and reply." "Turn back," came the cry from within. "Here is no ear for you. I have sunk my hearing in the deafness of mortals."

True address from God directs man into the place of lived speech, where the voices of the creatures grope past one another, and in their very missing of one another succeed in reaching the eternal partner.

Responsibility

The idea of responsibility is to be brought back from the province of specialized ethics, of an "ought" that swings free in the air, into that of lived life. Genuine responsibility exists only where there is real responding.

Responding to what?

To what happens to one, to what is to be seen and heard and felt. Each concrete hour allotted to the person, with its content drawn from the world and from destiny, is speech for the man who is attentive. Attentive, for no more than that is needed in order to make a beginning with the reading of the signs that are given to you. For that very reason, as I have already indicated, the whole apparatus of our civilization is necessary to preserve men from this attentiveness and its consequences. For the attentive man would no longer, as his custom is, "master" the situation the very moment after it stepped up to him: it would be laid upon him to go up to and into it. Moreover, nothing that he believed he possessed as always available would help him, no knowledge and no technique, no system and no programme; for now he would have to do with what cannot be classified, with concretion itself. This speech has no alphabet, each of its sounds is a new creation and only to be grasped as such.

It will, then, be expected of the attentive man that he faces creation as it happens. It happens as speech, and not as speech rushing out over his head but as speech directed precisely at him. And if one were to ask another if he too heard and he said he did, they would have agreed only about an experiencing and not about something experienced.

But the sounds of which the speech consists—I repeat it in order to remove the misunderstanding, which is perhaps still possible, that I referred to something extraordinary and larger than life—are the events of the personal everyday life. In them, as they now are, "great" or "small," we are addressed, and those which count as great, yield no greater signs than the others.

Our attitude, however, is not yet decided through our becoming aware of the signs. We can still wrap silence about us—a reply characteristic of a significant type of the age—or we can step aside into the accustomed way; although both times we carry away a wound that is not to be forgotten in any productivity or any narcotism. Yet it can happen that we venture to respond, stammering perhaps—the soul is but rarely able to attain to surer articulation—but it is an honest stammering, as when sense and throat are united about what is to be said, but the throat is too horrified at it to utter purely the already composed sense. The words of our response are spoken in the speech, untranslatable like the address, of doing and letting—whereby the doing may behave like a letting and the letting like a doing. What we say in this way with the being is our entering upon the situation, into the situation, which has at this moment stepped up to us, whose appearance we did not and could not know, for its like has not yet been.

Nor are we now finished with it, we have to give up that expectation: a situation of which we have become aware is never finished with, but we subdue it into the substance of lived life. Only then, true to the moment, do we experience a life that is something other than a sum of moments. We respond to the moment, but at the same time we respond on its behalf, we answer for it. A newly-created concrete reality has been laid in our arms; we answer for it. A dog has looked at you, you answer for its glance, a child has clutched your hand, you answer for its touch, a host of men moves above you, you answer for their need.[2]

Morality and Religion

Responsibility which does not respond to a word is a metaphor of morality. Factually, responsibility only exists when the court is there to which I am responsible, and "self-responsibility" has reality only when the "self" to which I am responsible becomes transparent into the absolute. But he who practises real responsibility in the life of dialogue does not need to name the speaker of the word to which he is responding—he knows him in the word's substance which presses on and in, assuming the cadence of an inwardness, and stirs him in his heart of hearts. A man can ward off with all his strength the belief that "God" is there, and he tastes him in the strict sacrament of dialogue.

Yet let it not be supposed that I make morality questionable in order to glorify religion. Religion, certainly, has this advantage over morality, that it is a phenomenon and not a postulate, and further that it is able to include composure as well as determination. The reality of morality, the demand of the demander, has a place in religion, but the reality of religion, the unconditioned being of the demander, has no place in morality. Nevertheless, when religion does itself justice and asserts itself, it is much more dubious than morality, just because it is more actual and inclusive. Religion as risk, which is ready to give itself up, is the nourishing stream of the arteries; as system, possessing, assured and assuring, religion which believes in religion is the veins' blood, which ceases to circulate. And if there is nothing that can so hide the face of our fellowman as morality can, religion can hide from us as nothing else can the face of God. Principle there, dogma here, I appreciate the "objective" compactness of dogma, but behind both there lies in wait the—profane or holy—war against the situation's power of dialogue, there lies in wait the "once-for-all" which resists the unforeseeable moment. Dogma, even when its claim of origin remains uncontested, has become the most exalted form of invulnerability against revelation. Revelation will tolerate no perfect tense, but man with the arts of his craze for security props it up to perfectedness.

Notes

Dialogue

1. There is a typical example here, which could be multiplied many times, of a play of words in the German which cannot be reproduced in the English. "This is not superstition (*Aberglaube*), but perverse knowledge (*Aberwissen*)." And of course this is more than a *play* of words, since this perverse knowledge leads direct to gnosis, which is very different from the theme, faith.—Trans. Note.

2. The significance of *responsibility* (and the point of the whole section, indeed of the whole of *Dialogue*) is brought out more acutely in the German than in the English. *Wort, Antwort, antworten, verantworten,* etc., are part of a closely interrelated situation in which speech and response, answering for and being responsible for, and so on, are more intimately connected than the English version can hope to show. If the reader will remember that "responsibility" carries in itself the root sense of being "answerable," then the significance of the "word" in actual life will not be lost. Buber's teaching about the "word" always carries a strict reference to "lived life," and is very far from being an abstraction, theological or other.—Trans. Note.

2

The Social Dimensions of Man

Distance and Relation*

1

The question I wish to raise is that of the principle of human life, that is, its beginning.

This cannot be thought of here as a beginning in time. It is not sensible to try to discover when and how a certain species of life, instead of being content like the rest with the perception of things and conditions, began to perceive its own perceiving as well. The only way is to consider, in all its paradox and actuality, the category of being characterized by the name of man, in order to experience its ground and its beginning.

It would be quite wrong to make the reality of the spirit the starting point of the question. The one way to expose the principle of a being is first to contrast its reality with that of other known beings. But the reality of the spirit is not given to us apart from man: all the spiritual life which is given to us has its reality in him. Nature alone presents itself to us for this act of contrasting—nature which certainly includes man but which, as soon as we penetrate to his essentiality, is compelled to loosen its grasp and even to relinquish for our separate consideration this child which from its standpoint is an aberration. This separate consideration takes place thereafter not within nature, but starts from nature.

Starting from nature—that is, in this case, starting from the association of "living beings" to which man, so far as he is a part of nature, must be reckoned as belonging—does not mean noting those characteristics which distinguish man from the others, but it means examining the ground of being of those characteristics as a whole. Only in this way shall we learn both the fact and the reason for the fact that those distinguishing characteristics as a whole constitute not only a special group of beings but a special way of being, and thus constitute a special category of being. The act of contrasting, carried out properly and adequately, leads to the grasp of the principle.

*Reprinted from *The Knowledge of Man*, trans. Ronald Gregor Smith (London: George Allen and Unwin, Ltd., 1965), pp. 59–71.

57

In this way we reach the insight that the principle of human life is not simple but twofold, being built up in a twofold movement which is of such kind that the one movement is the presupposition of the other. I propose to call the first movement "the primal setting at a distance" and the second "entering into relation." That the first movement is the presupposition of the other is plain from the fact that one can enter into relation only with being which has been set at a distance, more precisely, has become an independent opposite. And it is only for man that an independent opposite exists.

The double principle cannot be demonstrated in the first instance in man's "inner life," but in the great phenomena of his connection with an otherness which is constituted as otherness by the event of "distancing." When the principle has been demonstrated in this way its working out in the inner life of the human person will become clear.

Modern biology speaks of an animal's environment (*Umwelt*), by which is understood the total world of objects accessible to its senses, as conditioned by the circumstances of life which are peculiar to this animal. An animal—something of this kind is said—perceives only the things which concern it in the total situation available to it, and it is those things which make its world (*Umwelt*). But it seems questionable whether the concept of a world is rightly used here, whether we are justified in regarding the context described as an environment as a kind of world, and not simply as a kind of realm. For by "world" we must mean that which is extended substantially beyond the realm of the observer who is *in* the world and as such is independent. Even a "world of the senses" is a world through being composed not of sense data alone, but through what is perceived being completed by what can be perceived, and it is the unity of these two which constitutes the proper "world" of the senses. An animal's organism gathers, continuously or continually, the elements which meet the necessities and wants of its life, in order to construct from them the circle of its existence. Wherever swallows or tunny wander, their bodily being (*Leiblichkeit*) carries out this selection from "nature," which as such is completely unknown to them, and on which they in turn have an effect, again as on something which they neither know nor can know. An animal's "image of the world," or rather, its image of a realm, is nothing more than the dynamic of the presences bound up with one another by bodily memory to the extent required by the functions of life which are to be carried out. This image depends on, it clings to, the animal's activities.

It is only man who replaces this unsteady conglomeration, whose constitution is suited to the lifetime of the individual organism, by a unity which can be imagined or thought by him as existing for itself.

With soaring power he reaches out beyond what is given him, flies beyond the horizon and the familiar stars, and grasps a totality. With him, with his human life, a world exists. The meeting of natural being with the living creature produces those more or less changing masses of usable sense data which constitute the animal's realm of life. But only from the meeting of natural being with man does the new and enduring arise, that which comprehends and infinitely transcends the realm. An animal in the realm of its perceptions is like a fruit in its skin; man is, or can be, in the world as a dweller in an enormous building which is always being added to, and to whose limits he can never penetrate, but which he can nevertheless know as one does know a house in which one lives—for he is capable of grasping the wholeness of the building as such. Man is like this because he is the creature (*Wesen*) through whose being (*Sein*) "what is" (*das Seiende*) becomes detached from him, and recognized for itself. It is only the realm which is removed, lifted out from sheer presence, withdrawn from the operation of needs and wants, set at a distance and thereby given over to itself, which is more and other than a realm. Only when a structure of being is independently over against a living being (*Seiende*), an independent opposite, does a world exist.

The view could be put forward that this giving of independence to a world is the result of agelong developments of mankind, and that it can therefore not be constitutive of man as such. But it cannot concern us when and how the category of man has been realized; our concern is its ground. When a world exists, and to the extent to which it exists, there exists the man who conditions it, and he is there not in the sense of a species of living creatures, but of a category which has moved into reality. No matter where you meet man on his way, he always holds over against himself to some degree, in some way, that which he does not know as well as that which he knows, bound up together in one world, however "primitive." This is of course true of his connection with time no less than of his connection with space. An animal's actions are concerned with its future and the future of its young, but only man imagines the future: the beaver's dam is extended in a time-realm, but the planted tree is rooted in the world of time, and he who plants the first tree is he who will expect the Messiah.

Now the second movement has been added to the first: Man turns to the withdrawn structure of being (*Seiende*) and enters into relation with it. "First" and "second" are not to be taken in the sense of a temporal succession; it is not possible to think of an existence over against a world which is not also an attitude to it as a world, and that means the outline of an attitude of relation. This is to say no more than that an animal does not know the state of relation because one cannot stand in a relation to something that is not perceived as contrasted and existing for itself. The rainmaker who deals with the cloud that is sailing up beyond the orbit of his sight acts within the same category as the physicist who has worked out the existence of the still unseen planet, and communicates with it at his desk.

We may characterize the act and the work of entering into relation with the world as such—and, therefore, not with parts of it, and not with the sum of its parts, but with it as the world—as synthesizing apperception, by which we establish that this pregnant use of the concept involves the function of unity: by synthesizing apperception I mean the apperception of a being as a whole and as a unity. Such a view is won, and won again and again, only by looking upon the world as a world. The conception of wholeness and unity is in its origin identical with the conception of the world to which man is turned. He who turns to the realm which he has removed from himself, and which has been completed and transformed into a world—he who turns to the world and looking upon it steps into relation with it, becomes aware of wholeness and unity in such a way that from then on he is able to grasp being as a wholeness and a unity; the single being has received the character of wholeness and the unity which are perceived in it from the wholeness and unity perceived in the world. But a man does not obtain this view simply from the "setting at a distance" and "making independent." These would offer him the world only as an object, as which it is only an aggregate of qualities that can be added to at will, not a genuine wholeness and unity. Only the view of what is over against me in the world in its full presence, with which I have set myself, present in my whole person, in relation—only this view gives me the world truly as whole and one. For only in such an opposition are the realm of man and what completes it in spirit, finally one. So it has always been, and so it is in this hour.

What has been indicated here must not be misunderstood as meaning that I "establish" the world, or the like. Man's act of setting at a distance is no more to be understood as primary than his act of relation which is bound up with it. Rather is this the peculiarity of human life, that here and here alone a being has arisen from the whole, endowed and entitled to detach the whole as a world from himself and to make it an opposite to himself, instead of cutting out with his senses the part he needs from it, as all other beings do, and being content with that. This endowment and this entitlement of man produce, out of the whole, the being of the world, and this being can only mean that it is there for man as something that is for itself, with which he is able to enter into relation.

We must now look afresh at the twofold nature of the principle. Though the two movements are bound together in it very closely and with many strands, yet they are not to be understood as just two aspects of the same event or process. There is no kind of parallelism here, nothing that would make the carrying out of the one movement bring about the carrying out of the other. Rather it must be firmly maintained that the first creates the presupposition for the second—not its source, but its presupposition. With the appearance of the first, therefore, nothing more than room for the second is given. It is only at this point that the real history of the spirit begins, and this history takes its eternal rise in the extent to which the second movement shares in the intimations of the first, to the extent of their mutual interaction, reaction, and co-operation. Man can set at a distance without coming into real relation with what has been set at a distance. He can fill the act of setting at a distance with the will to relation, relation having been made possible only by that act; he can accomplish the act of relation in the acknowledgment of the fundamental actuality of the distance. But the two movements can also contend with one another, each seeing in the other the obstacle to its own realization. And finally, in moments and forms of grace, unity can arise from the extreme tension of the contradiction as the overcoming of it, which is granted only now and in this way.

2

He who, with his eyes on the twofold principle of human life, attempts to trace the spirit's course in history must note that the great phenomena on the side of acts of distance are preponderantly universal, and those on the side of acts of relation preponderantly personal, as indeed corresponds to their connection with one another. The facts of the movement of distance yield the essential answer to the question, How is man possible; the facts of the movement of relation yield the essential answer to the question, How is human life realized. The first question is strictly one about category; the second is one of category and history. Distance provides the human situation; relation provides man's becoming in that situation.

This difference can be seen in two spheres, within the connection with things and within the connection with one's fellow men.

An animal also makes use of things. In fact it is in animals that we can observe using in the exact sense, when they turn something, on which they happen, round and round until they reach the possibility of using it for the attainment of a definite purpose, whether preconceived or arising at that moment. Monkeys make use of a stick they have found in order to force an opening which they could not have made with the arm, they make use of a stone to crack nuts. But they do not set aside any of these things, which for the moment have become tools, in order to use them the next day in a similar fashion; clearly none of them persists in their consciousness as a thing in which the faculty of the lever or the hammer dwells. These things are to hand, as occasion arises, in their realm; they never receive their place in a world. Only man, as man, gives distance to things which he comes upon in his realm; he sets them in their independence as things which from now on continue to exist ready for a function and which he can make wait for him so that on each occasion he may master them again, and bring them into action. A suitable piece of metal which has once been used as an auger does not cease to be an auger: it persists in the quality which has now been made known, this very piece of metal, this specific It with its known capacity now persists there; it is at one's disposal. Every change made in the stuff of things which is intended to make them more suitable for fulfilling a purpose, every strengthening and refining, every differentiation and combination, every technique is built on this elementary basis—that a person sets aside something which he finds, and makes it into something for itself, in which state, however, having become a tool, it can always be found again, and always as this same tool ready to carry out this same work. A monkey can swing the branch of a tree as a weapon; but man alone is capable of providing the branch with a separate existence, in that it is thenceforth established as a "weapon" and awaits man's pleasure to be used again. Whatever is done to it after that to shape it into a proper cudgel, there is no further essential change: technique only fulfils what has been given by the primary choice and assignment, by a primary nomos.

But now something new and essentially different can enter the situation.

Let us think of a tribe which is close to nature, and which already knows the axe, a simple but reliable stone-axe. Then it occurs to a lad to scratch a curved line on his axe with the aid of a sharper stone. This is a picture of something and of nothing: it may be a sign, but even its author does not know of what. What was in his mind? Magic—to give the tool a more powerful effect? Or simply a play with the possibility presented by the empty space on the shaft? The two things are not mutually exclusive, but they mingle—the magical intention concentrates the play in more solid forms, the free play loosens the form decided on by magic and changes it—but even together these do not suffice to explain the unheard-of fact that a work has been carried out without any model, reaching beyond the technical purpose. We have to turn to the principle of human life in its twofold character in order to establish what has happened. Man sets things which he uses at a distance, he gives them into an independence in which function gains duration, he reduces and empowers them to be the bearers of the function. In this way the first movement of the principle is satisfied, but the second is not. Man has a great desire to enter into personal relation with things and to imprint on them his relation to them. To use them, even to possess them, is not enough, they must become his in another way, by imparting to them in the picture-sign his relation to them.

But the picture-sign grows to be a picture; it ceases to be accessory to a tool and becomes an independent structure. The form indicated by even the clumsiest ornament is now fulfilled in an autonomous region as the sediment of man's relation to things. Art is neither the impression of natural objectivity nor the expression of spiritual subjectivity, but it is the work and witness of the relation between the *substantia humana* and the *substantia rerum*, it is the realm of "the between" which has become a form. Consider great nude sculptures of the ages: None of them is to be understood properly either from the givenness of the human body or from the will to expression of an inner state, but solely from the relational event which takes place between two entities which have gone apart from one another, the withdrawn "body" and the withdrawing "soul." In each of the arts there is something specifically corresponding to the relational character to be found in the picture. Music, for example, can be understood in terms of categories only when it is recognized that music is the ever renewed discovering of tonal being in the movement of "distancing" and the releasing of this tonal being in the movement of relation by bodying it forth.

3

The twofold principle of human life can be still more fully clarified in men's relation to one another.

In an insect state the system of division of labour excludes not merely every variation, but also every granting of a function in the precise sense of an individual award. In human society at all its levels persons confirm one another in a practical way to some extent or other in their personal qualities and capacities, and a society may be termed human in the measure to which its members confirm one another. Apart from the technique of the tool and from the weapon, what has enabled this creature, so badly equipped "by nature," to assert himself and to achieve lordship of the earth is this dynamic, adaptable, pluralistic form of association,

which has been made possible by the factor of mutual individual completion of function and the corresponding factor of mutual individual
recognition of function. Within the most closely bound clan there still
exist free societies of fishers, free orders of barter, free associations of
many kinds, which are built upon acknowledged differences in capacity
and inclination. In the most rigid epochs of ancient kingdoms the family
preserved its separate structure, in which, despite its authoritative quality, individuals affirmed one another in their manifold nature. And everywhere the position of society is strengthened by this balance of
firmness and looseness. Man has always stood opposed to natural
powers as the creature equipped with the tool which awaits him in independence, who forms his associations of independent single lives. An
animal never succeeds in unravelling its companions from the knot of
their common life, just as it never succeeds in ascribing to the enemy an
existence beyond his hostility, that is, beyond its own realm. Man, as
man, sets man at a distance and makes him independent; he lets the life
of men like himself go on round about him, and so he, and he alone, is
able to enter into relation, in his own individual status, with those like
himself. The basis of man's life with man is twofold, and it is one—the
wish of every man to be confirmed as what he is, even as what he can
become, by men; and the innate capacity in man to confirm his fellow
men in this way. That this capacity lies so immeasurably fallow constitutes the real weakness and questionableness of the human race: actual humanity exists only where this capacity unfolds. On the other
hand, of course, an empty claim for confirmation, without devotion for
being and becoming, again and again mars the truth of the life between
man and man.

The great characteristic of men's life with one another, speech, is dou-
bly significant as a witness to the principle of human life. Men express
themselves to men in a way that is different, not in kind or degree but
essentially, from the way animals express themselves to their companions. Man and many animals have this in common, that they call out to
others; to speak to others is something essentially human, and is based
on the establishment and acknowledgment of the independent otherness of the other with whom one fosters relation, addressing and being
addressed on this very basis.[1] The oldest form of word, along with—
and perhaps even before—the "holophrastic" characterization of situations by means of words in the form of sentences, which signified the
situations for those who had to be informed, may have been the individual's name: when the name let the companion and helper at a distance
know that his presence, his and none other, was needed in a given situation. Both the holophrase and the name are still signals, yet also words;

for—and this is the second part of the witness of speech to the principle of human life—man sets also his calls at a distance and gives them independence, he stores them, like a tool he has prepared, as objects which are ready for use, he makes them into words which exist by themselves. Here in speech the addressing of another as it were cancels out, it is neutralized—but in order to come again and again to life, not indeed in those popular discussions which misuse the reality of speech, but in genuine conversation. If we ever reach the stage of making ourselves understood only by means of the dictograph, that is, without contact with one another, the chance of human growth would be indefinitely lost.

Genuine conversation, and therefore every actual fulfilment of relation between men, means acceptance of otherness. When two men inform one another of their basically different views about an object, each aiming to convince the other of the rightness of his own way of looking at the matter, everything depends so far as human life is concerned, on whether each thinks of the other as the one he is, whether each, that is, with all his desire to influence the other, nevertheless unreservedly accepts and confirms him in his being this man and in his being made in this particular way. The strictness and depth of human individuation, the elemental otherness of the other, is then not merely noted as the necessary starting point, but is affirmed from the one being to the other. The desire to influence the other then does not mean the effort to change the other, to inject one's own "rightness" into him; but it means the effort to let that which is recognized as right, as just, as true (and for that very reason must also be established there, in the substance of the other) through one's influence take seed and grow in the form suited to individuation. Opposed to this effort is the lust to make use of men by which the manipulator of "propaganda" and "suggestion" is possessed, in his relation to men remaining as in a relation to things, to things, moreover, with which he will never enter into relation, which he is indeed eager to rob of their distance and independence.

Human life and humanity come into being in genuine meetings. There man learns not merely that he is limited by man, cast upon his own finitude, partialness, need of completion, but his own relation to truth is heightened by the other's different relation to the same truth—different in accordance with his individuation, and destined to take seed and grow differently. Men need, and it is granted to them, to confirm one another in their individual being by means of genuine meetings. But beyond this they need, and it is granted to them, to see the truth, which the soul gains by its struggle, light up to the others, the brothers, in a different way, and even so be confirmed.

4

The realization of the principle in the sphere between men reaches its height in an event which may be called "making present." As a partial happening something of this is to be found wherever men come together, but in its essential formation I should say it appears only rarely. It rests on a capacity possessed to some extent by everyone, which may be described as "imagining" the real: I mean the capacity to hold before one's soul a reality arising at this moment but not able to be directly experienced. Applied to intercourse between men, "imagining" the real means that I imagine to myself what another man is at this very moment wishing, feeling, perceiving, thinking, and not as a detached content but in his very reality, that is, as a living process in this man. The full "making present" surpasses this in one decisive way: something of the character of what is imagined is joined to the act of imagining, that is, something of the character of an act of the will is added to my imagining of the other's act of will, and so on. So-called fellow feeling may serve as a familiar illustration of this if we leave vague sympathy out of consideration and limit the concept to that event in which I experience, let us say, the specific pain of another in such a way that I feel what is specific in it, not, therefore, a general discomfort or state of suffering, but this particular pain as the pain of the other. This making present increases until it is a paradox in the soul when I and the other are embraced by a common living situation, and (let us say) the pain which I inflict upon him surges up in myself, revealing the abyss of the contradictoriness of life between man and man. At such a moment something can come into being which cannot be built up in any other way.

The principle of human life which we have recognized suggests how making present may be understood in its ontological significance. Within the setting of the world at a distance and the making it independent, yet also essentially reaching beyond this and in the proper sense not able to be included in it, is the fact of man's himself being set at a distance and made independent as "the others." Our fellow men, it is true, live round about us as components of the independent world over against us, but in so far as we grasp each one as a human being he ceases to be a component and is there in his self-being as I am; his being at a distance does not exist merely for me, but it cannot be separated from the fact of my being at a distance for him. The first movement of human life puts men into mutual existence which is fundamental and even. But the second movement puts them into mutual relation with me which happens from time to time and by no means in an even way, but depends on our carrying it out. Relation is fulfilled in a full making present when

I think of the other not merely as this very one, but experience, in the particular approximation of the given moment, the experience belonging to him as this very one. Here and now for the first time does the other become a self for me, and the making independent of his being which was carried out in the first movement of distancing is shown in a new highly pregnant sense as a presupposition—a presupposition of this "becoming a self for me," which is, however, to be understood not in a psychological but in a strictly ontological sense, and should therefore rather be called "becoming a self with me." But it is ontologically complete only when the other knows that he is made present by me in his self and when this knowledge induces the process of his inmost self-becoming. For the inmost growth of the self is not accomplished, as people like to suppose today, in man's relation to himself, but in the relation between the one and the other, between men, that is, pre-eminently in the mutuality of the making present—in the making present of another self and in the knowledge that one is made present in his own self by the other—together with the mutuality of acceptance, of affirmation and confirmation.

Man wishes to be confirmed in his being by man, and wishes to have a presence in the being of the other. The human person needs confirmation because man as man needs it. An animal does not need to be confirmed, for it is what it is unquestionably. It is different with man: Sent forth from the natural domain of species into the hazard of the solitary category, surrounded by the air of a chaos which came into being with him, secretly and bashfully he watches for a Yes which allows him to be and which can come to him only from one human person to another. It is from one man to another that the heavenly bread of self-being is passed.

Elements of the Interhuman*

The Social and the Interhuman

It is usual to ascribe what takes place between men to the social realm, thereby blurring a basically important line of division between two essentially different areas of human life. I myself, when I began nearly fifty years ago to find my own bearings in the knowledge of society, making use of the then unknown concept of the interhuman,[1] made the same error. From that time it became increasingly clear to me that we have to do here with a separate category of our existence, even a separate dimension, to use a mathematical term, and one with which we are so familiar

---

*Reprinted from *The Knowledge of Man*, trans. Ronald Gregor Smith (London: George Allen and Unwin, Ltd., 1965), pp. 72–88.

that its peculiarity has hitherto almost escaped us. Yet insight into its peculiarity is extremely important not only for our thinking, but also for our living.

We may speak of social phenomena wherever the life of a number of men, lived with one another, bound up together, brings in its train shared experiences and reactions. But to be thus bound up together means only that each individual existence is enclosed and contained in a group existence. It does not mean that between one member and another of the group there exists any kind of personal relation. They do feel that they belong together in a way that is, so to speak, fundamentally different from every possible belonging together with someone outside the group. And there do arise, especially in the life of smaller groups, contacts which frequently favour the birth of individual relations, but, on the other hand, frequently make it more difficult. In no case, however, does membership in a group necessarily involve an existential relation between one member and another. It is true that there have been groups in history which included highly intensive and intimate relations between two of their members—as, for instance, in the homosexual relations among the Japanese Samurai or among Doric warriors—and these were countenanced for the sake of the stricter cohesion of the group. But in general it must be said that the leading elements in groups, especially in the later course of human history, have rather been inclined to suppress the personal relation in favour of the purely collective element. Where this latter element reigns alone or is predominant, men feel themselves to be carried by the collectivity, which lifts them out of loneliness and fear of the world and lostness. When this happens—and for modern man it is an essential happening—the life between person and person seems to retreat more and more before the advance of the collective. The collective aims at holding in check the inclination to personal life. It is as though those who are bound together in groups should in the main be concerned only with the work of the group and should turn to the personal partners, who are tolerated by the group, only in secondary meetings.

The difference between the two realms became very palpable to me on one occasion when I had joined the procession through a large town of a movement to which I did not belong. I did it out of sympathy for the tragic development which I sensed was at hand in the destiny of a friend who was one of the leaders of the movement. While the procession was forming, I conversed with him and with another, a goodhearted "wild man," who also had the mark of death upon him. At that moment I still felt that the two men really were there, over against me, each of them a man near to me, near even in what was most remote from me; so different from me that my soul continually suffered from this difference, yet by virtue of this very difference confronting me with authentic being. Then the formations started off, and after a short time I was lifted out of all confrontation, drawn into the procession, falling in with its aimless step; and it was obviously the very same for the two with whom I had just exchanged human words. After a while we passed a café where I had been sitting the previous day with a musician whom I knew only slightly. The very moment we passed it the door opened, the musician stood on the threshold, saw me, apparently saw me alone, and waved to me. Straightway it seemed to me as though I were taken out of the procession and of the presence of my marching friends, and set there, confronting the musician. I forgot that I was walking along with the same step; I felt that I was standing over there by the man who had called out to me, and without a word, with a smile of understanding, was answering him. When consciousness of the facts returned to me, the procession, with my companions and myself at its head, had left the café behind.

The realm of the interhuman goes far beyond that of sympathy. Such simple happenings can be part of it as, for instance, when two strangers exchange glances in a crowded streetcar, at once to sink back again into the convenient state of wishing to know nothing about each other. But also every casual encounter between opponents belongs to this realm, when it affects the opponent's attitude—that is, when something, however imperceptible, happens between the two, no matter whether it is marked at the time by any feeling or not. The only thing that matters is that for each of the two men the other happens as the particular other, that each becomes aware of the other and is thus related to him in such a way that he does not regard and use him as his object, but as his partner in a living event, even if it is no more than a boxing match. It is well known that some existentialists assert that the basic factor between men is that one is an object for the other. But so far as this is actually the case, the special reality of the interhuman, the fact of the contact, has been largely eliminated. It cannot indeed be entirely eliminated. As a crude example, take two men who are observing one another. The essential thing is not that the one makes the other his object, but the fact that he is not fully able to do so and the reason for his failure. We have in common with all existing beings that we can be made objects of observation. But it is my privilege as man that by the hidden activity of my being I can establish an impassable barrier to objectification. Only in partnership can my being be perceived as an existing whole.

The sociologist may object to any separation of the social and the interhuman on the ground that society is actually built upon human relations, and the theory of these relations is therefore to be regarded as the very foundation of sociology. But here an ambiguity in the concept "relation" becomes evident. We speak, for instance, of a comradely relation between two men in their work, and do not merely mean what happens between them as comrades, but also a lasting disposition which is actualized in those happenings and which even includes purely psychological events such as the recollection of the absent comrade. But by the sphere of the interhuman I mean solely actual happenings between men, whether wholly mutual or tending to grow into mutual relations. For the participation of both partners is in principle indispensable. The sphere of the interhuman is one in which a person is confronted by the other. We call its unfolding the dialogical.

In accordance with this, it is basically erroneous to try to understand the interhuman phenomena as psychological. When two men converse together, the psychological is certainly an important part of the situation, as each listens and each prepares to speak. Yet this is only the hidden accompaniment to the conversation itself, the phonetic event fraught with meaning, whose meaning is to be found neither in one of the two partners nor in both together, but only in their dialogue itself, in this "between" which they live together.

Being and Seeming

The essential problem of the sphere of the interhuman is the duality of being and seeming.

Although it is a familiar fact that men are often troubled about the impression they make on others, this has been much more discussed in moral philosophy than in anthropology. Yet this is one of the most important subjects for anthropological study.

We may distinguish between two different types of human existence. The one proceeds from what one really is, the other from what one wishes to seem. In general, the two are found mixed together. There have probably been few men who were entirely independent of the impression they made on others, while there has scarcely existed one who was exclusively determined by the impression made by him. We must be content to distinguish between men in whose essential attitude the one or the other predominates.

This distinction is most powerfully at work, as its nature indicates, in the interhuman realm—that is, in men's personal dealings with one another.

Take as the simplest and yet quite clear example the situation in which two persons look at one another—the first belonging to the first type, the second to the second. The one who lives from his being looks at the other just as one looks at someone with whom he has personal dealings. His look is "spontaneous," "without reserve"; of course he is not uninfluenced by the desire to make himself understood by the other, but he is uninfluenced by any thought of the idea of himself which he can or should awaken in the person whom he is looking at. His opposite is different. Since he is concerned with the image which his appearance, and especially his look or glance, produces in the other, he "makes" this look. With the help of the capacity, in greater or lesser degree peculiar to man, to make a definite element of his being appear in his look, he produces a look which is meant to have, and often enough does have, the effect of a spontaneous utterance—not only the utterance of a psychical event supposed to be taking place at that very moment, but also, as it were, the reflection of a personal life of such-and-such a kind.

This must, however, be carefully distinguished from another area of seeming whose ontological legitimacy cannot be doubted. I mean the realm of "genuine seeming," where a lad, for instance, imitates his heroic model and while he is doing so is seized by the actuality of heroism, or a man plays the part of a destiny and conjures up authentic destiny. In this situation there is nothing false; the imitation is genuine imitation and the part played is genuine; the mask, too, is a mask and no deceit. But where the semblance originates from the lie and is permeated by it, the interhuman is threatened in its very existence. It is not that someone utters a lie, falsifies some account. The lie I mean does not take place in relation to particular facts, but in relation to existence itself, and it attacks interhuman existence as such. There are times when a man, to satisfy some stale conceit, forfeits the great chance of a true happening between I and Thou.

Let us now imagine two men, whose life is dominated by appearance, sitting and talking together. Call them Peter and Paul. Let us list the different configurations which are involved. First, there is Peter as he wishes to appear to Paul, and Paul as he wishes to appear to Peter. Then there is Peter as he really appears to Paul, that is, Paul's image of Peter, which in general does not in the least coincide with what Peter wishes Paul to see; and similarly there is the reverse situation. Further, there is Peter as he appears to himself, and Paul as he appears to himself. Lastly, there are the bodily Peter and the bodily Paul. Two living beings and six ghostly appearances, which mingle in many ways in the conversation between the two. Where is there room for any genuine interhuman life?

Whatever the meaning of the word "truth" may be in other realms, in the interhuman realm it means that men communicate themselves to one another as what they are. It does not depend on one saying to the other everything that occurs to him, but only on his letting no seeming creep in between himself and the other. It does not depend on one letting himself go before another, but on his granting to the man to whom he communicates himself a share in his being. This is a question of the authenticity of the interhuman, and where this is not to be found, neither is the human element itself authentic.

Therefore, as we begin to recognize the crisis of man as the crisis of what is between man and man, we must free the concept of uprightness from the thin moralistic tones which cling to it, and let it take its tone from the concept of bodily uprightness. If a presupposition of human life in primeval times is given in man's walking upright, the fulfillment of human life can only come through the soul's walking upright, through the great uprightness which is not tempted by any seeming because it has conquered all semblance.

But, one may ask, what if a man by his nature makes his life subservient to the images which he produces in others? Can he, in such a case, still become a man living from his being, can he escape from his nature?

The widespread tendency to live from the recurrent impression one makes instead of from the steadiness of one's being is not a "nature." It originates, in fact, on the other side of interhuman life itself, in men's dependence upon one another. It is no light thing to be confirmed in one's being by others, and seeming deceptively offers itself as a help in this. To yield to seeming is man's essential cowardice, to resist it is his essential courage. But this is not an inexorable state of affairs which is as it is and must so remain. One can struggle to come to oneself—that is, to come to confidence in being. One struggles, now more successfully, now less, but never in vain, even when one thinks he is defeated. One must at times pay dearly for life lived from the being; but it is never too dear. Yet is there not bad being, do weeds not grow everywhere? I have never known a young person who seemed to me irretrievably bad. Later indeed it becomes more and more difficult to penetrate the increasingly tough layer which has settled down on a man's being. Thus there arises the false perspective of the seemingly fixed "nature" which cannot be overcome. It is false; the foreground is deceitful; man as man can be redeemed.

Again we see Peter and Paul before us surrounded by the ghosts of the semblances. A ghost can be exorcized. Let us imagine that these two find it more and more repellent to be represented by ghosts. In each of them the will is stirred and strengthened to be confirmed in their being as what they really are and nothing else. We see the forces of real life at work as they drive out the ghosts, till the semblance vanishes and the depths of personal life call to one another.

Personal Making Present

By far the greater part of what is today called conversation among men would be more properly and precisely described as speechifying. In general, people do not really speak to one another, but each, although turned to the other, really speaks to a fictitious court of appeal whose life consists of nothing but listening to him. Chekhov has given poetic expression to this state of affairs in *The Cherry Orchard,* where the only use the members of a family make of their being together is to talk past one another. But it is Sartre who has raised to a principle of existence what in Chekhov still appears as the deficiency of a person who is shut up in himself. Sartre regards the walls between the partners in a conversation as simply impassable. For him it is inevitable human destiny that a man has directly to do only with himself and his own affairs. The inner existence of the other is his own concern, not mine; there is no direct relation with the other, nor can there be. This is perhaps the clearest expression of the wretched fatalism of modern man, which regards degeneration as the unchangeable nature of *Homo sapiens* and the misfortune of having run into a blind alley as his primal fate, and which brands every thought of a breakthrough as reactionary romanticism. He who really knows how far our generation has lost the way of true freedom, of free giving between I and Thou, must himself, by virtue of the demand implicit in every great knowledge of this kind, practise directness—even if he were the only man on earth who did it—and not depart from it until scoffers are struck with fear, and hear in his voice the voice of their own suppressed longing.

The chief presupposition for the rise of genuine dialogue is that each should regard his partner as the very one he is. I become aware of him, aware that he is different, essentially different from myself, in the definite, unique way which is peculiar to him, and I accept whom I thus see, so that in full earnestness I can direct what I say to him as the person he is. Perhaps from time to time I must offer strict opposition to his view about the subject of our conversation. But I accept this person, the personal bearer of a conviction, in his definite being out of which his conviction has grown—even though I must try to show, bit by bit, the wrongness of this very conviction. I affirm the person I struggle with: I struggle with him as his partner, I confirm him as creature and as creation, I confirm him who is opposed to me as him who is over against me. It is true that it now depends on the other whether genuine dialogue, mutuality in speech arises between us. But if I thus give to the other who confronts me his legitimate standing as a man with whom I am ready to enter into dialogue, then I may trust him and suppose him to be also ready to deal with me as his partner.

But what does it mean to be "aware" of a man in the exact sense in which I use the word? To be aware of a thing or a being means, in quite general terms, to experience it as a whole and yet at the same time without reduction or abstraction, in all its concreteness. But a man, although he exists as a living being among living beings and even as a thing among things, is nevertheless something categorically different from all things and all beings. A man cannot really be grasped except on the basis of the gift of the spirit which belongs to man alone among all things, the spirit as sharing decisively in the personal life of the living man, that is, the spirit which determines the person. To be aware of a man, therefore, means in particular to perceive his wholeness as a person determined by the spirit; it means to perceive the dynamic centre which stamps his every utterance, action, and attitude with the recognizable sign of uniqueness. Such an awareness is impossible, however, if and so long as the other is the separated object of my contemplation or even observation, for this wholeness and its centre do not let themselves be known to contemplation or observation. It is only possible when I step into an elemental relation with the other, that is, when he becomes present to me. Hence I designate awareness in this special sense as "personal making present."

The perception of one's fellow man as a whole, as a unity, and as unique—even if his wholeness, unity, and uniqueness are only partly developed, as is usually the case—is opposed in our time by almost everything that is commonly understood as specifically modern. In our time there predominates an analytical, reductive, and deriving look between man and man. This look is analytical, or rather pseudo analytical, since it treats the whole being as put together and therefore able to be taken apart—not only the so-called unconscious which is accessible to relative objectification, but also the psychic stream itself, which can never, in fact, be grasped as an object. This look is a reductive one because it tries to contract the manifold person, who is nourished by the microcosmic richness of the possible, to some schematically surveyable and recurrent structures. And this look is a deriving one because it supposes it can grasp what a man has become, or even is becoming, in genetic formulae, and it thinks that even the dynamic central principle of the individual in this becoming can be represented by a general concept. An effort is being made today radically to destroy the mystery between man and man. The personal life, the ever near mystery, once the source of the stillest enthusiasms, is levelled down.

What I have just said is not an attack on the analytical method of the human sciences, a method which is indispensable wherever it furthers knowledge of a phenomenon without impairing the essentially different knowledge of its uniqueness that transcends the valid circle of the method. The science of man that makes use of the analytical method must accordingly always keep in view the boundary of such a contemplation, which stretches like a horizon around it. This duty makes the transposition of the method into life dubious; for it is excessively difficult to see where the boundary is in life.

If we want to do today's work and prepare tomorrow's with clear sight, then we must develop in ourselves and in the next generation a gift which lives in man's inwardness as a Cinderella, one day to be a princess. Some call it intuition, but that is not a wholly unambiguous concept. I prefer the name "imagining the real," for in its essential being this gift is not a looking at the other, but a bold swinging—demanding the most intensive stirring of one's being—into the life of the other. This is the nature of all genuine imagining, only that here the realm of my action is not the all-possible, but the particular real person who confronts me, whom I can attempt to make present to myself just in this way, and not otherwise, in his wholeness, unity, and uniqueness, and with his dynamic centre which realizes all these things ever anew.

Let it be said again that all this can only take place in a living partnership, that is, when I stand in a common situation with the other and expose myself vitally to his share in the situation as really his share. It is true that my basic attitude can remain unanswered, and the dialogue can die in seed. But if mutuality stirs, then the interhuman blossoms into genuine dialogue.

Imposition and Unfolding

I have referred to two things which impede the growth of life between men: the invasion of seeming, and the inadequacy of perception. We are now faced with a third, plainer than the others, and in this critical hour more powerful and more dangerous than ever.

There are two basic ways of affecting men in their views and their attitude to life. In the first a man tries to impose himself, his opinion and his attitude, on the other in such a way that the latter feels the psychical result of the action to be his own insight, which has only been freed by the influence. In the second basic way of affecting others, a man wishes to find and to further in the soul of the other the disposition toward what he has recognized in himself as the right. Because it is the right, it must also be alive in the microcosm of the other, as one possibility. The other need only be opened out in this potentiality of his; moreover, this opening out takes place not essentially by teaching, but by meeting, by existential communication between someone that is in actual being and someone that is in a process of becoming. The first way has been most powerfully developed in the realm of propaganda, the second in that of education.

The propagandist I have in mind, who imposes himself, is not in the least concerned with the person whom he desires to influence, as a person; various individual qualities are of importance only in so far as he can exploit them to win the other and must get to know them for this purpose. In his indifference to everything personal the propagandist goes a substantial distance beyond the party for which he works. For the party, persons in their difference are of significance because each can be used according to his special qualities in a particular function. It is true that the personal is considered only in respect of the specific use to which it can be put, but within these limits it is recognized in practice. To propaganda as such, on the other hand, individual qualities are rather looked on as a burden, for propaganda is concerned simply with *more*—more members, more adherents, an increasing extent of support. Political methods, where they rule in an extreme form, as here, simply mean winning power over the other by depersonalizing him. This kind of propaganda enters upon different relations with force; it supplements it or replaces it, according to the need or the prospects, but it is in the last analysis nothing but sublimated violence, which has become imperceptible as such. It places men's souls under a pressure which allows the illusion of autonomy. Political methods at their height mean the effective abolition of the human factor.

The educator whom I have in mind lives in a world of individuals, a certain number of whom are always at any one time committed to his care. He sees each of these individuals as in a position to become a unique, single person, and thus the bearer of a special task of existence which can be fulfilled through him and through him alone. He sees every personal life as engaged in such a process of actualization, and he knows from his own experience that the forces making for actualization are all the time involved in a microcosmic struggle with counterforces. He has come to see himself as a helper of the actualizing forces. He knows these forces; they have shaped and they still shape him. Now he puts this person shaped by them at their disposal for a new struggle and a new work. He cannot wish to impose himself, for he believes in the effect of the actualizing forces, that is, he believes that in every man what is right is established in a single and uniquely personal way. No other way may be imposed on a man, but another way, that of the educator, may and must unfold what is right, as in this case it struggles for achievement, and help it to develop.

The propagandist, who imposes himself, does not really believe even in his own cause, for he does not trust it to attain its effect of its own power without his special methods, whose symbols are the loudspeaker and the television advertisement. The educator who unfolds what is there believes in the primal power which has scattered itself, and still scatters itself, in all human beings in order that it may grow up in each man in the special form of that man. He is confident that this growth needs at each moment only that help which is given in meeting, and that he is called to supply that help.

I have illustrated the character of the two basic attitudes and their relation to one another by means of two extremely antithetical examples. But wherever men have dealings with one another, one or the other attitude is to be found in more or less degree.

These two principles of imposing oneself on someone and helping someone to unfold should not be confused with concepts such as arrogance and humility. A man can be arrogant without wishing to impose himself on others, and it is not enough to be humble in order to help another unfold. Arrogance and humility are dispositions of the soul, psychological facts with a moral accent, while imposition and helping to unfold are events between men, anthropological facts which point to an ontology, the ontology of the interhuman.

In the moral realm Kant expressed the essential principle that one's fellow man must never be thought of and treated merely as a means, but always at the same time as an independent end. The principle is expressed as an "ought" which is sustained by the idea of human dignity. My point of view, which is near to Kant's in its essential features, has another source and goal. It is concerned with the presuppositions of the interhuman. Man exists anthropologically not in his isolation, but in the completeness of the relation between man and man; what humanity is can be properly grasped only in vital reciprocity. For the proper existence of the interhuman it is necessary, as I have shown, that the semblance not intervene to spoil the relation of personal being to personal being. It is further necessary, as I have also shown, that each one means and makes present the other in his personal being. That neither should wish to impose himself on the other is the third basic presupposition of the interhuman. These presuppositions do not include the demand that one should influence the other in his unfolding; this is, however, an element that is suited to lead to a higher stage of the interhuman.

That there resides in every man the possibility of attaining authentic human existence in the special way peculiar to him can be grasped in the Aristotelian image of entelechy, innate self-realization; but one must note that it is an entelechy of the work of creation. It would be mistaken to speak here of individuation alone. Individuation is only the indispensable personal stamp of all realization of human existence. The self as such is not ultimately the essential, but the meaning of human existence given in creation again and again fulfils itself as self. The help that men give each other in becoming a self leads the life between men to its height. The dynamic glory of the being of man is first bodily present in the relation between two men each of whom in meaning the other also means the highest to which this person is called, and serves the self-realization of this human life as one true to creation without wishing to impose on the other anything of his own realization.

Genuine Dialogue

We must now summarize and clarify the marks of genuine dialogue.

In genuine dialogue the turning to the partner takes place in all truth, that is, it is a turning of the being. Every speaker "means" the partner or partners to whom he turns as this personal existence. To "mean" someone in this connection is at the same time to exercise that degree of making present which is possible to the speaker at that moment. The experiencing senses and the imagining of the real which completes the findings of the senses work together to make the other present as a whole and as a unique being, as the person that he is. But the speaker does not merely perceive the one who is present to him in this way; he receives him as his partner, and that means that he confirms this other being, so far as it is for him to confirm. The true turning of his person to the other includes this confirmation, this acceptance. Of course, such a confirmation does not mean approval; but no matter in what I am against the other, by accepting him as my partner in genuine dialogue I have affirmed him as a person.

Further, if genuine dialogue is to arise, everyone who takes part in it must bring himself into it. And that also means that he must be willing on each occasion to say what is really in his mind about the subject of the conversation. And that means further that on each occasion he makes the contribution of his spirit without reduction and without shifting his ground. Even men of great integrity are under the illusion that they are not bound to say everything "they have to say." But in the great faithfulness which is the climate of genuine dialogue, what I have to say at any one time already has in me the character of something that wishes to be uttered, and I must not keep it back, keep it in myself. It bears for me the unmistakable sign which indicates that it belongs to the common life of the word. Where the dialogical word genuinely exists, it must be given its right by keeping nothing back. To keep nothing back is the exact opposite of unreserved speech. Everything depends on the legitimacy of "what I have to say." And of course I must also be intent to raise into an inner word and then into a spoken word what I have to say at this moment but do not yet possess as speech. To speak is both nature and work, something that grows and something that is made, and where it appears dialogically, in the climate of great faithfulness, it has to fulfill ever anew the unity of the two.

Associated with this is that overcoming of semblance to which I have referred. In the atmosphere of genuine dialogue, he who is ruled by the thought of his own effect as the speaker of what he has to speak, has a destructive effect. If instead of what has to be said, I try to bring attention to my *I*, I have irrevocably miscarried what I had to say; it enters the dialogue as a failure, and the dialogue is a failure. Because genuine dialogue is an ontological sphere which is constituted by the authenticity of being, every invasion of semblance must damage it.

But where the dialogue is fulfilled in its being, between partners who have turned to one another in truth, who express themselves without reserve and are free of the desire for semblance, there is brought into being a memorable common fruitfulness which is to be found nowhere else. At such times, at each such time, the word arises in a substantial way between men who have been seized in their depths and opened out by the dynamic of an elemental togetherness. The interhuman opens out what otherwise remains unopened.

This phenomenon is indeed well known in dialogue between two persons; but I have also sometimes experienced it in a dialogue in which several have taken part.

About Easter of 1914 there met a group consisting of representatives of several European nations for a three-day discussion that was intended to be preliminary to further talks.[2] We wanted to discuss together how the catastrophe, which we all believed was imminent, could be avoided. Without our having agreed beforehand on any sort of modalities for our talk, all the presuppositions of genuine dialogue were fulfilled. From the first hour immediacy reigned between all of us, some of whom had just got to know one another; everyone spoke with an unheard-of unreserve, and clearly not a single one of the participants was in bondage to semblance. In respect of its purpose the meeting must be described as a failure (though even now in my heart it is still not a certainty that it had to be a failure); the irony of the situation was that we arranged the final discussion for the middle of August, and in the course of events the group was soon broken up. Nevertheless, in the time that followed, not one of the participants doubted that he shared in a triumph of the interhuman.

One more point must be noted. Of course it is not necessary for all who are joined in a genuine dialogue actually to speak; those who keep silent can on occasion be especially important. But each must be determined not to withdraw when the course of the conversation makes it proper for him to say what he has to say. No one, of course, can know in advance what it is that he has to say; genuine dialogue cannot be arranged beforehand. It has indeed its basic order in itself from the beginning, but nothing can be determined, the course is of the spirit, and some discover what they have to say only when they catch the call of the spirit.

But it is also a matter of course that all the participants, without exception, must be of such nature that they are capable of satisfying the presuppositions of genuine dialogue and are ready to do so. The genuineness of the dialogue is called in question as soon as even a small number of those present are felt by themselves and by the others as not being expected to take any active part. Such a state of affairs can lead to very serious problems.

I had a friend whom I account one of the most considerable men of our age. He was a master of conversation, and he loved it: his genuineness as a speaker was evident. But once it happened that he was sitting with two friends and with the three wives, and a conversation arose in which by its nature the women were clearly not joining, although their presence in fact had a great influence. The conversation among the men soon developed into a duel between two of them (I was the third). The other "duelist," also a friend of mine, was of a noble nature; he too was a man of true conversation, but given more to objective fairness than to the play of the intellect, and a stranger to any controversy. The friend whom I have called a master of conversation did not speak with his usual composure and strength, but he scintillated, he fought, he triumphed. The dialogue was destroyed.

On the Psychologizing of the World*

What we are speaking of is something that does not exist outside of us but within our lives. From out of our lives it must ever again be set right, from out of our lives testimony to it must ever again be given if we wish to penetrate into the depths of the subject.

"Psychologizing of the world" is the inclusion of the world in the soul, the transference of the world into the soul, but not just any such transference but only that which goes so far that the essential is thereby

*Reprinted from *A Believing Humanism: My Testament 1902–65* (New York: Simon and Schuster, 1967), pp. 144–53.

disturbed. This essential is the facing of I and world. That the world faces me and that between us the real happens, this essential basic relation from which our life receives its meaning is injured if the world is so far removed within the soul that its non-psychic reality is obliterated, that this fundamental relation of I to world ceases to be able to be a relation of I to Thou. (In place of world we can also say here Being.) After this essential disturbance the world is perhaps only something in me with which I can certainly concern myself, as with other things in me to which, however, I cannot legitimately, cannot in full truth say *Thou*.

This fact of psychologizing can also be called by a philosophical expression, psychologism. What is in question here, however, is not a world view, as psychologism is otherwise, but a fact that exists in almost every man of today.

The reality in which the non-perverted man finds himself is the reality of an immediate connection of I and world, a connection, however, which signifies no fusion, but a connection of relation. It is founded upon the I and the world as entities clearly separate from each other. The arch of relationship rises, as it were, on these two clearly individual pillars. This natural relation is easily obscured in the course of development, on the one side in that human thought removes the world into the soul (cosmic phenomena are grasped as psychic, they are a function, dependent upon the soul of man), on the other side in that the soul is removed into the world and appears as its product, as something that has grown out of it, as understandable on the basis of its evolution.

This double game of human thought is furthered by one fact: namely that however separately the two pillars stand opposite each other, there still exists a mutual inclusion of I and world. *Psychologism* in its easiest form regards the world as an idea. *Cosmologism* regards the soul as an element, a product of the world. In the face of this fact, we must still say: The world is, of course, also my *idea, i.e.,* I *also* possess it as idea; only what is essential in it does not enter into my idea—the world's character of being does not enter into it. And conversely, if the soul is conceived from the standpoint of the world, what is essential in the soul (the I) remains outside, is not included in the world. (Instead of speaking substantively of the I, we can also say the I's character as self.) It is so that this mutual inclusion, soul-world and world-soul, exists; but the essence of the one and of the other remain thereby untouched.

Now the question arises: are these two aspects which at a certain level of development of man appear on the scene and belong to each other, are they things between which we must choose, are they opposites for which no third thing exists that overarches this opposition, overcomes it? Must this rendering being fictitious exist, although a relation of the world to the soul is thereby made impossible? I do not believe so. Today, to be sure, we can only hint at this third that can liberate us from the two; it is not yet graspable even in the form of a provisional image.

The perspective that sees the inclusion of I and world as a whole and embeds this whole in the real being (the perspective that sees the reality so truly that this inclusion has its place in it), is a greater apprehension of reality than that to which we are accustomed. The reality into which the concepts of the psychic and the cosmic can enter is the *pneumatic reality* (according to a religious valuation). This reality understood as existing being, as existing being into which all that is psychic and all that is cosmic and all that is opposite and all that is inclusive of the two is embedded, this *ontologism* we can, with all foresight and self-limitation, set up for a moment as a third to the two—psychologism and cosmologism— a third which unites them. But careful! Exact knowledge of the limitation of what one says! What we are discussing is a problem, not an answer. Perhaps there are, for all that, hints of an answer or presentiments in it.

The Concept of the Soul: Is man really composed of soul and body? Does man really feel himself consisting of two kinds of things? Not *I!* Naturally two aspects exist, I perceive myself by my senses as well as from within me without my senses. But these are only two ways of seeing oneself. Are they really two kinds of things? From where does this division arise? From the fact of death and our relation to it. We are inclined to take the edge off death. We are inclined to say that this duality just simply comes apart. But we *know* of death only that it is the end of our conceivable being. We probably must also know, however, that we cannot die; yet we may not make the not-being-able-to-die conceptual otherwise than that it is the mystery itself, that it takes place in the mystery. But nowhere here do we find a legitimization of the division.

Nonetheless we know of psychic phenomena—thinking, feeling, willing, etc.—what are they? Are they like the body? Are the physical and the psychic alike in that the latter, *like* the body, belongs to the I as long as life is preserved? And, really, *there* is a going apart.

If we grasp the body I-wise and the soul I-wise, then they are only two aspects. But is not one of these interior aspects beyond the I?—Yes, indeed. If we regard more deeply what we call the psychic phenomena in their essence, then we find that all of them and their connection point to something that cannot be understood from the standpoint of the I, that transcending even the phenomena of solitude, of apparent individuality, in reality point to something beyond the individual. Even though a great number of phenomena appear thus, as though they stood outside of the relationship between the I and the other, these phenomena also have only arisen dynamically from out of the fact of relationship and are only comprehensible through this fact.

Concept of the Spirit: Spirit and soul are both, as it were, planes of relationship. Neither is to be understood as the I; they are to be regarded as various forms of relationship in its being removed to the I. Soul is to be understood from the relationship between man and world, spirit from the relationship between man and that which is not world, between man and the Being that does not manifest itself in the world, that does not enter into the worldly manifestation. But both, soul and spirit, are not to be understood from the isolated individual, not to be understood as the *I*, but only from the relationship between I and worldly or nonworldly being. Characteristic of both is the dynamic, i.e., that they stand in a continually developing double movement, in the unfolding or realization of the relationship and in the I's withdrawing-into-itself or being-withdrawn from the relationship. (The spirit is different in this from the soul; the spirit points to something from which it stems, points to something new which arises ever again, what exists from of old in a nonindividuated, unconditioned manner. That is too delicate to be able to say more about it.) The character of the soul as I is thereby broken: in so far as the soul is comprehended as I, it is comprehended in amputation, in abstraction, not in the whole existence.

"Psychologizing of the world" thus means abstraction, attempt at a complete detachment of the soul from its basic character of relationship. This derives from the fact that the spirit in its condition of highest differentiation is inclined to bend back on itself, i.e., that the spirit to the extent of its individuation is inclined to forget, to deny that it does not exist *in* man (in I), but between man and what is not man (what is not world). Then Being is psychologized, installed within the soul of man. The world no longer confronts the soul. That is the soul-madness of the spirit. In place of the soul, which is a plane of relationship between man and world, an all-penetrating substance is created: all is transformed into soul. This fact is the true fall. Here first the fall takes place.

How does psychologism arise? We distinguish between philosophical and naïve psychologism.

Philosophical Psychologism: It is the foundation of the philosophical disciplines (that which determines the methods, lays the ground for the criteria). It is fundamental today even in cases where apparently another starting point can be or is chosen. Basically one ever again tries to go back to what he regards as the real, the undeniable, to the psychological. ("I do not mean something that exists outside the soul.") Even metaphysical views are psychologically legitimized. We are told to what psychic functions they correspond. It is also thus in the ethical, in the aesthetic realm. For example, in the aesthetic it is forgotten that we enter *into* a world when we go to the work of art, that we really come into something new; this *work*, this being is absorbed and it is asserted that it exists in us. One does not recognize that it *is* and that beforehand it just was not possessed by us. To transpose the relation into the receiving subject means to destroy the being.

Naïve Psychologism: There is remarkably little awareness of this. Man always imagines everything as happening through and in him. "The landscape is a state of the soul," says Amiel. That is a malformation of the genuine nature feeling. Something *other* is, but one forgets the duality and experiences the relationship so strongly that this is felt more strongly than the existence of the two individuals. Thus also God is played with (Rilke). In the Youth Movement the relation between man and reality is spoken of, but in so doing men are all inclined to regard this as something tied up with their person; all the conceptions in the youth movement take on a certain "my" character. (For example: discussion of a tragic occurrence between men is ever again interlaced with statements which begin, "*My* kind . . . *My* blood . . . *My* destiny, etc.") Somewhat similar is the fact that many men are determined in their inner focus by how they appear to other men, that they all refer back to the image that they produce in others. They do not live from the core out, not to the other from their own center, but from the image that they produce in others.[1]

And the erotic: almost throughout only differentiated self-enjoyment. The other man is not made present in his life, not accepted as the other life with its right. What is elementally perceived is what takes place in one's own soul. Even the attempts at the spiritual life, the religious life are soaked through with the same poison. The term expressionism is indicative: the important is seen not in the communication between me and the form to which I strive but in the expression of what takes place *in me*. Thereby the real connexion is destroyed. Only out of the belief in the not-I can I enter into a connexion; I must walk toward the other, beholding, hearkening, fulfilling him.

Active Form of Psychologism: Relation of present-day man to himself: How does man perceive himself? First of all through *self-experience:* this is met with in the natural growth of consciousness. What ascends between me and myself and becomes conscious in this level of relationship of the soul (between me and the world) in its dynamic (coming to each other, stripping apart, becoming alone) is self-experience gained through a natural growth of consciousness. Here no willfulness interferes. Secondly, *self-observation:* that is an interference; it wills to further the growth and thwarts it. It does not lead to deeper self-experience but disintegrates it. What one seemingly experiences thus is not the reality but something distorted. It is not experience but belaboring. One can only experience without willfulness. It is similar with *experience of the soul* (a happiness, a present, it gives an artist greatness) *and observation by the soul* (can be industriously exercised, yet yields only talent).

Scientific Form of Psychologism: It expresses itself in the analytical method, more exactly "analyticism," which applies this method as universally valid, which no longer knows, therefore, that it is a method and only *provisionally* usable and must always be ready to be given up. When the analysis longs for synthesis, it is not thus. When the man knows, now I must do this, I must, for example, seek a motive although I know that no motive exists, I must, for example, dissect the life of the soul although it is a unity, that is not analyticism. In this wise restriction, I would gladly emphasize this, I have often encountered the analytical method precisely in the representatives of the direction prevailing here[2] as true scientific method.

Here another word about the problematic of the province of psychotherapy. The sicknesses of the soul are sicknesses of relationship. They can only be treated completely if I transcend the realm of the patient and add to it the world as well. If the doctor possessed superhuman power, he would have to try to heal the relationship itself, to heal in the "between." The doctor must know that really he ought to do that and that only his boundedness limits him to the one side.

Psychology is the investigation of the soul in a set abstraction from the world (similar to the way that plane geometry deals with planes, although only solid objects exist). The limit of psychology is there where this set (assumed) abstraction abolishes itself on reality, where it touches on reality, on the relationship. What *share* can psychology have *in the overcoming of psychologism?* We can only grasp this overcoming if we understand that psychologism is a marginal phenomenon. This marginal phenomenon clearly develops into self-contradiction. If psychologism becomes so intensified that the man can simply no longer bring his capacity for external relationship (the inborn Thou[3]) to others, to the world, if his strength of relationship recoils backward into the I, if he has to encounter himself, if the double ever again appears to him, then that state exists that I call self-contradiction.[4] Attempt at flight is pseudo-religiousness (the double possesses a religious meaning). This phenomenon is the place of the turning.[5]

Community in a time like ours can only happen out of breakthrough, out of turning. Only the need aroused by the uttermost sundering, the marginal phenomenon, provides the motive force for this. Does psychology, the true, the genuine psychology, have a function in this? Only from the standpoint of psychology is the problematic of individuation manifest. Only when it comes to its borders, does it come on the un-psychological. Through the self-suspension of the shut-off levels of individuation, psychology can lead to a genuine apprehension of community and—deed. Genuine community begins in a time like this with the discovery of the metapsychic character of reality and rests upon the belief in this reality.

The *empirical community* is a dynamic fact. It does not take away from man his solitude but fills it, makes it positive. It thereby deepens the consciousness of responsibility of the individual—the place of responsibility is man's becoming solitary. The community does not have its meaning in itself. It is the abode where the divine has not yet consumed itself, the abode of the coming theophany. If one knows this, then one also knows that community in our time must ever again miscarry. The monstrous, the dreadful phenomenon of psychologism so prevails that one cannot simply bring about healing, rescue with a single blow. But the disappointments belong to the way. There is no other way than that of this miscarrying. That is the way of faithful faith.

Notes

Distance and Relation

1. Animals, especially domestic animals, are capable of regarding a man in a "speaking" way; they turn to him as one to whom they wish to announce themselves, but not as a being existing for himself as well, outside this addressing of him. On this remarkable frontier area, cf. Buber, *I and Thou*, pp. 96f., 125f., and *Between Man and Man*, p. 22f.—Ed.'s Note.

Elements of the Interhuman

1. "Das Zwischenmenschliche." See my Introduction to Werner Sombart, *Das Proletariat*, Vol. 1, in Die Gesellschaft: Sammlung Sozialpsychologischer Monographien, ed. by Martin Buber (1st ed.; Frankfurt am Main: Rütten & Loening, 1906).

2. I have set down elsewhere an episode from this meeting. See my essay "Dialogue." (This volume, preceding chapter.)

On the Psychologizing of the World

1. This is the origin of the typology of "being and seeming" which Buber develops in "Elements of the Interhuman."—M. F. (This volume, preceding essay.)

2. See Explanatory Comments, 1., [in *A Believing Humanism*, Simon and Schuster, 1967,] p. 240.

3. See Explanatory Comments, 2., [in *A Believing Humanism*,] p. 240f.

4. See Explanatory Comments, 3., [in *A Believing Humanism*,] p. 241.

5. "The turning" is a basic term not only in *I and Thou* but throughout Buber's thought from his earliest to his latest writings. It goes back to the *teshuvah* of the Hebrew Bible—the call of the prophets to turn back to God with one's whole existence, including one's relations to one's fellowmen, one's community, other peoples, and the world of nature.—M. F.

II

THE SOCIAL FRAMEWORK
OF CULTURAL CREATIVITY

In part II some of Buber's major writings that deal directly with the relations between human intersubjectivity and processes of cultural creativity are presented.

The common denominator of all these analyses is their very basis in the community, as the major social framework or situation in which such creativity can take place—mainly because it is only within the framework of community that the potential relation between intersubjectivity and cultural creativity can be realized.

But community as presented in these excerpts, and in all of Buber's writings, does not mean any sort of aggregation of people. Buber is interested in those communities which evince some distinct characteristics, which are described in the excerpts gathered in part I.

The most central characteristics of such communities are the combination of some grounding in concrete reality—often, as in the case of the biblical community or the Zionist movement, in primordial reality—and second, the community's openness to some center beyond such primordial givens. In all such communities a very crucial role is played by the distinct type of leadership which promulgates and articulates the relations between these primordial bases and the orientations beyond them.

In the excerpts brought under chapters 4, 5, and 6, Buber examines some of the more dramatic of such types of leadership and communities—the biblical community, the Hasidic one, and the national one as manifest in the Zionist movement. In the excerpt on precursors of utopianism he examines the kernels of such leadership and community in the modern world.

Although these various communities necessarily differ in the details of their composition and organizations, they all share the combination of such grounding in concrete social relations together with the openness to intersubjectivity as well as to a realm beyond them, the realm of the sacred, the transcendent. Intersubjectivity and a dialogue with the sacred—which, though they can be found in many concrete settings, are not necessarily tied to any such setting—provide the social frameworks most conducive to cultural creativity.

3

Community as the Basic Social Framework
of Human Creativity

A Translation of Buber's Preface to "Die Gesellschaft"*

DIE GESELLSCHAFT: SAMMLUNG SOZIALPSYCHOLOGISCHER MONOGRAPHIEN,
ED. M. BUBER[1]

Geleitwort zur Sammlung

This collection of monographs, Die Gesellschaft, addresses itself to the problem of the interhuman (*das Zwischenmenschliche*). Its subject matter, therefore, is the associative life of men in all its forms (*Formen*), objective structures (*Gebilde*),[2] and actions (*Aktionen*). The methodological perspective assumed in each of the monographs here presented is that of social psychology.

Das Zwischenmenschliche is that which occurs between (*zwischen*) men; in some ways it is not unlike an impersonal, objective process. The individual may very well experience *das Zwischenmenschliche* as his "action and passion," but somehow it cannot be fully ascribed or reduced to personal experience.[3] For *das Zwischenmenschliche* can only properly be apprehended and analyzed as the synthesis of the "action and passion" of two or more individuals: the "action and passion" of one are intertwined with those of another, each finding in this abiding tension opposition and complementarity.

Two or more individuals live with one another, that is to say, they stand to one another in a relation of interaction (*Wechselwirkung*), in a relation of reciprocal effect. Every relation of interaction between two or more individuals may be designated as an association or a society (*Gesellschaft*). The function of association is social life, or more properly, *das Zwischenmenschliche*.

What one could comprehend and analyze in his own sphere of existence, without having to postulate the existence of another intentional

---

*Appendix reprinted from P. Mendes-Flohr, *From Mysticism to Dialogue in Martin Buber's Transformation of German Social Thought* (Detroit: Wayne University Press, 1989), pp. 127–30.

93

being (*zwecksetzender Einzelwesen*),[4] is simply the human or the individual. The notion of *das Zwischenmenschliche*, on the other hand, assumes the existence of diverse, distinctly constituted intentional beings who live with and affect one another. We do not regress to the fact of individuation, the incontrovertible existence of individuated beings, and raise it anew as a problem; rather, we accept this fact and proceed from there.

Das Zwischenmenschliche occurs in specific forms and produces specific objectified structures. Pure forms of *das Zwischenmenschliche* are super- and subordination, cooperation and noncooperation, groupings, social rank, class organizations, and all types of economic and cultural associations, both natural and normative. The structures of *das Zwischenmenschliche* are the objectified expressions of human collectivity: values, elements of spiritual and economic mediation (*Mittlung*), the objective instruments of production, the social aspects of culture, and indeed all products of human association. To be sure, form and structure constitute the static aspects of *das Zwischenmenschliche*. Those features of social life that are not presented in constant temporal conjunction but unfold in time—action, transformation, and revolution —represent the dynamic aspect of *das Zwischenmenschliche*.

Sociology is the science of the forms of *das Zwischenmenschliche*. The objective structures of *das Zwischenmenschliche* are dealt with by ethics, political economy, political science, or the philosophy of law. The actions of *das Zwischenmenschliche* are the subject matter of historiography; that is, of economic, social, and cultural history.

None of these disciplines, if they do not wish totally to detach themselves from the roots of the lived life (*erlebtes Leben*), can dispense with psychology. The actual "psychological" problem of *das Zwischenmenschliche*, however, arises initially outside the purview of the various [traditional] disciplines and thus requires separate consideration and treatment. Social forms, structures, and actions are derivative expressions of psychic processes; they thus demand to be investigated in relation to these processes. Should one limit oneself to external images, structures, correlations, and causality, the essence of society would not be thoroughly disclosed. Only when one grasps society as essentially the experience of souls (*als das Erlebnis von Seelen*), does one advance to its abiding existential basis.

Social life arises out of feelings and urges, which beget, in turn, new feelings and urges. This all runs its courses within a psychic cycle and in this context is regarded as nothing but psychic. What happens between individuals happens between complexes of psychic elements; only as such is it understandable. The social forms have their ultimate significance in that they bring human psyches into a relationship of opposition and complementarity. Social structures are, as it were, the aggregation of the psychic energy of many, energy that is deposited in the psyches of many and wherein this energy retains a personal content and character. Social action is essentially the transformation of psychic life in rhythm, tempo, and intensity of expression. The problem of *das Zwischenmenschliche* is, thus, fundamentally one of social psychology: its object is social life, which is to be regarded as a psychical process.

What is the subject of this process? Where is the "I" who experiences this process? On what basis can this process be removed from the field of individual psychology?

That there is no social soul that exercises supremacy over individual souls is self-evident. Likewise, it is obvious that the "social-psychological" process takes place in those complexes we call individuals.[5] Given this fact, one tends to justify a special denotation of a genetic or methodological factor: the psychic processes considered here are only possible if the individual is in a state of sociation (*Vergesellschaftung*);[6] indeed, these processes can be observed only in this state.

Something else, though, is more significant. To be sure, the social-psychological process is enacted in the individual—however, the entire process is not realized by each individual. The process does not consist of many similar happenings, each having a human soul as its subject. Rather the process combines dissimilar happenings (*Geschehnisse*) that, when combined, complement one another and form the social-psychological process. The relationship, interaction, and community of these dissimilar happenings are none other than *das Zwischenmenschliche*.

The individual does not experience some exemplar of this process but only a part of it.[7] This, as it were, basic situation (*Grundverhältnis*) is frequently obscured by the fact that the variegated distribution of the social-psychological process is represented not by individuals but by groups. Upon closer scrutiny, however, one will note that within these groups a new and subtle distribution [of the social-psychological process] takes place. Occasionally, this "basic situation" is almost unnoticeable, as with mass phenomena. On the other hand, in polar relations as, for instance, that of a man and a woman, it is completely apparent. More than any other fact, this "basic situation" constitutes the legitimation of social psychology as a field of study.

The social-psychological problem can be considered and treated from two different approaches: either as the various fundamental forms (*Grundformen*) of the social-psychological process; that is, the usual classification is applied and the social ideas, feelings, and urgings are systematically ordered and analyzed. The analytic social psychology (*zergliedernde Sozialpsychologie*)[8] that is achieved in this manner can by its very nature be the work of a single individual only. The other way of approaching the problem, however, is to present the various forms, objective structures, and actions of *das Zwischenmenschliche* and demonstrate the essential social-psychological process in them. Since these aspects belong to the most varied realms of life, a cooperative collection—like this series, which marshals the efforts of experts from various fields—suggests itself as most appropriate for a total and integrated presentation. Should this succeed, the series may be considered as a preparatory work to "a descriptive social psychology" (*beschreibende Sozialpsychologie*)[9] . . .

Comments on the Idea of Community*

The ambiguity of the concept that is employed is greater here than anywhere else. One says, for example, that socialism is the passing of the control over the means of production from the hands of the entrepreneur into that of the collective; but everything depends on what one understands by collective. If it is what we are accustomed to call the state, i.e., an institution in which an essentially unstructured mass lets its business by conducted by a so-called representation, then in a socialist society essentially this will have changed, in that the workers will feel themselves to be represented by the possessors of the power of the disposal of the means of production. But what is representation? Is it not in the all too far-reaching allowing-oneself-to-be-represented that the worst defect of modern society lies? And in a socialist society will not the economic letting-oneself-be-represented be added to the political so that only then for the first time the almost unlimited being-represented and thereby the almost unlimited central accumulation of power will predominate? But the more a human group lets itself be represented in the determination of its common affairs and the more from outside, so much the less community life exists in it, so much the poorer in community does it become. For community—not the primitive but that which is possible and suitable for us men of today—proclaims itself above all in the common active handling of the common and cannot endure without it.

The primal hope of all history depends upon a genuine, hence thor-

---

*Reprinted from *A Believing Humanism: My Testament 1902–65* (New York: Simon and Schuster, 1967), pp. 87–92.

oughly *communally disposed* community of the human race. Fictitious, counterfeit, a planet-size lie would be the unity that was not established out of real communal living of smaller and larger groups that dwell or work together and out of their reciprocal relationships. Everything depends therefore upon the collective, into whose hands the control over the means of production will pass, making possible and demanding by its structure and its institutions real communal living of manifold groups, indeed that these groups themselves become the true subjects of the process of production; thus that the mass be as articulated and in its articulations (the various communes) be as powerful as the common economy of mankind affords; thus that the centralistic letting-oneself-be-represented only extend so far as the new order absolutely demands. The inner question of destiny does not take the form of a fundamental Either-Or: it is the question of the legitimating, ever-newly-drawn demarcation line, the thousandfold system of demarcation lines between the realms that it is necessary to centralize and those that it is necessary to liberate, between the law of unity and the claim of community. The unremitting testing of the current state of things from the standpoint of the claim of the community as that which is always liable to oppression by the central power, the vigilance concerning the *truth of the boundary,* ever changing according to the changing historical conditions, would be the task of the spiritual conscience of mankind, a high court of an unheard-of kind, the reliable representation of the living idea. The Platonic "guardians" await here a new form of manifestation.

The representative of the idea, I say, not a rigid principle but the living form [*Gestalt*] that now wants to become malleable to be shaped in the material of just this earth day. Community too may not become principle; it too, when it appears, shall satisfy not a concept but a situation. Realization of the idea of community, like the realization of any idea, does not exist once for all and generally valid but always only as the moment's answer to a moment's question.

For the sake of this, its life meaning, all sentimentality, all exaggeration and overenthusiasm must be kept far from our thinking about community. Community is never mood, and even where it is feeling, it is always the feeling of a *state of existence.* Community is the inner constitution of a common life that knows and embraces the parsimonious "account," the opposing "accident," the suddenly invading "care." It is commonness of need and only from this commonness of spirit, commonness of trouble and only from this commonness of salvation. Even that community that calls the spirit its master and salvation its promise, the "religious," is only community when it serves its master in the unselective, unexalted simple reality that it has not chosen for itself, that rather, just thus, has been sent; only when it prepares the way for its promise through the brambles of this pathless hour. Certainly, "works" are not required, but the work of faith is required. It is only truly a community of faith when it is a community of work.

The real essence of community is undoubtedly to be found in the—manifest or hidden—fact that it has a center. The real origin of community is undoubtedly only to be understood by the fact that its members have a common relationship to the center superior to all other relations: the circle is drawn from the radii, not from the points of the periphery. And undoubtedly the primal reality of the center cannot be known if it is not known as transparent into the divine. But the more earthly, the more creaturely, the more bound a character the circle takes, so much the truer, the more transparent it is. The "social" belongs to it. Not as a subdivision but as the world of authentication: in which the truth of the center proves itself. The early Christians were not satisfied with the communes that were next to or above the world, and they went into the desert so as to have no community except that with God and no more disturbing world. But it was shown to them that God does not will that man be alone with him, and above the holy impotence of solitude grew the brotherly order. Finally, overstepping the realm of Benedict, Francis established the bond with the creatures.

Yet a community does not need to be founded. When historical destiny had put a human band in a common nature- and life-space, there was space for the development of a genuine commune; and no altar of a city god was necessary in the center if the inhabitants knew themselves united for the sake of and through the Unnamable. A living and ever-renewed togetherness was given and needed only to be developed in the immediacy of all relationships. The common concerns were deliberated and decided in common—in the most favorable cases not through representatives but in the gathering in the marketplace, and the unification experienced in public radiated out into each personal contact. The danger of seclusion might threaten: the spirit expelled it, which thrived here as nowhere else and broke its great window into the narrow walls for the sake of a vision of people, humanity, cosmos.

But, objectors tell me, that is now quite irrecoverable. The modern city has no agora, and modern man has no time for the transactions of which he can be relieved by his chosen representatives. A concrete togetherness is already destroyed by the compulsion of quantity and the form of organization. Work joins one to other persons than leisure does, sport to others than politics; day and soul are tidily divided. But the ties are just factual, one pursues together the common interests and tendencies and has no use for "immediacy." Collectivity is no intimate crouching down together but a great economic or political union of forces, unproductive for romantic play of the imagination but comprehensible as numbers, expressing itself in actions and effects to which the individual may belong without intimacies but in consciousness of his energetic contribution. Those "bonds" that resist the inevitable development must dissolve. There is still the family, to be sure, which as a house-community appears to demand and to guarantee a measure of living life together, but it too will emerge out of the crisis into which it has entered as a union for a purpose, or it will disappear.

In opposition to this mixture of correct evidence and distorted conclusions, I espouse the rebirth of the commune. Rebirth, not restoration. It cannot be restored in fact, although it seems to me that each breath of neighborliness in the apartment building, each wave of a warmer comradeship during the rest period in the highly rationalized factory means a growth of communal-mindedness of the world, and although at times an upright village commune pleases me more than a parliament. It cannot be restored. But whether a rebirth of the commune takes place out of the waters and the spirit of the approaching transformation of society— by this, it seems to me, the lot of the human species will be determined. An organic communal being—and only such is suitable for a formed and articulated mankind—will never be erected out of individuals, only out of small and the smallest communities: a people is community to the extent that it is communally disposed.

If the family does not emerge from the crisis, which today appears like ruin, purified and renewed, then the form of statehood will end up by being only a furnace which will be fueled with the bodies of the generations. The commune which can be renewed in such a manner exists only as a residue. If I speak of a rebirth, I do not think of a continuing, but of a changed world situation. By the new communes—one could also call them the new fellowships—I mean the subject of the transformed economy, the collective into whose hands the control over the means of production shall pass. Once again: everything depends upon whether they will be made ready, whether they will be ready.

How much of economic and political autonomy will be accorded them—for they will necessarily be economic and political unities at the same time—is a technical question that one has to pose and to answer ever anew, but to pose and to answer from the standpoint of the more than technical knowledge that the inner might of a community is also conditional upon its outer strength. The relation of centralism and decentralization is a problem that, as has been said, is to be dealt with not fundamentally but, like everything that concerns the traffic of the idea with reality, with the great tact of the spirit, with the untiring weighing of the legitimate How Much. Centralization, yes, but only so much as must be centralized according to the conditions of the time and the place; if the high court that is summoned to the drawing and new drawing of the line of demarcation remains awake in its conscience, then the division between base and apex of the power pyramid will be entirely different from today's, even in states that call themselves communist, which certainly still means striving for community. A system of representation must also exist in the form of society that I have in mind; but it will not present itself, like those of today, in the seeming representation of amorphous masses of voters but in the work-tested representatives of economic communities. The represented will not be bound with their representatives in empty abstractions, through the phraseology of a party program, as today, but concretely, through common activity and common experience.

But the most essential must be that the process of the formation of community must continue into the relations of the communities to each other. Only a community of communities may be called a communal being.

The picture that I have hastily sketched will be put on the shelf of "utopian socialism" until the storm turns over the leaves again. Just as I do not believe in Marx's "gestation" of the new form of society, so I do not believe in Bakunin's virgin birth out of the womb of the revolution. But I believe in the meeting of image and destiny in the plastic hour.

The Forerunners*

I have pointed out [in earlier chapters of *Paths in Utopia*] that in "utopian" socialism there is an organically constructive and organically purposive or planning element which aims at a re-structuring of society, and moreover not at one that shall come to fruition in an indefinite future after the "withering away" of the proletarian dictator-state, but beginning here and now in the given conditions of the present. If this is correct it should be possible to demonstrate, in the history of utopian socialism, the line of evolution taken by this element.

In the history of utopian socialism three pairs of active thinkers emerge, each pair being bound together in a peculiar way and also to its generation: Saint-Simon and Fourier, Owen and Proudhon, Kropotkin and Gustav Landauer. Through the middle pair there runs the line of cleavage separating the first phase of this socialism—the phase of transi-

*Reprinted from *Paths in Utopia* (Boston: Beacon, 1958), pp. 16–23.

tion to advanced capitalism—from the second, which accompanies the rise of the latter. In the first each thinker contributes a single constructive thought and these thoughts—at first strange and incompatible with one another—align themselves together, and in the second Proudhon and his successors build up the comprehensive synthesis, the synthetic idea of restructure. Each step occupies its own proper place and is not interchangeable.

A few figures will help to make the relations between the generations clear. Saint-Simon was born twelve years before Fourier and died twelve years before him, and yet both belong to the generation which was born before the French Revolution and perished before 1848—save that the younger, Fourier, belongs by nature and outlook to the eighteenth century and the older, Saint-Simon, to the nineteenth century. Owen was born before the great Revolution, Proudhon at the time of the Napoleonic triumphs; thus they belong congenitally to different generations but, as they both died between 1848 and 1870, death united them once more in a single generation. The same thing is repeated with Kropotkin, who was born before 1848, and Landauer, before 1870: both died soon after the First World War.

Saint-Simon—of whom the founder of sociology as a science, Lorenz von Stein, justly says that he "half understood, half guessed at *society*" (that is, society as such in contradistinction to the State) "for the first time in its full power, in all its elements and contradictions"—makes the first and, for his epoch, the most important contribution. The "puberty-crisis" which mankind had entered meant for him the eventual replacement of the existing régime by "le régime industriel." We can formulate it in this way: the cleavage of the social whole into two essentially different and mutually antagonistic orders is to yield place to a uniform structure. Hitherto society had been under a "government," now it was to come under an "administration," and the administration was not, like the former, to be entrusted to a class opposed to society and made up of "legalists" and "militarists," but to the natural leaders of society itself, the leaders of its production. No longer was one group of rulers to be ousted by another group of rulers, as had happened in all the upheavals known to history; what remains necessary as a police force does not constitute Government in the old sense. "The producers have no wish to be plundered by any one class of parasites rather than by any other. . . . It is clear that the struggle must end by being played out between the whole mass of parasites on the one hand and the mass of producers on the other, in order to decide whether the latter shall continue to be the prey of the former or shall obtain supreme control of society." Saint-Simon's naïve demand of "messieurs" the workers that they should make the entrepreneurs their leaders—a demand which was to weld the active portion of the capitalists and the proletarians into one class— contains, despite its odd air of unreality, the intimation of a future order in which no leadership is required other than that provided by the social functions themselves; in which politics have in fact become what they are in Saint-Simon's definition: "the science of production," i.e. of the pre-conditions most favourable to this. In the nature of things governments cannot implement policies of this sort; "government is a continual source of injury to industry when it meddles in its affairs; it is injurious even where it makes efforts to encourage it." Nothing but an overcoming of government as such can lead society out of the "extreme disorder" in which it languishes; out of the dilemma of a nation which is "essentially industrial" and whose government is "essentially feudal"; out of division into two classes: "one that orders and one that obeys" (the Saint-Simonist Bazard expressed it even more pungently soon after the death of his master, in 1829: "two classes, the exploiters and the exploited"). The present epoch is one of transition not from one sort of régime to another, but from a sham order to a true order, in which "work is the fountain-head of all virtues" and "the State is the confederacy of all workers" (so runs the formula of the Saint-Simonists). This cannot be the affair of a single nation only, for it would be opposed by other nations; the "industrial system" must be established over all Europe and the feudal system, persisting in bourgeois form, annihilated. Saint-Simon calls this "Europeanism." He realizes, however, that altering the relationship between the leaders and the led is not the sole intention, but that the alteration must permeate the whole inner structure of society. The moment when the industrial régime is "ripe" (i.e. when society is ripe, for it can be "determined with reasonable exactitude by the fundamental circumstance that, in any given nation, the vast majority of individuals will by then have entered into more or less numerous industrial associations each two or three of which will be interconnected by industrial relationships. This will permit a general system to be built up, since the associations will be led towards a great common goal, as regards which they will be co-ordinated of themselves each according to its function." Here Saint-Simon comes very near to the idea of social restructuring. What he lacks is the conception of genuine organic social units out of which this re-structuring can be built; the idea of "industrial associations" does not provide what is required. Saint-Simon divined the significance of the small social unit for the rebuilding of society, but did not recognize it for what it was.

    It is just this social unit which is the be-all and end-all for Fourier. He thought he had discovered "the secret of association" and in this he saw—the formula dates from the same time, about 1820, when Saint-Simon gave his "industrial system" its final formulation—"the secret of the union of interests." Charles Gide has rightly pointed out that Fourier was here opposing the legacy of the French Revolution, which had contested the right of association and prohibited trades-unions; and opposing it because it was from the collapse of the cadres of the old corporations that the "anarchic" principle of free competition had derived, which, as Fourier's most important pupil—Considérant—had foretold in his manifesto of 1843 on the principles of socialism (by which the Communist Manifesto appears to have been influenced), would inevitably result in the exact opposite of what its introduction purposed, namely, in the "universal organization of great monopolies in all branches of industry." Fourier countered this with his "association communale sur le terrain de la production et de la consummation" (as Considérant again formulated it in 1848); which is to say the formation of local social units based on joint production and consumption. It is a new form of the "commune rurale," which latter is to be regarded as "l'élément alvéolaire de la société"—a conception not, of course, found in Fourier himself but only in his school that was also influenced by Owen (whom Fourier did not wish to read). Only free and voluntary association, so we are told in 1848, can solve the great organic problem of the future, "the problem of organizing a new order, an order in which individualism will combine spontaneously with 'collectism'" (*sic*). Only in this way can "the third and last emancipatory phase of history" come about, in which the first having made serfs out of slaves, and the second wage-earners out of serfs (we find this idea in Bazard as far back as 1829), "the abolition of the proletariat, the transformation of wage-earners into companions (associés)" will be accomplished. But one will scan Fourier's own expositions of his system and the drafts of his projects in vain for the concrete expression of his opposing principle. His "phalanstery" has been compared with a large hotel, and in fact it offers many similarities to those typical products of our age which meet the greatest possible part of their requirements with their own production —only that in this case production is managed by the guests themselves, and instead of the minimum conduct regulations as in the notices in hotel-rooms there is a law which regulates the daily round in all its details—a law that has various attractions and leaves one's powers of decision fundamentally untouched but is, in itself, meticulously exact. Although the supreme authority, the "Areopagus," issues no commands, but only gives instructions and each group acts according to its will, nevertheless this will simply "*cannot* deviate from that of the Areopagus, for he is the puissance d'opinion." Many things in this law may strike us as bizarre, but all the same it expresses some important and fruitful ideas, such as the alternation of various activities—a notion that foreshadows Kropotkin's "division of labour in time." On the other hand, and regarded precisely from this standpoint, the phalanstery is a highly unsocialistic institution. The division of labour in the course of a summer day leads the poor Lucas from the stables to the gardeners, from there to the reapers, the vegetable-growers, the manual workers, etc., while the same division of labour leads the rich Mondor from the "industrial parade" to the hunt, from there to fishing, to the library, greenhouses and so on. When we read that the poor have to enjoy a "graduated state of wealth that the rich may be happy," or that "only through the utmost inequality of worldly possessions can this beautiful and magnanimous agreement be reached," i.e. the renunciation by the rich of a great part of their dividends in favour of work and talent—we realize that these units which bear the stamp of a mechanical fantasy have no legitimate claim to be considered as the cells of a new and legitimate order. Their uniformity alone (for despite their appearance of inner diversity they represent, item for item, the same pattern, the same machinery) renders them totally unsuitable for a restructuring of society. Fourier's "universal harmony" which embraces world and society means, in society itself, only a harmony between the individuals living together, not a harmony between the units themselves (although some people may, of course, imagine a "federation of phalanges"). The interconnection between the units has no place in his system, each unit is a world on its own and always the same world; but of the attraction which rules the universe we hear nothing as between these units, they do not fuse together into associations, into higher units, indeed they cannot do so because they are not, like individuals, diversified, they do not complement one another and cannot therefore form a harmony. Fourier's thought has been a powerful incentive to the Co-operative Movement and its labours, in particular to the Consumer Co-operatives; but the constructive thinking of "utopian socialism" has only been able to accept him by transcending his ideas.

Fourier's *chef d'oeuvre* appeared in 1822, the *Traité d'Association Domestique Agricole;* Saint-Simon's *Le Système Industriel* in 1821 and 1822; and from 1820 dates Robert Owen's *Report to the County of Lanark,* which appeared in 1821 and was the matured presentation of his "plan." But Fourier's *La Théorie des Quatre Mouvements et des Destinées Générales,* which contains his system in a nutshell, had already appeared in 1808; Saint-Simon's *De la Réorganisation de la Société Européenne* in 1814; Owen's *A New View of Society*—the theoretical foundation of his plans—in 1813 and 1814. If we go still further back in time we come to Saint-Simon's earliest work at the turn of the century, in which the impending crisis of humanity is already announced, and Fourier's article on universal harmony, which may be regarded as the first sketch of his doctrine. At the same time, however, we find Owen engaged in purely practical activity as the leader of the cotton-spinners in New Lanark, in which capacity he brought about some exemplary social innovations. Unlike that of Saint-Simon and Fourier his doctrine proceeds from practice, from experiment and experience. No matter whether he knew of Fourier's theories or not, Owen's teaching is, historically and philosophically speaking, a rejoinder to theirs, the empirical solution of the problem as opposed to the speculative one. The social units on which society is to be built anew can in this case be called organic; they are numerically limited communities based on agriculture and sustained by the "principle of united labour, expenditure and property, and equal privileges," and in which all members are to have "mutual and common interests." Already we see how Owen, as distinct from Fourier, presses forward to the simple pre-requisites for a genuine community where the rule is not necessarily and exclusively common ownership, but rather a binding together and "communizing" of property; not equality of expenditure, but rather equality of rights and opportunities. "Communal life," says Tönnies of the historical forms of "community," i.e. the "true and enduring forms of men's life together," is "*mutual* possession and enjoyment, and possession and enjoyment of *common* property." In other words, it is a common housekeeping in which personal possessions can stand side by side with common ones, save that through the building of a common economy (quite otherwise than in the scheme of Fourier) only a narrow margin is set between differences in personal possessions and that, as a result of mutuality, of mutual give and take, there arises that very condition which is here termed "mutual possession and enjoyment," i.e. the appropriate participation of all members in one another. Precisely this conception underlies Owen's plan. (Later he goes further and reckons common ownership and co-operative union among the basal foundations of his projected Colony.) He does not fail to appreciate that great educational activity is required for its realization. "Men have not yet been trained in principles that will permit them to act in union, except to defend themselves or to destroy others. . . . A necessity, however, equally powerful, will now compel men to be trained to act together to create and conserve." Owen knew that ultimately it was a matter of transforming the whole social order, and in particular the relationship between the rulers and the ruled. "The interest of those who govern has ever appeared to be, and under the present systems ever will appear to be, opposed to the

interest of those whom they govern." This must continue "while man
remains individualized," that is, while society refuses to build itself up
out of the real bonds between individuals. The change will reach completion in each single one of the village communities planned, before it
extends from them to the community as a whole. The Committee governing the individual village will "form a permanent, experienced local
government, never opposed to, but always in closest union with, each
individual governed." Certainly there remain at the outset the problems
of what Owen calls "the connection of the new establishments with the
Government of the country and with the old society," but from his ap-
pellation "the old society" it is clear that Owen is thinking of the new
society as growing out of the old and renewing it from within. At the
same time various stages in the evolution of the new society will have of
necessity to exist side by side. A characteristic example of this is given in
the Draft of Statutes (inspired by Owen) put forward by the "Association of All Classes of All Nations," founded in 1835, which, using a term
that had only just begun to be current in this sense, called itself "The
Socialists." Of the three divisions of this association the lower two have
only the function of Consumer Co-operatives; the third and highest, on
the contrary, is to establish a brotherhood and sisterhood which shall
form a single class of producers and consumers differentiated by age
alone, "without priests, lawyers, soldiery, buyers and sellers." This is
Utopia, to be sure, but a Utopia of that special kind without which no
amount of "science" can transform society.

The line of development leading from Saint-Simon to Fourier and
Owen rests on no sequence in time; the three men whom Engels names
as the founders of socialism worked in approximately the same period;
one could almost say that it is a development in contemporaneity. Saint-
Simon lays down that society should progress from the dual to the
unitary, the leadership of the whole should proceed from the social functions themselves, without the political order superimposing itself as an
essentially distinct and special class. To this Fourier and Owen reply that
this is only possible and permissible in a society based on joint production and consumption, i.e. a society composed of units in which the two
are conjoined, hence of smaller communities aiming at a large measure
of self-sufficiency. Fourier's answer affirms that each of these units is to
be constituted like the present society in respect of property and the
claims of the individual, only that the resultant society will be led
from contradiction to harmony by the concord of instinct and activity.
Owen's answer, on the other hand, affirms that the transformation of
society must be accomplished in its total structure as well as in each of its

cells: only a just ordering of the individual units can establish a just order in the totality. This is the foundation of socialism.

Notes

A Translation of Buber's Preface to Die Gesellschaft

1. Frankfurt am Main: Rütten & Loening, 1908. The "Geleitwort" that introduces the series appears in Volume I, *Das Proletariat*, by Werner Sombart; v–xiv. The present translation is of pages ix–xiv.

2. Cf. George Simmel, "The Problem of Sociology," in *Essays on Sociology, Philosophy and Aesthetics*, K. H. Wolff, ed. and trans. (New York: Harper Torchbooks, 1959), where Simmel speaks of "the embodiment of social energies into structures (*Gebilde*) that exist and develop outside the individual" (p. 312).

3. Cf. Simmel, "How is Society Possible?" in ibid: "The nexus by which each [individual] is interwoven with the life and activities of every other . . . is transformed into a teleological nexus as soon as it is considered from the perspective of the . . . individual" (p. 355).

4. Cf. G. Simmel, *Philosophie des Geldes* (Leipzig: Duncker and Humbolt, 1900), 7.

5. Cf. Simmel, "The Problem of Sociology," in *Essays*, op. cit.: "Certainly there is no doubt that all societal processes . . . have their seat in minds" (p. 329).

6. Cf. W. Dilthey, "Ideen über eine beschreibende und zergliedernde Psychologie," op. cit., in *Gesammelte Schriften*, V (Leipzig and Berlin: Teubner, 1914).

7. Precisely because of this fact, Simmel deems the question of social psychology and sociology as misleading. The understanding of social psychology prevalent at Simmel's time was based on a mechanical-functional model, a model that Simmel rejects because it fails to explain the objective, metaindividual character observed in the forms of sociation: see Paul Honigsheim, "The Time and Thought of the Young Simmel," in *Essays*, op. cit., 192–93.

8. Cf. Simmel, *Soziologie* (Leipzig: Duncker & Humbolt, 1908), 31.

9. Cf. ibid.

4

Biblical Leadership and Community

Biblical Leadership*

I do not imagine that you will expect me to give you any so-called character sketches of biblical leaders. That would be an impossible undertaking, for the Bible does not concern itself with character, nor with individuality, and one cannot draw from it any description of characters of individualities. The Bible depicts something else, namely, persons in situations. The Bible is not concerned with the difference between these persons; but the difference between the situations in which the person, the creaturely person, the appointed person, stands his test or fails is all-important to it.

But neither can it be my task to delve beneath the biblical account to a picture more trustworthy historically, to historical data out of which I could piece together a historically useful picture. This too is impossible. It is not that the biblical figures are unhistorical. I believe that we are standing at the beginning of a new era in biblical studies; whereas the past era was concerned with proving that the Bible did not contain history, the coming era will succeed in demonstrating its historicity. By this I do not mean that the Bible depicts men and women and events as they were in actual history; rather do I mean that its descriptions and narratives are the organic, legitimate ways of giving an account of what existed and what happened. I have nothing against calling these narratives myths and sagas, so long as we remember that myths and sagas are essentially memories which are actually conveyed from person to person. But what kind of memory is it which manifests itself in these accounts? I say again: memory; not imagination. It is an organic memory molding its material. We know of it today, because occasionally, though indeed in unlikely and indeed in incredible ways, the existence of great poets with such organic memories still extends into our time. If we want to distinguish between narrators, between a great narrator and one who is simply very talented, the best way is to consider how each of them handles

*Reprinted from *Israel and the World: Essays in a Time of Crisis* (New York: Schocken Books, 1948), pp. 119–33.

the events of his own life. The great narrator allows the events to drop into him as they happen, careless, trusting, with faith. And memory does its part: what has thus been dropped into it, it molds organically, unarbitrarily, unfancifully into a valid account and narrative; a whole on which admittedly a great deal of conscious work has then to be done, but the distinguishing mark was put upon it by the unarbitrarily shaping memory. The other narrator registers, he makes an inventory in what he also calls the memory, but which is really something quite different; he preserves the events while they are happening in order to be able to draw them forth unaltered when he needs them. Well, he will certainly draw them forth from the preservative after a fashion unaltered, and fit for use after a fashion, and then he may do with them what he can.

I said that the great poets show us in their way how the nascence of myths and sagas takes place. Each myth, even the myth we usually call the most fantastic of all, is creation around a memory core, around the kernel of the organically shaping memory. It is not that people to whom something like the exodus from Egypt has happened subsequently improvise events, allowing their fancy to add elements which they do not remember and to "embroider" on what happened; what happened continues to function, the event itself is still active and at work in their souls, but these souls, this community soul, is so made that its memory is formative, myth-creating, and the task before the biblical writers is then to work on the product of this memory. Nowhere is there any point where arbitrariness is observable or interference by alien elements; there is in it no juggling.

This being the case, we cannot disentangle the historical from the biblical. The power of the biblical writing, which springs from this shaping memory, is so great, the elemental nature of this memory so mighty, that it is quite impossible to extract any so-called historical matter from the Bible. The historical matter thus obtained would be unreal, amorphous, without significance. But it is also impossible to distil "the historical matter" from the Bible for another reason. In contrast to the sacred historiography of the other nations, there exists in the case of Israel no evidence from profane parallels by which one might correct the sacred documents; there is no historiography of another tendency than that which resides in this shaping memory; and this shaping memory stands under a law. It is this law which I shall try to elucidate by the examples with which I deal today.

In order to bring out still more clearly and exactly what I have in mind, I shall ask you to recall one of the nations with whom Israel came into historical contact and dispute; I do so for the purpose of considering the aspect under which this nation must have regarded one of the biblical leaders. Let us try to imagine how Abraham must have been regarded by one of the nations against whose kings he fought, according to Gen. 14, a chapter whose fundamental historical character seems to me beyond doubt. Undoubtedly Abraham was a historical figure to this nation in the same sense in which we usually speak about history today. But he was no longer Abraham. That which is important for us about Abraham, that which makes him a biblical character, a "Father," that which is the reason why the Bible tells us about Abraham, that is no longer embraced under this aspect, the significance of the figure has vanished. Or, take for instance the Egyptians and Moses, and imagine how an Egyptian historian would have described Moses and his cause. Nothing essential would have been left; it would be a skeleton taking the place of the living person.

All we can do therefore is to refer to the Bible, to that which is characteristic of the biblical leader as the Bible, without arbitrariness, tells of him and thinks of him, under the law of *its* conception of history, *its* living of history, which is unlike everything which we are accustomed to call history. But from this law, from this biblical way of regarding leader and leadership, different from all other ways in which leader and leadership have been regarded, from this have we—from this has Judaism—arisen.

As I now wish to investigate the question of the essence of biblical leadership, I must exclude from the inquiry all those figures who are not *biblical* leaders in the strict sense of the term: and this means, characteristically enough, I must exclude all those figures who appear as continuators, all those who are not called, elected, appointed anew, as the Bible says, directly by God, but who enter upon a task already begun without such personal call—whether it is a disciple to whom the person who is not permitted to finish the task hands over his office, breathing as it were toward his disciple the spirit that breathes upon him; or whether it is a son who succeeds an elected, originally anointed king, without receiving any other anointing than the already customary official one, which is thus no longer the anointing that comes upon a person and turns him into another man.

Thus I do not consider figures like Joshua and Solomon because the Bible has such figures in common with history—they are figures of universal history. Joshua is a great army leader, a great conqueror, but a historical figure like any other, only with special religious affiliations added, which, however, do not characterize his person. Solomon is an Oriental king, only a very wise one; he does his task, he builds the Temple, but we are not shown that this task colors and determines him. What has happened here is simply that the completion of a task, the completion of a task already intended and already begun, has been taken over by a disciple or a successor. The task of Moses, which he had already begun but was not allowed to finish, was taken over by Joshua; the task of David, which he was not allowed to finish, was taken over by Solomon. In this connection I recall the words that David and God exchanged in the second book of Samuel on the proposed building of the Temple and the prohibition against David's carrying it out: "It is not for you," says God, reproving David as he had reproved Moses when he told Moses that it was not for him to bring into their land the people whom he had led out of Egypt. The work is taken away from him, and taken away from him, moreover, in view of his special inner and outer situations; another man has nothing more to do than to bring the work to its conclusion.

Only the elected, only those who begin, are then comprised under the biblical aspect of leadership. A new beginning may also occur within a sequence of generations, as for instance within those which we call the generations of the patriarchs; this is clearly seen in the case of Jacob, with whom something new begins, as the particular way in which revelation comes to him indicates.

I would like first to attempt a negative characterization of the essential features of biblical leadership. It goes beyond both nature and history. To the men who wrote the Bible, nature, as well as history, is of God; and that in such a way that the biblical cosmogony relates each separately; in the first chapter the creation of the world is described as the coming of nature into being; and then in the second chapter this same creation of the world is described as the rise of history. Both are of God, but then the biblical event goes beyond them, God goes beyond them, not in the sense that they—nature and history—come to be ignored by God, but in the sense that time and again God's hand thrusts through them and interferes with what is happening—it so chooses, so sends, and so commands, as it does not seem to accord with the laws of nature and history to send, to choose, and to command.

I shall here show only by two particularly clear examples what I mean by this. First of all, it is the weak and the humble who are chosen. By nature it is the strong, those who can force their cause through, who are able and therefore chosen to perform the historical deeds. But in the Bible it is often precisely the younger sons who are chosen—from Abel, through Jacob, Joseph and Moses, to David; and this choosing is accompanied by a rejection, often a very emphatic rejection, of the older sons; or else those who are chosen were born out of wedlock, or of humble origin. And if it happens that a strong man like Samson appears, a man who has not all these limitations, then his strength is not his own, it is only loaned, not given, and he trifles it away, squanders it, in the way in which we are told, to get it back only in order to die.

A different but no less telling expression of what is meant by this peculiar election against nature is represented by the battle and victory of Gideon. The Bible makes him do the strangest thing any commander ever did. He has an army of ten thousand men, and he reduces its numbers again and again, till only three hundred men remain with him; and with these three hundred he gives battle and conquers.

It is always the same story. The purpose of God is fulfilled, as the Bible itself says in one place, not by might, nor by power, but "by my spirit."

It is "against nature" that in one way or another the leaders are mostly the weak and the humble. The way in which they carry out their leadership is "contrary to history." It is the moment of success which determines the selection of events which seem important to history. "World history" is the history of successes; the heroes who have not succeeded but who cannot be excluded from it on account of their very conspicuous heroism serve only as a foil, as it were. True, the conquered have also their place in "world history"; but if we scrutinize how it treats the conquerors and the conquered, what is of importance to history becomes abundantly clear. Granted that one takes Croesus together with Cyrus, that Herodotus has a use for him; nevertheless, in the heart of history only the conquerors have value. It murmurs a low dirge over the overpowered heroes, but its paean for those who stand firm, who force their cause through, for those who are crowned with success, rings out loud. This is current history, the history which we are accustomed to identify with what happens, with the real happenings in the world, in spite of the fact that this history is based only on the particular principle of picking and choosing, on the selection made by the historian, on the so-called historical consciousness.

The Bible knows nothing of this intrinsic value of success. On the contrary, when it announces a successful deed, it is duty-bound to announce in complete detail the failure involved in the success. When we consider the history of Moses we see how much failure is mingled in the one great successful action, so much so that when we set the individual events which make up his history side by side, we see that his life consists of one failure after another, through which runs the thread of his success. True, Moses brought the people out of Egypt; but each stage of this leadership is a failure. Whenever he comes to deal with this people, he is defeated by them, let God ever so often interfere and punish them. And the real history of this leadership is not the history of the exodus, but the history of the wandering in the desert. The personal history of Moses' own life, too, does not point back to his youth and to what grew out of it;

it points beyond, to death, to the death of the unsuccessful man, whose work, it is true, survives him, but only in new defeats, new disappointments, and continual new failures—and yet his work survives also in a hope which is beyond all these failures.

Or let us consider the life of David. So far as we are told of it, it consists essentially of two great stories of flight. Before his accession to the throne there are the manifold accounts of his flight from Saul, and then follows an interruption which is not trifling in terms of length and its value for profane history, but which in the account appears paltry enough, and after this there is the flight from Absalom, painted for us in detail. And even where the Bible recounts David's triumph, as for instance with the entry of the Ark into Jerusalem, this triumph is clearly described as a disgrace in a worldly sense; this is very unlike the language of "world history." What Michal, his wife, says to David of his triumph, how he ought to have felt ashamed of himself behaving as he did in front of his people—that is the language of profane history, i.e. of history *par excellence*. To history such a royal appearance is not permitted, and, rightly so, seeing that history is what it is.

And, finally, this glorification of failure culminates in the long line of prophets whose existence is failure through and through. They live in failure; it is for them to fight and not to conquer. It is the fundamental experience of biblical leadership, of the leadership described by one of them, a nameless prophet whose words are preserved in the second part of the Book of Isaiah where he speaks in the first person of himself as "the servant of the Lord," and says of God:

> *He hath made my mouth like a sharp sword,*
> *In the shadow of His hand hath He hid me;*
> *And He hath made me a polished shaft,—*
> *In his quiver hath He concealed me!* (Isa. 49:2).

This existence in the shadow, in the quiver, is the final word of the leaders in the biblical world; this enclosure in failure, in obscurity, even when one stands in the blaze of public life, in the presence of the whole national life. The truth is hidden in obscurity and yet does its work; though indeed in a way far different from that which is known and lauded as effective by world history.

Biblical leadership falls into five basic types, not according to differences in the personality and character of the leader—I have already said that personality and character do not come into consideration—but according to the difference in the successive situations, the great stages in the history of the people which the Bible describes, the stages in the dialogue between God and the people. For what the Bible understands by history is a dialogue in which man, in which the people, is spoken to and fails to answer, yet where the people in the midst of its failure continually rises up and tries to answer. It is the history of God's disappointments, but this history of disappointments constitutes a way, a way that leads from disappointment to disappointment and beyond all disappointments; it is the way of the people, the way of man, yes, the way of God through mankind. I said that there are five basic types in accordance with the successive stages of the situations in the dialogue: first, the Patriarch; second, the Leader in the original sense of one who leads the wandering; third, the so-called Judge; fourth, the King, but of course not the king who is a successor, a member of a dynasty, but the founder of the dynasty, called the first anointed; fifth, the Prophet. All these constitute different forms of leadership in accordance with the different situations.

First the Patriarch. This is a current conception which is not quite correct. No rulership is here exercised, and, when we understand the conception in its accurate sense, we cannot here speak of any leadership, for there is as yet no people to lead. The conception indicates a way along which the people are to be led beginning with these men. They are Fathers. It is for them to beget a people. It is the peculiar point in biblical history where God, as it were, narrows down his original plan for the whole of mankind and causes a people to be begotten that is called to do its appointed work toward the completion of the creation, the coming of the kingdom. The fathers of this people are the men of whom I speak. They are Fathers, nothing else. Patriarch expresses too much. They are the real fathers, they are those from whom this tribe, this people, proceeds; and when God speaks to them, when God blesses them, the same thing is always involved: conception and birth, the beginning of a people. And the great story which stands in the middle of the story of the patriarchs—the birth and offering of Isaac—makes exactly this point, in a paradoxical manner. Kierkegaard has presented this paradox very beautifully in the first part of his book *Fear and Trembling*. This paradoxical story of the second in the line of the patriarchs, of his being born and very nearly being killed, shows what is at stake: a begetting, but the begetting of a people standing at the disposal of God; a begetting, but a begetting commanded by God.

We have a people, and the people is in bondage. A man receives the charge to lead it out. That is he whom I have described as the Leader in the original meaning of the word. It is he who serves in a human way as a tool for the act which God pronounces, "I bore you on eagles' wings, and brought you unto myself" (Exod. 19:4). I have already spoken of his life. But in the middle of his life the event takes place in which Moses, after the passage through the Red Sea, intones the song in which the people joins, and which is the proclamation of a King. The words with which the song ends proclaim it: "King shall the Lord be for ever and ever" (Exod. 15:18). The people has here chosen God himself for its King, and that means that it has made a vital and experienced truth out of the tradition of a divine kingdom which was common to all Semitic peoples but which never had been taken quite seriously. The Hebrew leaders are so much in earnest about it that after the land has been conquered they undertake to do what is "contrary to history": they try to build up a society without a ruling power save only that of God. It is that experiment in primitive theocracy of which the Book of Judges tells, and which degenerates into anarchy, as is shown by the examples given in its last part.

The so-called Judge constitutes the third type of leadership. This type is to be understood as the attempt made by a leading group among the people that are dominated by the desire to make actual the proclamation of God as king, and try to induce the people to follow them. This attempt miscarries time and again. Time and again the people, to use the biblical phrase, falls away from God. But we can also express this in the language of history: time and again the people fall apart; it is one and the same thing whichever language we use. The attempt to establish a society under no other dominion than God's—this too can be expressed in the language of history, or if one likes, in the language of sociology: the attempt to establish a society on pure voluntarism fails over and over again. The people falls away. This is always succeeded by an invasion by one of the neighboring peoples, and Israel, from a historical point of view fallen apart and disunited, does not stand firm. But in its conquered state it again makes itself subject to the will of God, resolves anew to accept God's dominion, and again a divine mission occurs; there is always a leader whom the spirit lays hold of as it laid hold of Moses. This leader, whose mission it is to free the people, is "the Judge," or more correctly, "he who makes right"; he makes this right exist in the actual world for the people, which after its return to God now again has right on its side, by defeating the enemy. This is the rhythm of the Book of Judges; it might almost be called a tragic rhythm, were it not that the word tragic is so foreign to the spirit of biblical language.

But in this Book of Judges there is also something being prepared. The experience of failure, of the inability to bring about this intended, naïve, primitive theocracy becomes ever deeper, ever stronger grows the demand for a human kingdom. Judges itself is in its greater part written from an anti-monarchical standpoint. The Kings of the peoples file be-

fore one in a way determined by this point of view, which reaches its
height in that ironic fable of Jotham's (Judg. 9). But in its final chapters
the Book of Judges has to acknowledge the disappointment of the the-
ocratic hope, because the people is as it is, because men are as they are.
And so kingship is demanded under Samuel. And it is granted by God. I
said before, the way leads through the disappointments. Thus the demand of the people is as it were laid hold of and consecrated from above;
for by the anointing of the King a man is transformed into the bearer of a
charge laid upon him. But this is no longer—as was the case with the
Judge—a single charge the completion of which brings his leadership
to an end; it is a governor's charge which goes beyond individual acts,
indeed beyond the life of individual men. Anointing may also imply
the beginning of a dynasty, when the king is not rejected by God, as
Saul was.

The kingdom is a new stage in the dialogue, a new stage of attempt
and failure, only in this stage the account lays the burden of the failure
on the king and not any longer, as in the Book of Judges, on the whole
people. It is no longer those who are led but the leader himself who fails,
who cannot stand the test of the charge, who does not make the anointing come true in his own person—a crucial problem in religious history.
The history of the great religions, and in general all great history, is
bound up with the problem: How do human beings stand the test of
what is here called anointing?

The history of the kings is the history of the failure of him who has
been anointed to realize the promise of his anointing. The rise of messia-
nism, the belief in the anointed king who realizes the promise of his
anointing, is to be understood only in this context.

But now in the situation of the failure of kings the new and last type of
leader in biblical history arises, the leader who above all other types is
"contrary to history," the Prophet, he who is appointed to oppose the
king, and even more, history. When God says to Jeremiah, "I have made
thee . . . a brazen wall against the whole land" (Jer. 1:18), it is really so;
the prophet stands not only against the ruler but against the people itself. The prophet is the man who has been set up against his own natural
instincts that bind him to the community, and who likewise sets himself
up against the will of the people to live on as they have always lived,
which, naturally, for the people is identical with the will to live. It goes
without saying that not only the rulers but also the people treat the
prophet as their enemy in the way in which, as a matter of history, it falls
to the lot of such men to be treated. These experiences of suffering which
thus come upon the prophet join together to form that image of the ser-

vant of the Lord, of his suffering and dying for the sake of God's purpose.

When the Bible then tries to look beyond these manifestations of leadership to one which no longer stands amidst disintegration and failure, when the idea of the messianic leader is conceived, it means nothing else by it than that at last the answer shall be given: from out of mankind itself the word shall come, the word that is spoken with the whole being of man, the word that answers God's word. It is an earthly consummation which is awaited, a consummation in and with mankind. But this precisely is the consummation toward which God's hand pushes through that which he has created, through nature and through history. This is what the messianic belief means, the belief in the real leader, in the setting right of the dialogue, in God's disappointment being at an end. And when a fragment of an apocryphal gospel has God say to Jesus: "In all the prophets have I awaited thee, that thou wouldst come and I rest in thee, for thou art My rest," this is the late elaboration of a truly Jewish conception.

The biblical question of leadership is concerned with something greater than moral perfection. The biblical leaders are the foreshadowings of the dialogical man, of the man who commits his whole being to God's dialogue with the world, and who stands firm throughout this dialogue. The life of those people to whom I have referred is absorbed in this dialogue, whether the dialogue comes about through an intervention, as in Abraham's talk with God about Sodom, or Moses' after the sin of the golden calf; or whether it comes about through a resistance they offer against that which comes upon them and tries to overpower them; but their resistance ends in submission, which we find documented from Moses to Jeremiah; or whether the dialogue comes about through the struggle for a purpose and a task, as we know from that dialogue which took place between David and God; whatever the way, man enters into the dialogue again and again; imperfect entry, but yet one which is not refused, an entry which is determined to persevere in the dialogical world. All that happens is here experienced as dialogue, what befalls man is taken as a sign, what man tries to do and what miscarries is taken as an attempt and a failure to answer, as a stammering attempt to respond as well as one can.

Because this is so, biblical leadership always means a process of being-led. These men are leaders insofar as they allow themselves to be led, that is, insofar as they accept that which is offered them, insofar as they take upon themselves the responsibility for that which is entrusted to them, insofar as they make real that which has been laid upon them from outside of themselves, make it real with the free will of their own being, in the "autonomy" of their person.

So long as we remember this, we can make the lives of these leaders clear. Almost always what we see is the taking of a man out of the community. God lifts the man out of the community, cuts him off from his natural ties; from Abraham to Jeremiah he must go forth out of the land in which he has taken root, away to the place where he has to proclaim the name of God; it is the same story, whether it is a wandering over the earth like Abraham's, or a becoming utterly alone in the midst of the people like the prophets'. They are drawn out of their natural community; they fight with it, they experience in this community the inner contradiction of human existence. All this is intensified to the utmost precisely in the prophets. The great suffering of the prophets, preserved for us by Jeremiah himself in a small number of (in the highest sense of the word) autobiographical sayings is the ultimate expression of this condition.

But this ever widening gulf between leader and community, the ever greater failure of the leader, the leader's ever greater incompatibility with "history"—this means, from the biblical standpoint, the gradual overcoming of history. What we are accustomed to call history is from the biblical standpoint only the façade of reality. It is the great failure, the refusal to enter into the dialogue, not the failure in the dialogue, as exemplified by biblical man. This great refusal is sanctioned with the imposing sanction provided by so-called history. The biblical point of view repudiates with ever increasing strength this two-dimensional reality, most strongly in the prophets; it proclaims that the way, the real way, from the Creation to the Kingdom is trod not on the surface of success, but in the deep of failure. The real work, from the biblical point of view, is the late-recorded, the unrecorded, the anonymous work. The real work is done in the shadow, in the quiver. Official leadership fails more and more, leadership devolves more and more upon the secret. The way leads through the work which history does not write down, and which history cannot write down, work which is not ascribed to him who did it, but which possibly at some time in a distant generation will emerge as having been done, without the name of the doer—the secret working of the secret leadership. And when the biblical writer turns his eyes toward the final messianic overcoming of history, he sees how the outer history becomes engulfed, or rather how both the outer history and the inner history fuse, how the secret which the leadership had become rises up out of the darkness and illumines the surface of history, how the meaning of biblical history is consummated in the whole reality.

The Land*

According to the account in the Book of Numbers[1] and the parallel narrative in the Book of Deuteronomy,[2] Moses sends spies from Kadesh to Canaan. They bring back good and bad tidings. Shaken by the unfavourable part of the reports, the people lament, speak of appointing themselves a new head and returning to Egypt; those who offer them opposition are in danger of being stoned. At this point YHVH intervenes; He wishes to destroy the people, and to let the offspring of Moses serve for the making of a fresh one. Moses intercedes and wins forgiveness for them, but the sinful generation is condemned to perish in the wilderness; "forty years" must pass ere Israel enters Canaan.

Now the people suddenly resolve to depart for Canaan at once. Against the will of Moses and without the Ark of the Covenant, they make a sortie against the Amalekites and Canaanites living in the mountains, and are defeated.

It is scarcely possible to win any historical core of fact out of the narrative, save that the Amalekites, who had been compelled to relinquish Kadesh to the incursors, had united themselves with the neighbouring tribes and prevented further advances, for an entire generation as it would seem. Yet the story seems to hold an implication that Kadesh, where Israel obviously stayed for a long time, was the station at which the people became directly aware of Canaan as the goal of their wanderings.

Here Kadesh should not be understood as meaning a single spot, but the entire group of level valleys lying south of Palestine on the way between Akaba and Beersheba, which link up with the place of that name: valleys surrounded by hills, where springs gush forth, so that sometimes the water bursts from the clefts and crannies of the rocks. The land is rich in water and fruitful for the greater part, here and there, indeed, of a "paradisical fruitfulness."[3] To this day the soil, which is several feet deep, still provides the Arabs who till it with rich harvests of grain when there has been a good rainy season.[4] The district has noteworthy remains of Syro-Canaanite culture, dating from the second half of the second millenium B.C., including a fortress which is supposed[5] to have been already standing when Moses and his hosts came there; and the presence of which makes it possible to explain the biblical description of Kadesh as a "town" or fortified place.[6]

The people may have fixed on this spot, which was so suitable for the

*Reprinted from *Moses* (Oxford: The East and West Library, Phaidon Press, Ltd.), pp. 172–81.

purpose, as the centre of their movements, where, presumably on the Midianite model,[7] Moses remained with the Ark and the armed Levite guard, while the tribes swarmed forth. The fruitful soil was tilled, as had already been done by the "Fathers,"[8] with primitive but productive methods; and the herds were driven to pasture in the neighbourhood.[9] The Hebrews had returned not only "to the place of the Fathers"[10] but also to their form of life.

But is the urge to Canaan to be attributed, as some think, to the fact that the rapid increase of the people made it necessary to find more room? Or was Kadesh regarded from the very beginning as no more than a station, the prolonged sojourning in which was an outcome of the historical circumstances? Is the promise to Moses of a "good broad land"[11] to be explained as due to a later shaping of the Exodus tradition, or ought we to understand it as an essential motive in Moses' own actions? When Moses departed from Egypt, did he wish only to liberate the tribes? Or did he wish to lead them to settle as well? Was the memory of the Canaan of the Fathers at work in him as a hope and aspiration? In the religious field he had sought and found, in a passionately remembered past, the basis of the future which he wished to build. Was this equally true in the field of actual history?

In our own times critical investigation is once again beginning to recognize[12] that "the element of the promising of the land in the legends of the Fathers is not in itself a free creation of the Yahvist, a predating, perchance, of the needs of the tradition of the Occupation of the Land, but belongs to old and indeed to the oldest traditions." In other words: it will not do to view the stories of the Fathers as no more than a pseudo-historical justification of the claim to Canaan.[13] It has been emphatically pointed out[14] that the Fathers owed their position in the Israelite traditional sagas primarily to their function as recipients of revelation, and at the same time to the relations of the divinities revealing themselves to them "to genealogically confirmed associations, to clans and tribes";[15] as well as to the fact that this type of religion contained within itself "a tendency to the social and the historical," which "corresponds to the conditions of life in nomadic tribes."[16]

But from the fact that each of the Fathers has a separate designation for the God who revealed Himself to him—Shield of Abraham, Fear of Isaac, Paladin of Jacob—it would be quite wrong to conclude that three different gods are meant. He who receives a tradition from the father or the inaugurator regarding the latter's God will certainly identify the God who appears to himself with the God of that tradition; yet at the same time he will give expression to the fact of his own immediate and personal relationship, which is so basically important for him and his circle, by employing some fresh appellative. "Isaac recognizes the God of Abraham, who, however, was also his, Isaac's, own God, in a peculiar fashion deriving from his own personal biography, and so forth."[17]

If that is so, we must ascertain in how far it is still possible for us to examine the texts available to us with regard to a common concrete content of that revelation—and further, a content which contains an implicit trend towards the social and historical. We are entitled to regard the promising of the Land as such a content. These men announce that a God has led them hither in order that they, like some herald in the name of the king, may proclaim His name over the holy cities of this land, as a sign that He is about to come in order to claim them as having been his own from the beginning, and to take possession of them.[18] [19] That God promises them in specific connection with this that he wishes to "give" it to their offspring as the community of those who confess Him and serve Him. This is actually, as far as I can see, something so pregnant as to be without parallel in the history of religion; yet there is a primal lushness and freshness about it, such as cannot be synthesized in the laboratories of tendentious literature.

And it is very understandable historically that such a revelation continues to exert an effect. No distinction can be drawn between the "God of the Fathers" and the One who revealed Himself to Moses. Aye, the identity of the two, and with that identity the fulfilment of the ancient promise, cannot be imagined or supposed save together with the tremendous meaning of this revelation for Moses, which sets his personal activity into motion. Moses discovers himself as the agent and carrier of this fulfilment. It is of necessity part of the message which he brings to the people.

I tend to doubt whether the settlement of the people, with all its full concrete implications, can have become clear to him until this point. As far as can be judged, the tribes in Egypt were in all likelihood restricted to cattle-raising in the main, and the period of forced labour is scarcely likely to have served them as a preparation for agriculture; neither in Midian nor afterwards in Egypt could Moses ever have come to realize all the external and internal transformations that were bound to be involved in a transfer to a predominantly agrarian form of life. I tend to suppose that this can have begun to become clear to him only at Kadesh, with the beginning of the people's experience in some measure of tilling the soil.

As the thought of the land became more concrete, however, Moses would also have begun to consider the necessity of legal provisions such as might serve to regulate the new form of life in a fashion that could secure the conditions of a just social life, which he may well have known from nomadic tribal traditions and his own experience with the people, against grave disturbance. And here as well he would have had to start out from his basic idea, that of the real and direct rule of God, which would necessarily have led to the postulate that God owns all land.

The name Kadesh means "sanctuary";[20] since ancient times[21] it had been called "Fountain of Judgment"; it was a holy well. When I sat under the ancient oak in the grove above one of the sources of the Jordan in the extreme north of Palestine, at that unmistakable place of judgment which the Arabs still call "The Hill of the Judge" near Dan (which itself is also a name meaning "Judge"), I began to comprehend what Kadesh must have been in the far south of the country, and what had happened there. Moses, as had been the custom of the Fathers, had laid claim in the name of YHVH to the time-old hallowed place—we do not know anything about the god or spirit to which it had been dedicated. There he must not merely have pronounced judgment but must also have "set up law and judgment"[22]; that is clearly the duty and function of every leader of a people in such a situation, where he cannot draw on a fixed legal tradition adapted to the given conditions of life. Yet far beyond all the requirements of the moment, his mind may well have meditated on what must become precept in order that the at that time as yet unrealized people of God might become a reality under more favourable conditions.

Research in principle treats Israelite land law as predominantly post-Mosaic, because Moses in the wilderness cannot very well be supposed to have concerned himself with the entirely different type of organization to be found in the life of a settled people. Historically, however, it is quite thinkable that a legislator, who has in mind a fundamental transformation of the economic structure of a people, should also draft a legal system corresponding to that change, even though along very general lines only. To which it should be added that even the very modest agricultural attempts at Kadesh might already be sufficient to make the promulgation of certain provisions appear necessary to the leader, who is intent on the inner cohesion of the community.

In addition, it must be remembered that no innovations were involved as far as the world of the Ancient Orient was concerned. We know, for example, that in the old Arabian civilization "God, King and People was the juridical formula for the State" (in which formula the king functions as representative of the god, and as intermediary); and that in connection with this the soil was considered to be the property of the god.[23] Though the documents which have become known to us have to be dated many hundreds of years after Moses, it is scarcely possible to doubt the high age of the basic idea, particularly when we meet with cognate concepts at Babylon in the middle of the Third Millenium B.C.

As can so frequently be found in Israel's treatment of ancient Oriental spiritual values, the land law of the Bible transformed what was already existent into a realistic view which does not rest satisfied with any mere symbolism. Yet at the same time it elevated this pre-existent material into a higher sphere of meaning and word, while basing itself upon the principle expressed in the words of God[24]: "For the earth (the land) is mine; for you are dwellers and sojourners with me." To-day this sentence is once again recognized as "very ancient."[25] It is found in a text which, as a whole, belongs to a late literary period and is composed of various stylistic shreds;[26] but this certainly does not justify us in refusing to attribute it to Moses. The Israelites must, it would seem, have described their relations to Egypt in such terms; and the warning, found recurring even in the oldest part of biblical law,[27] not to oppress the "dweller," since they themselves had been in his situation when in Egypt, and therefore know his "soul," clearly has very deep roots in the historical memory of the people. Just as the children of Israel have left the service of Egypt for the service of YHVH, so from having been dwellers in Egypt they have become dwellers with YHVH. The introductory words "for the earth is mine" are also reminiscent of the words of the Eagle Speech: "For the whole earth is mine." On both occasions God lays claim to the earth; on one occasion, however, namely in the Eagle Speech, in respect of his rule over the peoples of the earth; and on the other, in the words about sojourners, in respect of possession of the soil, the soil of Canaan. [Buber gives the name "Eagle Speech" to the speech of God to Moses in which He exhorts Israel to keep His covenant. He refers to His bringing the Israelites out of Egypt: "I bore you upon eagles' wings and brought you unto me." Exod. 19:4.]

However, another motif seems to have become associated with the sense of these ancient words, and in it the belief of Moses in the one Lord, an early and powerful belief, is given expression.

In the, at all events, very old legal stratum of the so-called Book of the Covenant the command is found[28] to "let fall" the cultivated land, fields, vineyards and olive-groves, in the seventh year of their cultivation, and to "forsake" their yield so that "the needy ones of your people may eat therefrom"; what they leave over may be consumed by the "beasts of the field." The scanty and "somewhat abrupt"[29] formulation seems to be something like a preliminary note calling for later elucidation and precise definition. At the same time it is marked with that vivid force of expression which is so often characteristic of such notes. At the beginning of the section in which the "dwellers" passage is to be found[30] the underlying idea of the law is expressed more precisely, and in three respects: first that the seventh year is a "Sabbath unto YHVH" like the seventh day; second, that it should be a Sabbath for the soil, in which the latter should lie fallow and thus find rest like Man on the seventh day; third, that what it yields shall belong to all and sundry in common, freeman and bonds, Israelite and sojourner, man and beast. Here we obviously have the "better and more complete text";[31] or more precisely the expansion of that first sketch. The relationship between these two should not be taken as meaning that in the beginning there was a practical economic and social humanitarian provision, which was afterwards expanded and extended into the religious sphere by a later theology. Rather was the seventh year in Israel the period since time immemorial of a "fallow-lying which was sacral in intention, for the duration of which the right of usufruct enjoyed by the Israelite clans in the soil and land which fell to their lot was invalidated, and the sole and exclusive right of possession of Yahveh once more becomes manifest."[32] "The idea of the equality of all creatures"[33] is certainly characteristic of the Sabbatical year, as it is of the Sabbath itself; but it is as creatures of the one Creator that they are all equal to one another; and as on the day dedicated to YHVH, so in the year dedicated to Him, they receive the same rights in one or the other sphere, in one or the other form. And here the thought is certainly at work "that the soil shall be free for a time, so that it should not be subjected to the will of human beings, but left to its own nature; in order that it may be no man's land."[34] But just because it belongs to God, the soil must be made free again and again. Here the cosmic, the social and the religious aspects are still in their roots united; they cannot yet be separated from each other.

The epoch in which such a unity was still possible can be fixed. For this reason it has justly been said[35] that the establishment of the institution of the Sabbatical year "is thinkable only at a time when the Israelite tribes had not yet entirely foresaken the semi-nomadism of their early days and, though they have already begun to engage in agriculture, to be sure, have not yet made it the centre of gravity of their economic life." It is true that "for this stage the final period before and the initial period after their occupation of Palestine can equally well be thought of." But the earlier, Kadesh that is, is indicated by the as yet undiminished concentration of the wandering hosts and the intensity of the initiative of Moses; and at no later time can anything similar be found that will bear comparison with these two.

The view has been expressed in various quarters[36] "that the abolition of the preceding legal situation in respect of land during the seventh year was originally a complete one," as complete as in the later law regarding the year of Jubilee (which, incidentally, is not to my mind late in its nucleus, and certainly not merely "theoretical," but was rather intended to afford an extension of the period of restoration, because the one originally provided for was not observed). Hence, according to this view, in the Sabbatical year there was a fresh allotment of landed areas to the single families, such as can still be found taking place annually among certain Arab semi-nomads after a fashion reminiscent of the biblical terminology.[37]

If this assumption is correct, and so it seems to me, then it was the purpose of the Sabbatical year to lead to a renewal of the organization of the society, in order to start afresh. The renewal of the land in the fallow period and the renewal of the people in the restoration of the original equality are associated. "The unconditional connection of the people was intended to preserve the consciousness of common ownership of land and soil."[38] But this consciousness necessarily had to strike deep roots; it had to be nourished in its deeps by a knowledge of the life of the earth, on which the life of human beings is dependent.

So we are entitled to assume that Moses continued his Sabbatical train of thought and, while making use of the economic tradition of the semi-nomads, conceived the idea of overcoming the continually-expanding social harm for ever by ensuring the restoration, in each ensuing Sabbatical year, "of the normal situation of the national community of Israel after all the deviations and wrong developments of the preceding six years."[39]

The "normal situation" in question is that particular one in which the people found itself when it entered into the *melek* covenant and was prepared to fulfil it, that is, to bring about a genuine community; and it is this particular situation which Moses wishes to establish afresh again and again in despite of all "deviations and wrong developments" which might occur. What an isolated social contemplation might regard as a restoration of a normal situation, to a view including the religious element it becomes manifest as a renewal of the Covenant in the seventh year, the year of "letting fall," during which the old Mosaic law is read out loud at the Feast of Tabernacles before the assembled people in later days.[40] It becomes manifest as "a reconducting of the national community to the ideal basis of their existence, a renewed obligation of all members of the people to the will of Yahve, without which the union of the tribes into a national entity would not and could not have come about."[41]

Various scholarly hypotheses have been spun about Kadesh. Thus it has been supposed[42] that this had been the district of the Tribe of Levi since time untold, and that Moses was a priest of that tribe. "The cultic site at the Burning Bush, which presumably lay in the same valley," had been "held in high esteem far beyond the territory of Levi, among all the neighbouring tribes"; and at "the great festival of Yahwe" with which "was associated an annual fair and market standing under the protection of the truce of God," the priests of Levi functioned as "intermediaries and arbitrators between the tribes and the individuals."

An attractive picture, but here the historian goes an unwarranted distance from the texts which are available to him. What the latter provide is only that Moses made the fortified spot at the holy well of judgment into a centre of "Israel," at which he gave out the law and instructed the people. As the journey to Canaan became more and more plain as the task impending, first as immediately ahead and then, after the unfortunate issue of fighting, as a task for which they would have to equip themselves a long time in advance, Moses must have seen it as necessary to draft the fundamental principles of the land law on the basis of the experiences gained at Kadesh.

These had to be principles suitable for protecting the settled people from the dangers of settlement, from the inequality of land ownership that threatened the community with decomposition. No institution of the "once-for-all" kind seemed to be capable of prevailing here against the rapacity of those who possessed more. Here Moses, while supporting himself by the customs of the semi-nomads, brought from the deeps of his Sabbatical thought, in which time is rhythmically articulated, the principle of a regular restoration of the initial state of affairs, to be regulated by arranging the years according to the holy number, just as the days of the week had been arranged according to the holy number. And for Moses any effective arrangement is intimately bound up with consecration to YHVH; in fact it is the consecration which properly speaking establishes the order.

The Sabbath consecrated to YHVH establishes the unit of the week; the Sabbatical year consecrated to YHVH establishes the unit of seven years. As the Sabbath unites the busy household community in the common freedom of God, surmounting all the differences of the working days, so the Sabbatical year, surmounting all the differences which have ensued and accrued in the preceding six years, unites the busy national community in the common freedom of God. There the concrete foundations is the joint resting of human beings who have worked for six days; here it is the resting of the soil which has been tilled for six years. All the other provisions are bound up with this one. Just as those who have become slaves are liberated in the seventh year, which certain scholars[43] even identify with the Sabbatical year, so in the Sabbatical year, if those plausible assumptions were to be correct, the equality of ownership of the impoverished families with that of the enriched ones is reestablished; while the abolishment of, or the respite for, debts ameliorates the situation of the indebted individual, and enables him to fall back once again on his share of the family property. At the same time a great symbol of the common accessibility to all men of the nourishing earth is established by the equal right of all creatures to enjoy the usufruct of the earth in the Sabbatical year.

And above all this there hovers the consecration to YHVH, to whom the earth belongs and who, by means of that earth, nourishes His dwellers and sojourners. They ought not to thrust one another aside, they ought not to impoverish one another permanently or enslave one another; they must again and ever again become equal to one another in their freedom of person and free relation to the soil; they must rest together and enjoy the usufruct together; the times dedicated to God make them free and equal again and again, as they were at the beginning.

The land is given to them in common in order that in it and from it they may become a true national Community, a "Holy People." Such is the unfolding of the promise of Canaan to the Fathers, which had doubtless lived on in the Egyptian exile, even though almost forgotten. This earth, so YHVH had promised the Fathers, He would give to their "seed";[44] in order that they might become a *berakah,* a blessing power.[45]

Notes

The Land

1. Num. 13, 14.
2. Deut. 1:22–46.
3. Kuehtreiber, "Bericht ueber meine Reisen" (Zeitschrift des Deutschen Palaestina-Vereins 37, 1914), p. 11.
4. Cf. Woolley and Lawrence, *The Wilderness of Zin* (1914), p. 58ff.
5. Woolley, op. cit., p. 71.
6. Num. 20:16.
7. Cf. A. Klostermann, *Geschichte des Volkes Israel* (1896), p. 69.
8. Gen. 26:12.
9. Garstang, *The Heritage of Solomon* (1934), p. 177.
10. Gressmann, *Die Anfaenge Israels,* 2d ed., p. 106.
11. Exod. 3:8.
12. von Rad, "Das theologische Problem des Alttestamentlichen Schoepfungsglaubens," in: *Wesen und Werden des Alten Testaments* (1936), p. 139.
13. Galling, *Die Erwaehlungstraditionen Israels,* p. 65.
14. Alt, *Der Gott der Vaeter,* p. 57.
15. Ibid., p. 41.
16. Ibid., p. 46.
17. Buber, *The Teaching of the Prophets,* p. 40.
18. Gen. 12:8; 13:4; 21:33; 26:25.

19. Cf. Buber, op. cit., p. 36.

20. The Arabs of Sinai, to be sure, use the name *qadeis* for a spoon-shaped wooden vessel which they employ when drawing water out of an almost empty well (Woolley and Lawrence, *The Wilderness of Zin,* p. 53). This name is held to come from a word in the Hedjaz dialect. But it can be explained properly only as a folk-etymology of the name of the place, not as genuine etymology. Phythian-Adams, in *The Call of Israel,* p. 196, assumes quite incorrectly in this connection that the name has nothing to do with sanctity.

21. Gen. 14:7.

22. Exod. 15:25.

23. Rhodokanakis, "Die Bodenwirtschaft im alten Suedarabien" (Anzeigen der Wiener Akademie der Wissenschaften 53, 1916), p. 174.

24. Lev. 25:23.

25. von Rad, op. cit., p. 139.

26. Cf. Jirku, *Das israelitische Jubeljahr* (Reinhold-Seeberg-Festschrift, 1929), pp. 172ff.

27. Exod. 22:20; 23:9.

28. Exod. 23:10f.

29. Pedersen, *Israel, Its Life and Culture I–II* (1926), p. 544.

30. Lev. 25:2–7.

31. Pedersen, op. cit., p. 544.

32. Alt, *Die Urspruenge des israelitischen Rechts,* p. 65; cf. also von Rad, *Das formgeschichtliche Problem des Hexateuchs,* pp. 31f.

33. Menes, *Die vorisraelitischen Gesetze Israels* (1926), 39.

34. Pedersen, op. cit., p. 480.

35. Alt, op. cit., pp. 65f.

36. Fenton, *Early Hebrew Life* (1880), pp. 67ff.; Kennett, *Ancient Hebrew Life and Custom* (1933), p. 77; Alt, op. cit., p. 66.

37. Cf. Musil, *Arabia Petraea III,* pp. 293f.

38. Jirku, op. cit., p. 178.

39. Alt, op. cit., p. 66.

40. Deut. 31:10ff.

41. Alt, op. cit., p. 67.

42. Ed. Meyer, *Die Israeliten und ihre Nachbarstaemme,* pp. 80f.

43. Kugler, *Von Moses bis Paulus* (1922), pp. 42ff.; Kennett, op. cit., p. 77.

44. Gen. 12:7.

45. Ibid., 2.

5

Hasidic Community and Leadership

Introduction to *Tales of the Hasidim**

1

The purpose of this book is to introduce the reader to a world of legend-ary reality. I must call it legendary, for the accounts which have been handed down to us, and which I have here tried to put into fitting form, are not authentic in the sense that a chronicle is authentic. They go back to fervent human beings who set down their recollections of what they saw or thought they had seen, in their fervor, and this means that they included many things which took place but were apparent only to the gaze of fervor, and others which cannot have happened and could not happen in the way they are told, but which the elated soul perceived as reality and, therefore, related as such. That is why I must call it reality: the reality of the experience of fervent souls, a reality born in all inno-cence, unalloyed by invention and whimsy. These souls did not give an account of themselves but of what stirred them, and so, whatever we learn from this account is not only a fact in the psychological sense, but a fact of life as well. Something happened to rouse the soul, and it had such and such an effect; by communicating the effect, tradition also re-veals its cause; the contact between those who quicken and those who are quickened, the association between the two. That is true legend and that is its reality.

The men who are the subject of these tales, the men who quicken, are the zaddikim, a term which is usually translated by "the righteous," but which actually means "those who stood the test" or "the proven." They are the leaders of the hasidic communities. And the men who do the tell-ing,[1] whose tales constitute the body of transmitted legends, the men who were quickened, are the hasidim, "the devout," or, more accurately, those who keep faith with the covenant. They are the members of such communities. This book, then, purports to express and document the association between zaddikim and hasidim, and should be accepted as

---

*Reprinted from *Tales of the Hasidim* (New York: Schocken Books, 1947), pp. 1–34.

the expression and documentation of the life of the zaddikim with their hasidim.

2

The core of hasidic teachings is the concept of a life of fervor, of exalted joy. But this teaching is not a theory which can persist regardless of whether it is translated into reality. It is rather the theoretic supplement to a life which was actually lived by the zaddikim and hasidim, especially in the first six generations of the movement. . . .

The underlying purpose of all great religions and religious movements is to beget a life of elation, of fervor which cannot be stifled by any experience, which, therefore, must spring from a relationship to the eternal, above and beyond all individual experiences. But since the contacts a man makes with the world and with himself are frequently not calculated to rouse him to fervor, religious concepts refer him to another form of being, to a world of perfection in which his soul may also grow perfect. Compared to this state of perfect being, life on earth seems either only an antechamber, or mere illusion, and the prospect of a higher life has the task of creating fervor in the face of disappointing outer and inner experiences, of creating the fervent conviction that there is such a higher life, and that it is, or can gradually become, accessible to the human soul, under certain conditions beyond the bounds of earthly existence. Although faith in a life hereafter is integral to Judaism, there has always been a strong tendency to provide an earthly residence for perfection. The great Messianic concept of coming perfection on earth which everyone can actively help prepare for, could not, in spite of the power it exerted over souls, endow daily life with that constant, undaunted and exalted joy in the Now and Here, which can spring only from fulfilment in the present, not from hope in a future fulfilment. This was not altered when the Kabbalistic teaching of the transmigration of souls made it possible for everyone to identify his soul with that of a person of the Messianic generation, and thus have the feeling of participating in it. Only in the Messianic movements themselves, which always were based on the belief that perfection was just on the verge of being realized, did the fervor break through and permeate all of life. When the last of these movements, the Sabbatian movement, and its after-effects ended in renegacy and despair, the test for the living strength of religion had come, for here no mere softening of sorrow, but only a life of fervent joy could aid the Jew to survive. The development of hasidism indicates that the test was passed.

The hasidic movement did not weaken the hope in a Messiah, but it kindled both its simple and intellectual followers to joy in the world as it is, in life as it is, in every hour of life in this world, as that hour is. Without dulling the prick of conscience or deadening the sense of chasm between the ideal pattern of the individual limned by his Creator, and what he actually is, hasidism shows men the way to God who dwells with them "in the midst of their uncleannesses," a way which issues forth from every temptation, even from every sin. Without lessening the strong obligation imposed by the Torah, the movement suffused all the traditional commandments with joy-bringing significance, and even set aside the walls separating the sacred and the profane, by teaching that every profane act can be rendered sacred by the manner in which it is performed. It had nothing to do with pantheism, which destroys or stunts the greatest of all values: the reciprocal relationship between the human and the divine, the reality of the I and the You which does not cease at the rim of eternity. Hasidism did, however, make manifest the reflection of the divine, the sparks of God that glimmer in all beings and all things, and taught how to approach them, how to deal with them, how to "lift" and redeem them, and re-connect them with their original root. The doctrine of the Shekhinah, contained in the Talmud and expanded in the Kabbalah, of the Shekhinah as the Divine Presence which resides in this world, receives a new and intimate significance and applicability. If you direct the undiminished power of your fervor to God's world-destiny, if you do what you must do at this moment—no matter what it may be!—with your whole strength and with kavvanah, with holy intent, you will bring about the union between God and Shekhinah, eternity and time. You need not be a scholar or a sage to accomplish this. All that is necessary is to have a soul united within itself and indivisibly directed to its divine goal. The world in which you live, just as it is and not otherwise, affords you that association with God, which will redeem you and whatever divine aspect of the world you have been entrusted with. And your own character, the very qualities which make you what you are, constitutes your special approach to God, your special potential use for Him. Do not be vexed at your delight in creatures and things! But do not let it shackle itself to creatures and things; through these, press on to God. Do not rebel against your desires, but seize them and bind them to God. You shall not stifle your surging powers, but let them work at holy work, and rest a holy rest in God. All the contradictions with which the world distresses you are only that you may discover their intrinsic significance, and all the contrary trends tormenting you within yourself only wait to be exorcised by your word. All innate sorrow wants only to flow into the fervor of your joy.

But this joy must not be the goal toward which you strive. It will be vouchsafed you if you strive to "give joy to God." Your personal joy will rise up when you want nothing but the joy of God—nothing but joy in itself.

3

But how was man, in particular the "simple man," with whom the hasidic movement is primarily concerned, to arrive at living his life in fervent joy? How, in the fires of temptation, was he to recast the Evil Urge into an urge for what is good? How, in the wonted fulfilling of the commandments, was he to develop the rapturous bond with the upper worlds? How, in his meeting with creatures and things, grow aware of the divine sparks hidden within them? How, through holy kavvanah, illumine everyday life? We do, indeed, know that all that is necessary is to have a soul united within itself and indivisibly directed to its divine goal. But how, in the chaos of life on our earth, are we to keep the holy goal in sight? How retain unity in the midst of peril and pressure, in the midst of thousands of disappointments and delusions? And once unity is lost, how recover it? Man needs counsel and aid, he must be lifted and redeemed. And he does not need all this only in regard to his soul, for in some way or other, the domains of the soul are intertwined with the big and little cares, the griefs and despairs of life itself, and if these are not dealt with, how shall those loftier concerns be approached? A helper is needed, a helper for both body and soul, for both earthly and heavenly matters. This helper is called the zaddik. He can heal both the ailing body and the ailing soul, for he knows how one is bound up with the other, and this knowledge gives him the power to influence both. It is he who can teach you to conduct your affairs so that your soul remains free, and he can teach you to strengthen your soul, to keep you steadfast beneath the blows of destiny. And over and over he takes you by the hand and guides you until you are able to venture on alone. He does not relieve you of doing what you have grown strong enough to do for yourself. He does not lighten your soul of the struggle it must wage in order to accomplish its particular task in this world. And all this also holds for the communication of the soul with God. The zaddik must make communication with God easier for his hasidim, but he cannot take their place. This is the teaching of the Baal Shem and all the great hasidim followed it; everything else is distortion and the signs of it appear relatively early. The zaddik strengthens his hasid in the hours of doubting, but he does not infiltrate him with truth, he only helps him conquer and reconquer it for himself. He develops the hasid's own power for right prayer, he teaches him how to give the words of prayer the right direction, and he joins his own prayer to that of his disciple and therewith lends him courage, an increase of power—wings. In hours of need, he prays for his disciple and gives all of himself, but he never permits the soul of the hasid to rely so wholly on his own that it relinquishes independent concentration and tension, in other words, that striving-to-God of the soul without which life on this earth is bound to be unfulfilled. Not only in the realm of human passions does the zaddik point over and over to the limits of counsel and help. He does this also in the realm of association with God; again and again he emphasizes the limits of mediation. One man can take the place of another only as far as the threshold of the inner sanctum.

Both in the hasidic teachings and in the tales, we often hear of zaddikim who take upon themselves the sorrow of others, and even atone for others by sacrificing their own lives. But on the very rare occasions (as in the case of Rabbi Nahman of Bratzlav) when we read that the true zaddik can accomplish the act of turning to God for those nearest and dearest to him, the author immediately adds that this act done in place of the other facilitates the hasid's own turning to God. The zaddik helps everyone, but he does not relieve anyone of what he must do for himself. His helping is a delivery. He even helps the hasid through his death; those near him in the hour of his death receive "a great illumining."

Within these limits the zaddik has the greatest possible influence not only on the faith and mind of the hasid, but on his active everyday life, and even on his sleep, which he renders deep and pure. Through the zaddik, all the senses of the hasid are perfected, not through conscious directing, but through bodily nearness. The fact that the hasid looks at the zaddik perfects his sense of sight, his listening to him, his sense of hearing. Not the teachings of the zaddik but his existence constitutes his effectiveness; and not so much the circumstance that he is present on extraordinary occasions as that he is there in the ordinary course of days, unemphatic, undeliberate, unconscious; not that he is there as an intellectual leader but as the complete human being with his whole worldly life in which the completeness of the human being is tested. As a zaddik once said: "I learned the Torah from all the limbs of my teacher." This was the zaddik's influence on his true disciples. But his mere physical presence did not, of course, suffice to exert influence on the many, on the people at large, that influence which made hasidism a popular movement. To achieve this, he had to work with the people until they were ready to receive what he had to give them, to present his teachings in a form the people could accept as their own, he must "participate in the multitude." He had to mix with the people and, in order to raise them to the rung of what perfection they were capable of, he had to descend from his own rung. "If a man falls into the mire," says the Baal Shem, "and his friend wants to fetch him out, he must not hesitate to get himself a little dirty."

One of the great principles of hasidism is that the zaddik and the people are dependent on one another. Again and again, their relationship is compared to that between substance and form in the life of the individual, between body and soul. The soul must not boast that it is more holy than the body, for only in that it has climbed down into the body and works through its limbs can the soul attain to its own perfection. The body, on the other hand, may not brag of supporting the soul, for when the soul leaves, the flesh falls into decay. Thus the zaddikim need the multitude, and the multitude need the zaddikim. The realities of hasidic teaching depend on this inter-relationship. And so the "descending from the rung" is not a true descent. Quite the contrary: "If the zaddik serves God," says Rabbi Nahman of Bratzlav, "but does not take the trouble to teach the multitude, he will descend from his rung."

Rabbi Nahman himself, one of the most spiritual of all the zaddikim, felt a deep and secret sense of union between himself and "simple men." This union is the point of departure for his strange utterances about two months before he died. At first he was in a state of such spiritual exhaustion that he declared he was nothing but a "simple man." But when this state suddenly went over into the loftiest elation of spirit, he said that in such periods of descending, the zaddik was infused with vital strength which poured out from him into all the "simple men" in the world, not only those of Israel, but of all people. And the vital strength which flowed into him, hailed from "the treasure trove of gratuitous gifts" stored up in the land of Canaan from time immemorial, time before Israel, and this treasure trove, he added, consists of that secret substance which is also accorded to the souls of simple men and makes them capable of simple faith.

Here we come to the very foundation of hasidism, on which the life between those who quicken and those who are quickened is built up. The quintessence of this life is the relationship between the zaddik and his disciples, which unfolds the interaction between the quickener and the quickened in complete clarity. The teacher helps his disciples find themselves, and in hours of desolation the disciples help their teacher find himself again. The teacher kindles the souls of his disciples and they surround him and light his life with the flame he has kindled. The disciple asks, and by his manner of asking unconsciously evokes a reply, which his teacher's spirit would not have produced without the stimulus of the question.

Two "miracle tales" will serve to demonstrate the lofty function of discipleship.

Once, at the close of the Day of Atonement, the Baal Shem is greatly troubled because the moon cannot pierce the clouds and so he cannot say the Blessing of the New Moon, which in this very hour, an hour when Israel is threatened with grave danger, is to have a particularly salutary effect. In vain he strains his soul to alter the state of the sky. Then his hasidim, who know nothing of all this, begin to dance just as every year at this time, in joyful elation at the service performed by their master, a service like that of the high priest in the Temple of Jerusalem. First they dance in the outer room of the Baal Shem's house, but in their elation they enter his room and dance around him. At last, at the peak of ecstasy, they beg him to join the dance and draw him into the circle. And then the moon breaks through the heavy clouds and shines out, a marvel of flawless light. The joy of the hasidim has brought about what the soul of the zaddik, straining to the utmost of its power, was not able to effect.

Among the disciples of Rabbi Dov Baer the Great Maggid, the greatest disciple of the Baal Shem, Rabbi Elimelekh was the man who kept alive the core of the tradition and preserved the school as such. Once, when his soul rose up to heaven, he learned that with his holiness he was rebuilding the ravaged altar in the sanctuary of heavenly Jerusalem, which corresponds to the sanctuary of Jerusalem on this earth. At the same time, he learned that his disciples were helping him in this task of restoration. In a certain year, two of these were absent from the Festival of Rejoicing in the Law, Rabbi Jacob Yitzhak, later the rabbi of Lublin (the "Seer"), and Rabbi Abraham Joshua Heshel, later the rabbi of Apt. Heaven had told Elimelekh that Jacob Yitzhak would bring the Ark into the sanctuary, and that Abraham Joshua Heshel would bring the tables of the law. Yet now they were both missing! Then the zaddik said to his son: "Eighteen times over I can cry: 'Rise up, O Lord!' (as Israel, in the day of old, called toward the Ark, which was to precede them into battle)—and it will be of no use."

In this second story, the disciples participate in the work of the zaddik as individuals, in the first they take part in it as a "holy community." This form of collective effect is undoubtedly the more significant, though we have many and varied tales concerning the participation of individuals. The community of hasidim who belong to a zaddik, especially the close-knit circle of those who are constantly with him, or—at least—visit him regularly, is felt as a powerful dynamic unit. The zaddik unites with this circle both in prayer and in teaching. They are his point of departure in praying, for he does not pray merely as one speaking for them, but as their focus of strength in which the blaze of the community-soul is gathered, and from which this blaze is borne aloft fused with the flame of his own soul. On the sabbath when, at the third meal, he expounds the Scriptures and reveals what is hidden, his teaching is directed toward them: they are the field of force in which his words make manifest the spirit in expanding circles, like rings widening on the waters. And this meal itself! We can approach an understanding of its tension and bliss only when we realize that all—each giving himself utterly—are united into an elated whole, such as can only form around an elated center, which through its very being, points to the divine center of all being. This is a living connection which sometimes expresses itself strangely and even grotesquely, but the grotesque in itself is so genuine that it bears witness to the genuineness of the impulses. For hasidism must not be interpreted as an esoteric movement but one charged with primitive vitality which—as all primitive vitality—sometimes vents itself rather crudely. It is this very vitality which lends peculiar intensity to the relationship of one hasid toward another. Their common attachment to the zaddik and to the holy life he embodies binds them to one another, not only in the festive hours of common prayer, and of the common meal, but in all the hours of everyday living. In moments of elation, they drink to one another, they sing and dance together, and tell one another abstruse and comforting miracle tales. But they help one another too. They are prepared to risk their lives for a comrade, and this readiness comes from the same deep source as their elation. Everything the true hasid does or does not do mirrors his belief that, in spite of the intolerable suffering men must endure, the heartbeat of life is holy joy, and that always and everywhere, one can force a way through to that joy— provided one devotes one's self entirely to his deed.

There are many distorted aspects of hasidism which are by no means inherent only in the later stages of the movement. Side by side with the fervent love for the zaddik we find a coarsened form of reverence on the part of those who regard him as a great magician, as one who is an intimate of heaven and can right all that is wrong, who relieves his hasidim of straining their own souls and secures them a desirable place in the hereafter. Though the hasidim of a zaddik were often united by a feeling of true brotherliness, they frequently held aloof from and sometimes were even hostile to the followers of other zaddikim. A like contrast obtained between the free life in religion of a hasidic community and their thick-skinned opportunism in regard to the powers of the state. Sometimes, dull superstition settled down side by side with the innocent fantasy of the elated spirit and made shallows of its depths, and sometimes crass fraud made its appearance and abused it. Most of these phenomena are familiar to us through the history of other religious movements that sprang from the vitality of the people; others become understandable when we consider the pathological premises of life in exile. My aim was not to go into all this, but to show what it was that made hasidism one of the most significant phenomena of living and fruitful faith that we know, and—up to this time—the last great flowering of the Jewish will to serve God in this world and to consecrate everyday life to him.

In the very beginnings of the movement, hasidism disintegrated into separate communities whose inner life had small connection, and early in its history individual zaddikim display problematic traits. But every hasidic community still contains a germ of the kingdom of God, a germ—no more than that, but no less, and often this germ lives and grows even in substance which has fallen prey to decay. And even the zaddik who has squandered the spiritual inheritance of his forbears has hours in which his forehead gives forth a glow as though the primordial light had touched it with radiance.

4

In a crisis of faith, when faith is renewed, the man who initiates and leads the renewal is frequently not a spiritual character in the ordinary sense of the world, but one who draws his strength from an extraordinary union between the spiritual and tellurian powers, between heavenly and earthly fire, but it is the sublime which determines the earth-sustained frame. The life of such a man is a constant receiving of fire and transforming it into light. And this, which is and occurs within himself, is the cause of his twofold effect on the world: he restores to the element of earth those whom preoccupation with thought has removed from it, and those who are burdened with the weight of earth he raises to the heights of heaven.

Israel ben Eliezer of Mezbizh (Miedzyboz), called the Baal Shem Tov (1700–1760), the founder of hasidism, was such a man. He first appears merely as one in a series of Baale Shem, of "Masters of the Name," who knew a Name of God that had magic force, were able to invoke it, and with this art of theirs helped and healed the men who came to them—manifestations of a form of magic which was absorbed by religion. The actual basis for their work was their ability to perceive intrinsic connections between things, connections which lay beyond the bounds of time and space (apparent only to what we usually call intuition) and their peculiar strengthening and consolidating influence on the soul-center of their fellowmen, which enabled this center to regenerate the body and the whole of life—an influence of which the so-called "suggestive powers" are nothing but a distortion. Certain aspects of Israel ben Eliezer's work constitute a continuation of the work of the Baale Shem, but with one marked difference which even expresses itself in the change of the epithet "Baal Shem" to "Baal Shem Tov." This difference and what it signifies are unambiguously stressed in the legendary tradition.

In various versions we are told how either Rabbi Gershon, the Baal Shem's brother-in-law, who first despised him as an ignorant man but later became his faithful disciple, or one of the descendants of the Baal Shem went to a great rabbi who lived far away—in Palestine or in Germany—and he told him about Rabbi Israel Baal Shem. "Baal Shem?" said the rabbi questioningly. "I don't know any such person." And in the case of the Baal Shem's brother-in-law, the rejection is more pronounced, for when Rabbi Gershon speaks of the Baal Shem as his teacher, he receives the reply: "Baal Shem? No, there is no teacher by that name." But when Rabbi Gershon quickly rights his first words by giving the full name "Baal Shem Tov," the rabbi he is visiting assumes an entirely different attitude. "Oh!" he exclaims. "The Baal Shem Tov! He, to be sure, is a very great teacher. Every morning I see him in the temple of paradise." The sage refuses to have anything to do with common miracle men, but the Baal Shem Tov—that is quite another matter, that is something new. The addition of one word altered the meaning and the character of the epithet. "Shem Tov" is the "Good Name." The Baal Shem Tov, the possessor of the Good Name, is a man who, because he is as he is, gains the confidence of his fellowmen. "Baal Shem Tov" as a general designation refers to a man in whom the people have confidence, the confident of the people. With this, the term ceases to designate a rather doubtful vocation and comes to apply to a reliable person and, at the same time, transforms what was, after all, a category of magic, into one religious in the truest sense of the word. For the term "Baal Shem Tov" signifies a man who lives with and for his fellowmen on the foundation of his relation to the divine.

There is a story that Rabbi Yitzhak of Drohobycz, one of the ascetic "hasidim" who first rebelled against the Baal Shem, was full of hostility for the innovator because he had heard that he gave people amulets containing slips of paper inscribed with secret names of God. On the occasion of a meeting, he asked the Baal Shem about it. He opened one of the amulets and showed the questioner that on the slip there was nothing but his own name and that of his mother, "Israel ben Sarah." Here the amulet has completely lost its magical attributes. It is nothing but a sign and pledge of the personal bond between the helper and the one who is given help, a bond based on trust. The Baal Shem Tov helps those who trust him. He is able to help them because they trust him. The amulet is the permanent symbol of his direct influence at the given moment. It contains his name and thus represents him. And through this pledge of personal connection, the soul of the recipient is "lifted." The power at work here is the union of the tellurian and spiritual within the Baal Shem and, proceeding from this union, the relationship between him and his hasidim which involves both domains.

This sheds light on his attitude toward the "Men of Spirit" he wishes to win for the hasidic movement, and on the fact that most of them are willing to subject themselves to him. According to one legendary version, for instance, the greatest of his disciples, the actual founder of the hasidic school of teaching, Rabbi Dov Baer, the Maggid (wandering preacher) of Mezritch (Miedzyrzecze), comes to him to be cured of his illness. His physical suffering is only eased, but he is healed of "teaching without soul." This instance clearly demonstrates that Nature, at work in the person of the helper, guides the spirit, which has strayed too far from her, back into her domain, the only milieu in which the soul can thrive through ceaseless contact with her. And the "Great Maggid," whose powers as thinker are far superior to those of the Baal Shem, bows to the infinitely rare and decisive phenomenon: the union of fire and light in a human being. The same holds for another important exponent of hasidic teachings in the second generation, for Rabbi Jacob Joseph of Polnoye (Polonnoje). He was not an independent thinker, such as the Maggid, but well versed in the teachings, and thus enabled to receive and expound the teachings of the Baal Shem who drew him from his ascetic remoteness into a simple life with his fellowmen. There are various versions of how the Baal Shem won him over, but they all have two traits in common: he does not reveal himself directly, but manifests himself through his particular manner of concealment, and he tells him stories (he always likes to tell stories) which stir the hearer just because of their primitive character and apparent lack of intellectual quality, and finally make him see and accept them as a reference to his own secret needs. Here again, in the telling of simple stories and parables which, however, evoke a strong personal application, the connection between spirit and nature becomes manifest, a union which makes it possible for images to serve as symbols, that is as spirit which assumes form in Nature herself. What both of these disciples have to say about the teachings of the Baal Shem, and about their association with him, is characteristic in the same sense: he taught the Maggid (among other things) how to understand the language of birds and trees, and—so the rabbi of Polnoye tells his son-in-law—it was his "holy custom" to converse with animals. The Gaon of Vilna, the great opponent of hasidism, who was responsible for the ban pronounced upon it, the man who wished to proceed against the hasidim "as Elijah proceeded against the prophets of Baal," accused the Baal Shem of "having led astray" the Maggid of Mezritch "through his magic arts." What seemed magic was the union within a person of heavenly light and earthly fire, of spirit and nature. Whenever this union appears incarnate in human form, this person testifies—with the testimony of life—for the divine unity of spirit and nature, reveals this unity anew to the world of man which again and again becomes estranged from it, and evokes ecstatic joy. For true ecstasy hails neither from spirit nor from nature, but from the union of these two.

5

Not many of the immediate disciples of the Baal Shem stand in the limelight of legendary tradition. It is as though, for the time being, the power of ecstatic vision, which was his to so great a degree, narrowed and concentrated on a few persons beloved by their people, while of the others there are only isolated, though frequently very characteristic tales. Not until the third generation[2] does the House of Study of the Great Maggid become the focus for a long series of zaddikim, each entirely different from the other, whose memory legend preserved and embroidered with veneration. But aside from this, we are struck by a complete change in tone the moment we turn from the stories which concern the Baal Shem to those which deal with his disciples and are not immediately connected with his own life. The three men around whom legend has primarily crystallized, the Maggid of Mezritch, Pinhas of Koretz, and Yehiel Mikhal of Zlotchov, were, above all, teachers—the first as the head of the hasidic mother-school; the second in a small closed circle which developed hasidic wisdom along its own, independent lines; the third through the powerful influence he exerted in temporary contacts, wide in scope, but not followed up by continuous educational activities. Thus in the case of these three men legend is concerned chiefly with their teachings, while in the stories about the Baal Shem, his teachings only figure as one function, as one part of his life. In the third generation there is a noticeable change: the tales grow more varied, more vivid. They become more like the legends of the Baal Shem. Once more life is expressed in all its abundance—only that the secret of beginnings, the secret of primal magnitude is lacking.

Rabbi Dov Baer, the Maggid of Mezritch (died 1772), was a teaching thinker, or rather, the Baal Shem, who liberated him from his solitude, made a teaching thinker of him. From that time on, the task of teaching determined the deepest core of his thinking. It is significant that his favorite simile is that of the father adjusting himself to his little son who is eager to learn. He regards the world as God's self-adjustment to his little son: Man, whom he rears with tender care to enable him to grow up to his Father. Here then, under the influence of basic pedagogic experience, the Kabbalistic concept of the "contraction" of God to make room for the creation of the world ceases to be cosmogonic and enters the realm of the anthropological. It is this idea which spurs the Maggid to try to understand the world from the viewpoint of God's educational methods. But the fundamental prerequisite for all education is the strength and tenderness of the relationship between the educator and his pupil. Only one who experienced this like Rabbi Baer could do what he did, could—as Rabbi Shneur Zalman, the most all-inclusive among his disciples, tells us—unite the mercy of God with man's love of God, and the sternness of God with man's fear of God, in other words: set up the reciprocity of this relationship as the fundamental principle.

One must understand the tremendous seriousness the Maggid's own experience in receiving teaching had for his soul to appreciate not only the intensity with which he handles each of his disciples according to his particular character and his inner destiny, but also what is said of his manner of teaching. We are told that his disciples had very divergent interpretations of what he had said, but that the Maggid refused to decide for one or the other of these, because—no matter which of the seventy faces of the Torah one regards with a true spirit—one sees the truth. This sheds light on another aspect of the Maggid's method: When he spoke, he did not supply systematic connections, but threw out a single suggestion or a single parable without spinning it out and tying together the threads. His disciples had the task—and it was a task which absorbed them completely—of working over what had been said and supplying the missing links. Each did this for himself or they worked together. One of them wrote in a letter: "We were always content with one saying over a long period of time and kept it alive within us, pure and whole, until we heard another." The Maggid was concerned with waking the truth inherent in the spirit of his disciples, with "lighting the candles."

But we cannot grasp all this in its full significance until we remember that obviously the Maggid had always been a man given to ecstasy, only that, under the influence of the Baal Shem, this ecstasy was diverted from ascetic solitude to the active life of teaching disciples. From that moment on, his ecstasy assumed the shape of teaching. Many of his disciples have testified to the ecstatic character of his words. They say that he had only to open his lips and they all had the impression that he was no longer in this world, that the Divine Presence was speaking from his throat. And this phenomenon too cannot be understood until we probe down to the deepest depths accessible to us: It is apparent that with all the passion his soul was capable of, the Maggid put himself into the service of the will of God to lift his "little son" up to him. And to accomplish this service he regarded himself, his thinking as well as his teaching, only as a vessel for divine truth. To use his own words, he "changed the something back into the nothing." From this angle, we can understand that effect on his disciples which the youngest of them, later the "Seer of Lublin," described after his very first visit to the Maggid: "When I came before the master, before the Maggid, I saw him on his bed: something was lying there, which was nothing but simple will, the will of the Most High." That was why his disciples learned even more and greater things from his sheer being than from his words.

The founder of hasidism, the Baal Shem, had not been a teacher in the specific sense of the word. Compared to him, the Maggid represents the quintessence of what makes up the teacher, and that is the reason for his special influence. The Baal Shem had lived, wrought, helped, healed, prayed, preached, and taught. All this was one and the same thing, all was an organic part of unified, spontaneous life, and so teaching was only one among other natural manifestations of effective living. It was different with the Maggid. He was, of course, not a professional teacher, not a man with one specialized function. Only in eras when the world of the spirit is on the decline is teaching, even on its highest level, regarded as a profession. In epochs of flowering, disciples live with their master just as apprentices in a trade lived with theirs, and "learn" by being in his presence, learn many things for their work and their life both because he wills it, or without any willing on his part. That is how it was with the disciples of the Maggid. Over and over they say that he himself as a human being was the carrier of teaching, that, in his effect on them, he was a Torah personified. As far as he himself was concerned, however, the will to teach was the mainspring of his existence. He poured into his disciples all the strength of his life, recreated by contact with the Baal Shem. And all the work of his intellect, he put into the service of teaching. He did not write a book; neither had the Baal Shem. But if—unlike the Baal Shem—he permitted others to take down his words, he did this to transmit his teachings to future generations of disciples, as an indestructible prop.

The Great Maggid did not found an institute of learning. His spirit created only disciples, generations of disciples and disciples of disciples. No other religious movement of the modern era has produced so many and so varied independent personalities in so short a space of time.

Concerning the son of the Great Maggid, Rabbi Abraham, "the

Angel," who died only a few years after him (1776), Rabbi Pinhas of Koretz said that had he lived longer, all the zaddikim of his generation would have subjected themselves to him. And in the autobiography of one of his contemporaries who, on the ninth day of Av, the commemorative day of the destruction of the Temple, saw him lamenting for a night and a day, we read: "Then I realized that it was not for nothing that all called him an angel, for his was not the strength of one born of woman." But in one most significant respect, he cannot be considered a disciple of Rabbi Baer's, in this one respect he even leaves the teachings of the Baal Shem: he sets out to accomplish the "change of something into nothing" by returning to the way of ascetic solitude. Accordingly, he neither associates with the people at large, like the Baal Shem, nor with disciples, like the Baal Shem and the Great Maggid. He gave instruction in the Kabbalah to only one person, to Shneur Zalman, a man of his own age. In the preface to his posthumous book, he refers to the fact that the true teachings of the Baal Shem and the Great Maggid "grew dark and material before our eyes," in contrast to the steadfastness of a superior zaddik "who cannot descend to the lowest rung to uplift his generation." Here, as in other instances, the bodily descendants of a leading zaddik cease to transmit the teachings. As early as the second generation the problematic character of hasidic development becomes evident, in its most sublime aspect.

Rabbi Pinhas of Koretz (Korzec, died 1791) was the second among those who belonged to the Baal Shem's circle to become the focus of a tradition. He was not one of his disciples in the strict sense of the word, since he is said to have visited the Baal Shem only twice, the second time during the last days of his life. Apparently his contacts with Rabbi Israel ben Eliezer did not bring about any fundamental change in his views, but only confirmed and strengthened them. Yet he must certainly be included here. Although in his mention of the Baal Shem he does not designate him as his teacher, he and his school give important data about the Baal Shem and cite important utterances of his, for which we have no other source, and which therefore probably go back to oral transmission. One such utterance is the basis of one of the Rabbi Pinhas' major teachings: that we should "love" the evil-doer and hater "more" in order to compensate for the lack of the power of love he himself has caused in his place in the world. And other basic teachings of Rabbi Pinhas also derive from words of the Baal Shem. To gain a better understanding of the relationship, we must remember that the Baal Shem—as we glean from a number of indications—found kindred trends to which his influence afforded increased vitality and, frequently, a deeper rooting.

Among these kindred trends, those of Rabbi Pinhas (who was about thirty-two when the Baal Shem died) approximated his own most nearly, and he accepted him more as a companion than as a disciple.

Rabbi Leib, son of Sarah, the zaddik who wandered over the earth for secret purposes of his own, is said to have called Rabbi Pinhas the brain of the world. He was, at any rate, a true and original sage. In the period between the Baal Shem and his great-grandson Nahman of Bratzlav, he has no equal in fresh and direct thinking, in daring and vivid expression. What he says often springs from a profound knowledge of the human soul, and it is always spontaneous and great-hearted. In contrast to the Baal Shem and the Great Maggid, no ecstasies are reported of Rabbi Pinhas. Ecstasy wanes into the background and the mystic teachings are reduced to the precept of constant renewal through immersion in nothingness, a doctrine of dying and arising which, however, sponsors also sturdy living in tune with all the things of this earth, and a give-and-take community with one's fellowmen. Rabbi Pinhas' circle had no great influence on the outside world, but such as it is, it represents a unique and invaluable phenomenon, for its members were distinguished by the simple honesty of their personal faith, the unrhetorical telling of the teaching, a telling even tinged with humor, and by their loyal readiness to satisfy the demands put upon them, at the cost of their very lives.

One cannot consider Rabbi Pinhas apart from his most distinguished disciple, Rafael of Bershad. In the whole history of hasidism, rich in fruitful relationships between master and disciple, there is no other instance of so pure a harmony, of so adequate a continuation of the work. In reading the records, we sometimes hardly know what to ascribe to Pinhas and what to Rafael, and yet we have a number of utterances of the latter which bear the stamp of independent thinking. But more important than his independence is the matter of course devotion with which the disciple embodied his master's teachings in his life and—according to tradition—even in his death, which quietly and solemnly sealed the proclamation of the commandment of truth, for which the master had striven so many years.

Rabbi Yehiel Mikhal, the maggid of Zlotchov (died about 1786)[3] who first learned from the Baal Shem and, after his death, from the Great Maggid, was also a unique phenomenon, as yet insufficiently understood and difficult to understand. He came from a family of those ascetic mystic hasidim whom the new movement found ready to hand and tried to win for its own, because the earnestness of their faith which colored their whole attitude toward life rendered them particularly valuable for the task of renewal. Mikhal's father was that Rabbi Yitzhak of Drohobycz who had criticized the amulets of the Baal Shem. All manner of uncanny rumors were circulated about him, that he once did a favor to the "prince of the forest," for instance, or that he sent those of his new-born children who displeased him back to the upper world. (It was said that Mikhal remained alive only because his mother refused to let his father see his face, before he had promised to let him live.) Rabbi Yitzhak's mother, who was called "Yente, the prophetess," used to repeat the threefold "holy" of the choir of angels whose song she heard. To understand Mikhal, it is necessary to know his milieu. In spite of the fact that his father was close to the movement, he himself became a follower of the Baal Shem only after some hesitation. From what we are told it is quite evident that his father's suspicion lived on in him and was only gradually overcome. But he never wholly overcame his basic asceticism.

While he was still young, Mikhal became a great preacher, like his father before him, and went preaching from town to town. He fascinated and intimidated his audiences although he emphasized that the reproof in his sermons was directed toward himself as well as them. The Baal Shem chided him for imposing too heavy penances on sinners and apparently induced him to adopt a milder attitude. But even after his death they tell of souls who come to a younger zaddik to complain of Rabbi Mikhal who, as the chief justice of a court in heaven, censures unintentional earthly faults with the utmost severity because he, who remained pure, does not understand the temptations of men. Though he wholly accepted and absorbed the hasidic teachings and followed the trend of the Baal Shem in his doctrine of the Evil Urge as a helper and of the uplifting of sexuality, he never quite rid himself of asceticism, whose extreme forms, however, he emphatically rejected. According to a report, which all but crosses the border between the sublime and the ridiculous, he never warmed himself at the stove, for this would have been a concession to sloth, never bent down to his food, for this would have been yielding to greed, and never scratched himself, since this would have verged on voluptuousness. But Rabbi Mikhal's special endowment made for true hasidism in a very significant fashion. The most notable instance of this is that he carried on the tradition of those "first hasidim" of whom the Talmud says that they waited with praying until they had prepared the kavvanah within themselves. But he expanded this motif into something that embraced the whole community: in order to make his prayer representative for the community, he strove to unite with both the mightier and the humbler to form a single, continuous and powerful chain of prayer, and—taking as his point of departure the tradition of his father and a saying of the Baal Shem's—he also wanted to raise up the limp prayers which had not the strength to rise from the ground. This attitude, for which he incurred violent hostility, exerted an effective

influence on later generations who accorded him deep veneration. But
even a contemporary zaddik said of him that he was "a soul of the soul,"
and, in his own generation, played the same role as Rabbi Simeon ben
Yohai, the founder of the secret teachings, in his.

Like Rabbi Mikhal himself, two of his five sons figure in tales of
strange journeys of the soul to heaven. But a third, Rabbi Zev Wolf of
Zbarazh (died about 1802),[4] who was reputed to have been a very wild
child, was made of quite other stuff. Like his contemporary Rabbi
Moshe Leib of Sasov (who belonged to the fourth generation), he became one of the great friends of man and the earth. In contrast to his
father—though we must not forget that Rabbi Mikhal bade his sons
pray for their enemies—he obstinately refused to treat the wicked differently from the good. Wolf lavished his love on all human beings who
came his way and even on animals. He held that man should love all that
lives, and that this love must not be determined by the way the object of
his love behaves toward him. Among the disciples of Rabbi Mikhal was
Rabbi Mordecai of Neskhizh (Niesuchojce, died 1800), whom his
teacher took with him to visit the Great Maggid. He figures in a great
number of miracle tales, and it is told that even demons recognized his
power. The source of such a statement is actual power over the souls of
men, and in the case of Rabbi Mordecai such power definitely sprang
from the unity in his own soul. This unity, however, did not find adequate expression in power itself, but rather in the unity of his own life.
This is what the "Seer" of Lublin must have meant when he said that all
his activities were, in reality, one.

6

According to hasidic tradition, the Great Maggid had three hundred
disciples. About forty of these have come down to us an individuals with
their personal characteristics, the most of them also through their writings. Ten are represented in this volume [the first volume of *Tales of the
Hasidim*], but—as in the case of the Baal Shem's disciples—these ten do
not include all of those who were most significant as human beings,
because the legends about them, current among the people, do not suf-
fice to give a connected account of their lives. These ten are: Menahem
Mendel of Vitebsk (died 1788), whom the Maggid brought to the Baal
Shem when he was a boy; Aaron of Karlin (died 1772); Shmelke of
Nikolsburg (died 1778); Meshullam Zusya (yiddish Zishe) of Hanipol
(Annopol, died 1800); his younger brother, Elimelekh of Lizhensk
(Lezajsk, died 1809); Levi Yitzhak of Berditchev (died 1809); Shneur
Zalman of Ladi (died 1813); Shelomo of Karlin (died 1792); Israel of

Koznitz (Kozienice, died 1814); Jacob Yitzhak of Lublin (died 1815).

What makes Rabbi Menahem Mendel of particular importance in the history of hasidism is that he transplanted the movement to Palestine, where, to be sure, other zaddikim had settled before him. From the days of the Baal Shem, who, according to legend, had to turn back at the border, the focus of hasidic, as of the pre-hasidic, yearning for redemption, was "the Land." After having taken a leading part in the struggle against those who pronounced the ban, he translated this yearning into action by going to Palestine (1777) with three hundred of his hasidim. There he first settled near Safed, the ancient city of Kabbalists, and later in Tiberias. Thus he gave the movement a site which was not central in location but in spirit, and linked it organically with the past. And he brought the Land an element of new life. Concerning this, a grandson of his friend Shneur Zalman (who had not been able to accompany Mendel to Palestine) said that once, when the Land of Israel was on its highest rung, it had the power to uplift man, but that now that it had sunk so low, and strangely enough kept on sinking, it could no longer uplift man, that now man must uplift the Land, and only a man on so high a rung as Rabbi Mendel had been able to do this. In a letter from Palestine, Rabbi Mendel wrote that he regarded himself as an envoy to the palace of the king, dispatched by the governors of the provinces, that he must not for a moment lose sight of both the physical and spiritual welfare of the provinces. He remained in especially close and constant contact with the hasidim he had left behind in exile, so close that—as one of those who accompanied him writes—everything connected with them, everything taking place in their hearts, was manifest to him when he prayed before falling asleep.

From among all of his disciples, the Maggid chose Aaron of Karlin as his envoy, because he knew how to win souls as none other, even though his courting of them was linked with stern demands upon their whole attitude toward life. He died young, and in his funeral sermon his successor, Rabbi Shelomo of Karlin, said that the Lord had taken him before his time, because his power of converting men to God was so great that he deprived them of the freedom of choice which is of prime importance. When the Maggid heard of his death, he said: "He was our weapon in war. What shall we do now?" Rabbi Aaron did not wish to go contrary to the folk-character of the movement which not only persisted in the Karlin school but experienced a curious development there. Nevertheless, what he obviously wanted was to create an elite body dedicated to a life of faith. One main device by which he sought to accomplish this was the regulation of one day a week devoted to solitary meditation accompanied by fasting and the ritual bath. But this was to have nothing of the ascetic, for Rabbi Aaron regarded asceticism as a bait thrown out by Satan himself. His demands sprang from his own intrinsic experience. His "testament" expresses his deepest purpose for his own person: to prepare the proper kavvanah for the hour in which the soul departs from the body. His friend Shneur Zalman says of him that he was a veritable fountain of the love of God and that whoever heard him pray was seized by the love for God. But the picture becomes complete only through the words the same zaddik said about Rabbi Aaron's great fear of God after his death.[5] His love was only the flowering of his fear, for only through great fear—this was Rabbi Aaron's basic feeling—can one attain to great love. He who has not this fear does not love the great and terrible God himself, but only a small convenient idol. One of the sayings of his great-grandson who followed this trend is: "Fear without love is something imperfect; love without fear is nothing at all." And this world in which we live is the site where through fear one can attain to love, and where fear and love can fuse. That is why in another of his sayings we read: "This world is the lowest, and yet the loftiest of all."

Among the disciples of the Great Maggid, Rabbi Shmelke of Nikolsburg was the preacher par excellence, not a preacher who exhorted, as Rabbi Mikhal did in his youth, but a preacher per se. The sermon was his true element because he fervently believed that words inspired by God had the power to transform, and he never gave up this belief, even in the face of disappointments. He regarded the sermon as an action which lifts the prayer of the congregation to the highest level of purity. And so, in his sermons, he repeatedly demanded two things from those who prayed: first, that with the rivers of their love they wash away all separating walls and unite to one true congregation to furnish the site for the union with God; secondly, that they detach their prayers from individual wishes, and concentrate the full force of their being on the desire that God unite with his Shekhinah. This was the spirit in which he himself prayed and this holy intent of his lifted him to ecstasy, so that in the very midst of prayer, he abandoned the charted track of memory and custom and sang new melodies, never heard before. He left his Polish congregation for Nikolsburg in Moravia, which was utterly remote from the world of hasidism, and where a man such as he was bound to provoke constant annoyance. He exerted a profound influence on many a spirit that was still open and responsive, but the majority of those he stirred up from their usual ways did all they could to make his life in their community intolerable. We have various versions of the tale of how Rabbi Elimelekh, his younger friend in the Maggid's House of Study, visited him and in a coarse and pithy sermon told the burghers that they were not fit patients for so noble a doctor, that first he, Elimelekh, the barber, would have to subject them to drastic treatment. And the next instant, fixing now one, now the other with his gaze, he hurled at them the full description of all their secret vices and faults. Rabbi Shmelke never could have done that, if only because the weaknesses of individuals were not of sufficient importance in his eyes. His basic attitude to all men, including his foes, was love, the vast tide of love which he preached. His House of Study in Nikolsburg became one of the main centers of the movement. He exerted a great influence on his disciples and friends and through them on countless others.

In sharp contrast to Shmelke, Rabbi Meshullam Zusya, known as the Rabbi Reb Zishe, was a true man of the people. Here, in the narrow confines of an eastern ghetto, in a much later century, the "Fool of God" reappears, the singular character, known to us from the legends of Chinese Buddhists, from Sufis, and from the disciples of St. Francis of Assisi. Yet he may also be interpreted as the East European Jewish type of badhan, the jester who figures chiefly at weddings, but now sublimated into something holy. He is a human being who, because of his undamaged direct relationship with God, has quitted the rules and regulations of the social order, though he continues to participate in the life of his fellowmen. He does not sequester himself; he is only detached. His loneliness in the face of the eternal "Thou" is not the loneliness of the recluse, but of one who is composed and true to the world, a loneliness which includes intrinsic oneness with all living creatures. He leads his life among his fellows, detached and yet attached, regarding their faults as his own and rejoicing in them and in all creatures in the freedom of God. But since men are so made that they cannot endure an attitude such as this, which blocks their evasion of the eternal, they are content to jeer at the "fool." They make him suffer. They do not impose sharp and brief martyrdom, but life-long sorrows, and he delights in them. Yet men are also so made that such a destiny kindles them to the most sublime love, and it was with sublime love that Rabbi Zusya was loved by the people.

Rabbi Elimelekh, called the Rabbi Reb Melekh, was Zusya's brother and shared the wanderings of his youth. Year after year, they went on and on without a goal, making their lives an imitation of the journeying of the exiled Presence of God, watching for souls wakened or ready to be wakened. But then they parted ways. Zusya did, to be sure, settle down, but again and again he felt the urge to wander and into his old age he continued to be a boy who whistles a song for God. Elimelekh had the vocation to be a leader of men. He too knew the timeless world of ecstasy, but his clear and unerring reason taught him to protect himself against its dangers and enabled him to combine the life of the spirit with the activities of an organizer. Here again was a man who simultaneously headed the hasidic school and the hasidic congregation, and so Rabbi Elimelekh must be considered the true successor of the Great Maggid. While he did not approach him in originality of teaching, he was almost his equal in his power to build up, and even outstripped him in his intuitive knowledge of the many different types of people, their flaws and their needs, and the means to minister to these. In the legend-shaping memory of the people, he stands out as a doctor of souls, as a man who could exorcise demons, as a wonder-working counselor and guide.

Levi Yitzhak, the rav of Berditchev, the most original of the Maggid's disciples, and the one who came closest to the people, was very different from Elimelekh. He was akin to Zusya, but more of the stuff of this earth, and part and parcel of his nation. His ecstasy penetrated his strong and solid life. The transports of Rabbi Shmelke, whose devoted follower he was, passed over into him, only translated into something more substantial, as it were. In lieu of the strange new songs which broke from Rabbi Shmelke, Rabbi Yitzhak's whole body shook with uncontrollable tremors when he prayed. He liked to converse with crude and ignorant people, but even the worldliest of his words was holy and had for its purpose Yihudim, the uniting of the upper worlds. He was harsh enough when something displeased him about a man, but he was always willing to learn from others and had the greatest reverence for simplicity. Even his communings with God were colored by unvarnished intimacy. He confronted him not only as the passionate intercessor for Israel, he took him to account, made demands on him, and even ventured to hurl threats, a bitter and sublime jest which would have been blasphemy in another, but was irreproachable coming from the lips of this unique character. In his own fashion, however, he also praised God and often interrupted the flow of prescribed prayer by interpolating endearment for him.

Rabbi Shneur Zalman, the rav of Northern White Russia, who was called simply "the rav," or "the Tanya" after the title of his main work, intended to voyage to the Holy Land together with Rabbi Mendel of Vitebsk. But Mendel asked him to turn back—legend makes of it a command received in a dream vision—and the rav later founded the special Lithuanian school of hasidism, the Habad, a term made up of the initial letters of the three upper of the ten Sefirot which, according to the teachings of the Kabbalah, emanated from God: Hokhmah, wisdom; Binah, intelligence; Daat, knowledge. This very name, which detaches the specifically intellectual Sefirot out of the closely linked structure, points to the principle underlying this school: reason and intellect are to be reinstated as a way to find God. The Habad School represents an attempt to reconcile rabbinism with hasidism by incorporating both in a system of thought, a method which of necessity weakened certain fundamental concepts of hasidism. The very separating off of the spheres threatened to deprive hasidism of its strongest base: the teaching that sparks of God are inherent in all things and creatures, in all concepts and urges, sparks which desire us to redeem them and, linked with this teaching, the affirmation of the soul-body entity of man, provided he is able to turn all his stirrings toward God. The average man is no longer asked to transform "alien thoughts"; he is requested to turn away from them and this spells his renunciation of attaining all-embracing unity. The only ones who are not forbidden contact with the powers of temptation are the superior men. (Here, to be sure, the Habad teachings connect up with certain warnings of Rabbi Efraim of Sadylkov, the Baal Shem's grandson.) But in order to give the reason of the individual its due, the zaddik is deprived of the essential office which is his, according to the teachings of the Baal Shem and especially of the Great Maggid, the great office of cosmic helper and mediator. The things misused are discarded together with misuse itself. Yet in spite of everything, the special position of the Habad must not be interpreted as leading to schism. For the rav was exposed to the hostilities of the mitnagdim, the opponents of hasidism, no less, but even more, than the other zaddikim of his time. The anti-hasidic rabbis plotted against him and had him arrested again and again. He was confined in the fortress of Petersburg and subjected to lengthy cross-examination. What he was charged with were distorted teachings of the Baal Shem whose true intent he avowed. A certain zaddik said of the Habad—and he was not altogether wide of the mark—that it resembled a loaded gun in the hand of a man who can aim and who knows the target—only that the fuse was lacking. But even this branch movement with its rationalized mysticism (aided and abetted by the rational tendencies of the Lithuanian Jew) still manifests the old flight of the soul. The life of the zaddik with his hasidim is warmer and stronger than the chilly doctrine, and besides this the rav counted among his disciples distinguished men who again brought the teachings closer to the original tenets of hasidism. Surely the hasidic "flame" burned in the rav himself. We are told of certain traits in his life which give evidence of impassioned personal religiosity, and his clinging to God is documented by his melodies, particularly those known simply as "the rabbi's melodies." Sometimes these are linked with a Kabbalistic song, at others they revolve around "Tatenyu" (little father), a name by which God is addressed. Again and again, at a feast or in solitude, the Habad-hasidim sing them, expressing their fervor and renewing it by its expression.

Rabbi Shelomo of Karlin was instructed by his fellow-pupil Aaron of Karlin and later became his successor. He was a man of prayer in even a stricter sense than Levi Yitzhak, who prayed primarily in behalf of the people while Shelomo prayed only to pray. Rabbi Shelomo as none other accepted as his own the Baal Shem's doctrine that before praying man should prepare to die, because the intention of prayer demands the staking of his entire self. For him prayer was a stupendous venture to which one must give one's self up so completely that thought beyond that point is wholly impossible, that it is impossible to imagine what could take place afterwards. From his youth on, this capacity for self-surrender made his prayer indescribably forceful. Before presenting him to the Great Maggid, Rabbi Aaron told him about this youth who, on the eve of the Day of Atonement, spoke the words of the psalm: "How glorious is Thy name in all the earth," in such a way that not a single one of the fallen sparks remained unlifted. There is a significant story of how some of the hasidim of the "Tanya" came to see him and went into a long ecstasy over the way he recited a psalm before saying grace. The "Tanya" did, indeed, commend him with the words that he was "a hand's-breadth above the world," but it is also told that after Rabbi Mendel of Vitebsk's departure for Palestine, when a number of hasidim thought of joining Rabbi Shelomo, "the Tanya" deterred them with the very same words, saying: "How can you go to him? You know he is a hand's-breadth above the world!"—a statement which implied that while Shelomo's ecstasies were commendable, they were not beneficial. This furnishes a clue to what later happened between those two. During a crisis in the hasidic school of Karlin, brought about mostly by the Tanya's growing power of attraction, Rabbi Shelomo conceived the idea of settling in the region of Vitebsk, which had been Rabbi Mendel's main rallying point and which was now included in the Tanya's sphere of influence, and went to him, requesting his consent to this. The rav made three conditions which serve to characterize both men: Rabbi Shelomo was not to look down upon the scholars; he was not to look down upon "natural piety" (that is, piety which lacks ecstasy); and he must no longer declare that the zaddik has to carry the sheep (a phrase by which he designated the zaddik's function to mediate). Shelomo accepted the two first conditions but he rejected the third, and thus relinquished his plan. Later he visited the rav and the two had a lengthy discussion which—so the Habad-hasidim say—"could not be noted down" because of its "shocking" character. In the period of Poland's desperate battles of 1792, in the course of which Shelomo died, he prayed for Poland, while the Tanya (just as twenty years later during Napoleon's campaigns) prayed for Russia. According to tradition, which represents

Shelomo of Karlin as a reincarnation of the first, suffering Messiah who re-appears "from generation to generation," he was killed in the midst of prayer by a bullet a Cossack fired, but continued his work of prayer even after his death.

The Great Maggid's youngest disciple, Rabbi Israel, maggid of Koznitz, manifested a gentler, more composed form of Rabbi Shelomo's power of praying. Legend relates that the Baal Shem promised a book-binder and his wife the birth of a son in their old age, because they had gladdened his heart by their joyful celebration of the sabbath. The son, Rabbi Israel, was sickly all through life and often on the verge of death, but his prayers were so potent that the rows of devotees gazed at that frail form of his as though at a victorious general. When the Great Maggid died, Rabbi Israel attached himself to Rabbi Shmelke, after his death to Rabbi Elimelekh, and after his, to Rabbi Levi Yitzhak. At the very zenith of his life and his work, he still wished to be a disciple. When-ever he cited the words of the talmudic and later masters, he said their names with fear and trembling. On the eve of the Day of Atonement, the entire congregation, men, women, and children, used to come to his threshold and implore atonement with sobs and tears. And he himself came out to them weeping, prostrated himself in the dust, and cried: "I am more sinful than all of you!" Then they wept together and together they went to the House of Prayer to say the Kol Nidre prayer. The power of living prayer—of which he once said that its function was to waken and lift the dead prayers—radiated continually from his sick-bed. People came to him from all over: Jews, peasants, and nobles, to receive his blessing, to implore his mediation, or just to look on his face. No zaddik since the day of the Baal Shem had so many cures of the possessed placed to his credit. And legend even has him play an important role in the his-tory of his time. He is said to have predicted Napoleon's triumph and later his defeat—the outcome of the Russian expedition is traced back to the force of Rabbi Israel's prayers.

Rabbi Jacob Yitzhak of Lublin, a friend of Rabbi Israel and his fellow-pupil in the school of the Great Maggid and later in those of Rabbi Shmelke and Rabbi Elimelekh, also took part in the cosmic struggle. He was called "the Seer" because his intuition was even greater than that of his teacher, Rabbi Elimelekh. One of his disciples said: "If I may take the liberty of saying so, even the Rabbi Reb Melekh did not have the eyes of the Seer of Lublin." He is the only zaddik to whom the people accorded this by-name, which is, however, used in quite another sense than in the case of the biblical prophets. The prophet is the mouthpiece of the *will* of God. He does not see or predict a future reality. In fact, the future con-cerns him only in so far as it cannot yet be grasped and beheld as reality, in so far as it is still latent in the will of God and also in the free relationship of man to this divine will, and hence is, in a certain way, dependent on the inner decision of man. The seer in the hasidic meaning of the word, on the other hand, sees and sees only whatever reality is present in time and space, but his seeing reaches beyond the perception of the senses, beyond the grasp of intelligence on to what is in the process of becoming and back into the past which he recognizes in that and through that which is. Thus the rabbi of Lublin could read not only character and deeds, but the origin of souls (which according to the genealogy of souls, have their own law of propagation) and the migrations of the souls of his visitors. And he read this from their foreheads or even from the notes of request they handed him. Countless men came to him to have their souls illumined and suffused by the light of his eyes. And his disciples felt so secure in the shelter of his radiance that, while they dwelt in its pale, they forgot the exile and thought themselves in the Temple of Jerusalem. But he did not forget the exile. He was filled with ceaseless waiting for the hour of redemption and finally initiated and played the chief part in the secret rites which he and certain other zaddikim—among them Israel of Koznitz, who strove against Napoleon, and Mendel of Rymanov who sided with Napoleon—performed with the purpose of converting the Napoleonic wars into the pre-Messianic final battle of Gog and Magog. The three leaders in this mystic procedure all died in the course of the following year.[6] They had "forced the end": they died at its coming. The magic, which the Baal Shem had held in check, broke loose and did its work of destruction.

Barukh of Mezbizh (died 1811) grew up under the Great Maggid's care but lived his life remote from the master's other disciples. He was the younger of the two sons of Odel, the Baal Shem's daughter. His elder brother Efraim, whom his grandfather had still been able to educate himself, was a quiet sickly man. We know him almost only through the book in which he cites and interprets the teachings of the Baal Shem and tells the legendary anecdotes about him which—together with similar notes taken down by Rabbi Jacob Joseph of Polnoye—form the nucleus of a legendary biography. Beyond this, the book contains a description of his dreams in which the Baal Shem frequently appeared to him.

Barukh offers us quite another picture, one that is full of contradictions and yet an integrated whole. There has been much and legitimate mention of his interest in wealth and power, his pride and love of splendor, and what we know of these qualities of his would suffice to account for his quarrels with the most prominent zaddikim of his time, even if he had not almost always been the one to start them. And yet it would be a mistake to place him in the category of a later degenerate type of zaddik.

Many things we have from his own lips, and others told about him, prove that he led the life of a true and impassioned mystic. But his form of mystic life did not make for harmony with the world of man. It caused him to regard this world as an alien region in which he was an exile, and to consider it his duty to challenge and oppose it. His preference for the Song of Songs, which he recited with such fervor and abandon, helps us to gain insight into his soul, and no less important is the fact that he once designated God and himself as two strangers in an unknown land, two castaways who make friends with each other. But the picture of his soul which takes shape through these characteristics is complicated by the circumstance that Barukh liked to interpret the actions and incidents (even such as seem trivial to us) of his own life as the symbolizing of heavenly events, and wanted others to do likewise. A little deeper probing, however, makes it clear that, in the final analysis, he was concerned with something utterly different from the desire for recognition. Apparently he really meant what he once said: that he would rather be stricken dumb than "coin fine phrases," that is to say, to talk in a manner that would please his hearer rather than unbolt the gates of truth. By and large we must agree with what Rabbi Israel of Rizhyn, the Great Maggid's great-grandson, once said about him: "When a wise man went to the Rabbi Reb Barukh, he could spoon up the fear of God with a ladle, but the fool who visited him, became much more of a fool." And this, of course, does not hold for this one zaddik alone.

Notes

Introduction to Tales of the Hasidim

1. [In *Tales of the Hasidim*] I have prefaced the so-called "miracle tales," i.e., those in which the unreal aspects of reality are especially evident, with the phrase: "It is told."

2. In keeping with the contents of [the first volume of *Tales of the Hasidim*], this introduction deals only with the first three generations of zaddikim. . . .

3. The dates given for his death vary between 1781 and 1792.

4. The dates of his death given vary between 1800 and 1820.

5. See [in *Tales of the Hasidim*] the story of "The Little Fear and the Great Fear."

6. I have related these happenings in my book *Gog and Magog* (English title: *For the Sake of Heaven*).

6

National Community:
The Zionist Movement

The Land and Its Possessors*

[FROM AN OPEN LETTER TO GANDHI, 1939[1]]

A land which a sacred book describes to the children of that land is never merely in their hearts; a land can never become a mere symbol. It is in the hearts because it is in the world; it is a symbol because it is a reality. Zion is the prophetic image of a promise to mankind: but it would be a poor metaphor if Mount Zion did not actually exist. This land is called "holy"; but it is not the holiness of an idea, it is the holiness of a piece of earth. That which is merely an idea and nothing more cannot become holy; but a piece of earth can become holy.

Dispersion is bearable; it can even be purposeful, if there is somewhere an ingathering, a growing home center, a piece of earth where one is in the midst of an ingathering and not in dispersion, and whence the spirit of ingathering may work its way into all the places of the dispersion. When there is this, there is also a striving common life, the life of a community which dares to live today because it may hope to live tomorrow. But when this growing center, this ceaseless process of ingathering is lacking, dispersion becomes dismemberment. From this point of view, the question of our Jewish destiny is indissolubly bound up with the possibility of ingathering, and that is bound up with Palestine.

You ask: "Why should they not, like the other nations of the earth, make that country their National Home where they are born and where they earn their livelihood?" Because their destiny is different from that of all the other nations of the earth: it is a destiny, in truth and justice, no nation on earth would accept. Because their destiny is dispersion, not the dispersion of a fraction and the preservation of the main substance as in the case of other nations; it is dispersion without the living heart and

---

*Reprinted from *Israel and the World: Essays in a Time of Crisis* (New York: Schocken Books, 1948), pp. 227–33.

center; and because every nation has a right to demand the possession of a living heart. It is different, because a hundred adopted homes without one that is original and natural make a nation sick and miserable. It is different, because although the well-being and the achievement of the individual may flourish on stepmotherly soil, the nation as such must languish. And just as you, Mahatma, wish not only that all Indians should be able to live and work, but also that Indian substance, Indian wisdom and Indian truth should prosper and be fruitful, we wish the same for the Jews. For you there is no need of the awareness that the Indian substance could not prosper without the Indian's attachment to the mother-soil and without his ingathering therein. But we know what is essential: we know it because it is denied us or was so at least up to the generation which has just begun to work at the redemption of the mother-soil.

But painfully urgent as it is, this is not all: for us, for the Jews who think as I do, it is indeed not the decisive factor. You say, Mahatma Gandhi, that to support the cry for a national home which "does not much appeal to you," a sanction is "sought in the Bible." No—that is not so. We do not open the Bible and seek sanction in it, rather the opposite is true: the promises of return, of re-establishment, which have nourished the yearning hope of hundreds of generations give those of today an elementary stimulus, recognized by few in its full meaning but effective in the lives of many who do not believe in the message of the Bible. Still this, too, is not the determining factor for us who, although we do not see divine revelation in every sentence of Holy Scripture, yet trust in the spirit which inspired those who uttered them. What is decisive for us is not the promise of the Land, but the demand, whose fulfilment is bound up with the land, with the existence of a free Jewish community in this country. For the Bible tells us, and our inmost knowledge testifies to it, that once more than three thousand years ago our entry into this land took place with the consciousness of a mission from above to set up a just way of life through the generations of our people, a way of life that cannot be realized by individuals in the sphere of their private existence, but only by a nation in the establishment of its society: communal ownership of the land,[2] regularly recurrent leveling of social distinctions,[3] guarantee of the independence of each individual,[4] mutual aid,[5] a general Sabbath embracing serf and beast as beings with an equal claim to rest,[6] a sabbatical year in which the soil is allowed to rest and everybody is admitted to the free enjoyment of its fruits.[7] These are not practical laws thought out by wise men; they are measures which the leaders of the nation, apparently themselves taken by surprise and overpowered, have found to be the set task and condition for taking posses-

sion of the land. No other nation has ever been faced at the beginning of
its career with such a mission. Here is something which there is no forgetting and from which there is no release. At that time we did not carry
out that which was imposed upon us; we went into exile with our task
unperformed; but the command remained with us, and it has become
more urgent than ever. We need our own soil in order to fulfil it: we need
the freedom to order our own life: no attempt can be made on foreign
soil and under foreign statute. It cannot be that the soil and the freedom
for fulfilment are denied us. We are not covetous, Mahatma: our one
desire is that at last we may be able to obey.

Now you may well ask whether I speak for the Jewish people when I
say "we." No, I speak only for those who feel themselves entrusted with
the commission of fulfilling the command of justice given to Israel in the
Bible. Were it but a handful—these constitute the pith of the people, and
the future of the people depends on them; for the ancient mission of the
people lives in them as the cotyledon in the core of the fruit. In this connection, I must tell you that you are mistaken when you assume that in
general the Jews of today believe in God and derive from their faith guid-
ance for their conduct. Contemporary Jewry is in the throes of a serious
religious crisis. It seems to me that the lack of faith of present-day humanity, its inability truly to believe in God, finds its concentrated expression
in this crisis of Jewry; here all is darker, more fraught with danger, more
fateful than anywhere else in the world. Nor is this crisis resolved here in
Palestine; indeed we recognize its severity here even more than elsewhere
among Jews. But at the same time we realize that here alone it can be
resolved. There is no solution to be found in the lives of isolated and
abandoned individuals, although one may hope that the spark of faith
will be kindled in their great need. The true solution can only issue from
the life of a community which begins to carry out the will of God, often
without being aware of doing so, without believing that God exists and
that this is his will. It may issue from the life of the community, if believing people support it who neither direct nor demand, neither urge nor
preach, but who share the common life, who help, wait and are ready for
the moment when it will be their turn to give the true answer to the in-
quirers. This is the innermost truth of the Jewish life in the Land; perhaps it may be of significance for the solution of this crisis of faith not
only for Jewry but for all humanity. The contact of this people with this
land is not only a matter of sacred ancient history: we sense here a secret
still more hidden. You, Mahatma Gandhi, who know of the connection
between tradition and future, should not associate yourself with those
who pass over our cause without understanding or sympathy.

But you say—and I consider it to be the most significant of all the things you tell us—that Palestine belongs to the Arabs and that it is therefore "wrong and inhuman to impose the Jews on the Arabs."

Here I must add a personal note in order to make clear to you on what premises I desire to consider your thesis.

I belong to a group of people who from the time Britain conquered Palestine have not ceased to strive for the concluding of a genuine peace between Jew and Arab.

By a genuine peace we inferred and still infer that both peoples together should develop the land without the one imposing its will on the other. In view of the international usages of our generation, this appeared to us to be very difficult but not impossible. We were and still are well aware that in this unusual—yes, unprecedented—case, it is a question of seeking new ways of understanding and cordial agreement between the nations. Here again we stood and still stand under the sway of a commandment.

We considered it a fundamental point that in this case two vital claims are opposed to each other, two claims of a different nature and a different origin which cannot objectively be pitted against one another and between which no objective decision can be made as to which is just, which unjust. We considered and still consider it our duty to understand and to honor the claim which is opposed to ours and to endeavor to reconcile both claims. We could not and cannot renounce the Jewish claim; something even higher than the life of our people is bound up with this land, namely its work, its divine mission. But we have been and still are convinced that it must be possible to find some compromise between this claim and the other; for we love this land and we believe in its future; since such love and such faith are surely present on the other side as well, a union in the common service of the land must be within the range of possibility. Where there is faith and love, a solution may be found even to what appears to be a tragic opposition.

In order to carry out a task of such extreme difficulty—in the recognition of which we have to overcome an internal resistance on the Jewish side too, as foolish as it is natural—we were in need of the support of well-meaning persons of all nations, and hoped to receive it. But now you come and settle the whole existential dilemma with the simple formula: "Palestine belongs to the Arabs."

What do you mean by saying that a land belongs to a population? Evidently you do not intend only to describe a state of affairs by your formula, but to declare a certain right. You obviously mean to say that a people, being settled on the land, has so absolute a claim to that land that whoever settles on it without the permission of this people has committed a robbery. But by what means did the Arabs attain to the right of ownership in Palestine? Surely by conquest and in fact a conquest with intent to settle. You therefore admit that as a result their settlement gives them exclusive right of possession; whereas the subsequent conquests of the Mamelukes and the Turks which were conquests with a view to domination, not to settlement, do not constitute such a right in your opinion, but leave the earlier conquerors in rightful ownership. Thus settlement by conquest justifies for you a right of ownership of Palestine; whereas a settlement such as the Jewish—the methods of which, it is true, though not always doing full justice to Arab ways of life, were even in the most objectionable cases far removed from those of conquest—do not justify in your opinion any participation in this right of possession. These are the consequences which result from your axiomatic statement that a land belongs to its population. In an epoch when nations are migrating, you would first support the right of ownership of the nation that is threatened with dispossession or extermination; but were this once achieved, you would be compelled, not at once, but after a suitable number of generations had elapsed, to admit that the land "belongs" to the usurper. . . .

It seems to me that God does not give any one portion of the earth away, so that the owner may say as God says in the Bible: "For all the earth is Mine" (Exod. 19:5). The conquered land is, in my opinion, only lent even to the conqueror who has settled on it—and God waits to see what he will make of it.

I am told, however, I should not respect the cultivated soil and despise the desert. I am told, the desert is willing to wait for the work of her children: she no longer recognizes us, burdened with civilization, as her children. The desert inspires me with awe; but I do not believe in her absolute resistance, for I believe in the great marriage between man (adam) and earth (adamah). This land recognizes us, for it is fruitful through us: and precisely because it bears fruit for us, it recognizes us. Our settlers do not come here as do the colonists from the Occident to have natives do their work for them; they themselves set their shoulders to the plow and they spend their strength and their blood to make the land fruitful. But it is not only for ourselves that we desire its fertility. The Jewish farmers have begun to teach their brothers the Arab farmers to cultivate the land more intensively; we desire to teach them further: together with them we want to cultivate the land—to "serve" it, as the Hebrew has it. The more fertile this soil becomes, the more space there will be for us and for them. We have no desire to dispossess them: we want to live with them. We do not want to dominate them, we want to serve with them. . . .

Notes

The Land and Its Possessors

1. From a reply to Mahatma Gandhi, who in the course of an article (in *Harijan*) comparing the Jewish situation in Palestine with that of the Hindus in South Africa had questioned the validity of the Jewish claim to Palestine.—Ed.

2. Lev. 25:23.

3. Lev. 25:13.

4. Exod. 21:2.

5. Exod. 23:4f.

6. Exod. 23:12.

7. Lev. 25:2–7.

III

PROCESSES OF SOCIAL AND CULTURAL RENOVATION

In the excerpts from Buber's work brought together in this part, the major emphasis shifts from the great movements of cultural creativity to more dispersed creative situations of social regulation which can be found in the more routinized and formal frameworks of social life.

In these excerpts, the emphasis is not on the creation of new overall civilizational frameworks, but much more on the processes of continuous creation and recreation of common discourse, through which social renovation or regeneration can take place and the potentially stagnative tendencies inherent in any society can be counteracted. It is here that the basic characteristics of Buber's utopianism which distinguished him from the "classical" one are most clearly discernible—especially his denial of the validity of any total utopia, and the strong emphasis on the critical importance of partial, dispersed utopias.

It is only in these partial utopias that the renovating and regenerating forces of social authenticity can bear formation. Such regenerative possibilities are not limited to any specific social processes. They can be found—as the excerpts attest to—in processes of continuous reflexivity in the religious arena or in the continuous reconstruction of communal activities. They can also be found, as Buber's numerous writings on education attest to, in the educational arena (see, for instance, Buber's chapter on education in *Between Man and Man*, pages 83–103). All these processes share the basic characteristics of creative community, even if they do not create total utopias—perhaps because they do not create them.

7

Religious Renovation

The Teaching of the Tao*

Amid our theories of races and cultures, our time has lost sight of the old knowledge that the Orient forms a natural unity, expressed in its values and workings; that despite their differences the peoples of the East possess a common reality that sunders them in unconditional clarity from the destiny and genius of the West. The genetic explanation for this distinction, with which we are not here concerned, has its foundation, naturally, in the different conditions not only of space but also of time, for the spiritually determining epoch of the Orient belongs, in fact, to a moment of mankind other than that of the West.

Here I can only indicate the unity of the Orient through a single manifestation, which is, however, the most essential of all—that of the teaching.

In its primal state the spirit of the West is what all human spirit is in its primal state—magic. That is its essence, that it can encounter the thousandfold menace of the instorming freedom of nature with its constraint, the binding in which dwells magic power. Regulated word, ordered movement, magic speech, and magic gesture compel the demonic element under rule and order. All primitive technique and all primitive organization are magic; tools and arms, language and play, customs and bonds arise out of magical intention, and serve in their initial period a magical meaning from which their own life only gradually detaches itself and becomes independent.

This process of detaching and becoming independent is accomplished much more slowly in the Orient than in the West. In the West the magical endures in a living form only in the folk religiousness which has preserved the undifferentiated wholeness of life; in all other spheres the detachment is rapid and complete. In the Orient it is slow and incomplete: a magical character adheres for a long while to the products of the separation. The art of the Orient, for example, perseveres in many ways in its magical intention even after the attainment of artistic free-

*Reprinted from *Pointing the Way: Collected Essays,* trans. and ed. Maurice Friedman (New York: Harper and Bros., 1957), pp. 31–58.

dom and power; whereas in that of the West, reaching this height confers its own right and its own aim.

Among the three basic forces out of which the indicating spirit of the East (I do not consider here the forming spirit) builds itself, of which the Occident only possesses two creatively—called science and law—it is the third, called the teaching, that is able to detach itself most completely from the magical primal ground.

In order to understand the Orient it is necessary, in my view, to bring these three basic forces into the clearest possible contrast with one another.

"Science" includes all information about the "is," whether earthly or heavenly, these two being never and nowhere separated, but uniting into the sphere of being which is the subject of science.

"Law" includes all the commands of an "ought," human and divine, these two being never and nowhere separated from one another, but uniting into the sphere of ought which is the subject of law.

Science and law always belong together so that the "is" verifies itself in the "ought," the "ought" grounds itself on the "is." The growing cleavage between is and ought, between science and law, that characterizes the spiritual history of the Occident is alien to the Orient.

To science and law there belongs, as the third basic force of the Eastern spirit, the teaching.

The teaching includes no subjects, it has only *one* subject—itself: the one thing needful. It stands beyond "is" and "ought," information and command; it knows how to say only one thing, the needful that must be realized in genuine life. The needful is in no way accessible to an "is," and it is not obtainable through information; it is not already in existence either on earth or in heaven, rather it is possessed and lived. The genuine life is in no wise an ought, nor is it subject to a command. Authentic life is not taken over either from men or from God, rather it can be fulfilled only out of itself, and is nothing whatever other than fulfilment. Science rests upon the duality of demand and deed; the teaching rests wholly upon the unity of the one thing needful.

One can always transform fundamentally the meanings the words "is" and "ought" have in science and law, and describe the needful as an "is" that is accessible to no information and the genuine life as an "ought" that is subject to no command, and the teaching consequently is a synthesis of "is" and "ought." But if one does this, one should not thereby make this way of speaking—which is nonsense to science and law—idle, of no account, and presentable through replacing information and command by an "inner" information, and an "inner" command with which the teaching has to do. These phrases of a hackneyed rhetoric, used to explain belief, signify only confusion and delusion. The dialectic opposition of *inner* and *outer* can serve only symbolically for the elucidation of this experience; it cannot set the teaching in contrast to the other basic forces of the spirit. The teaching is not peculiar in that it concerns itself with the inner or receives its measure and sanction from it. To wish to narrow science and law for the sake of an "inner knowledge" that is not at all separable from the outer, for an "inner command" that is not separable from the outer would be senseless. What is peculiar to the teaching, rather, is that it is not concerned with the manifold and the individual but with the One, and that it therefore demands neither belief nor action, both of which are rooted in multiplicity and individuality. The teaching, in general, demands nothing; instead it simply proclaims itself.

This essential difference of the teaching from science and law is amply documented by history. The teaching forms itself independently of science and law until it finds its pure fulfilment in a central human life. Only in its decline that begins soon after this fulfilment does the teaching mingle with elements of science and law. Out of such intermixture there arises a religion: a product of the contamination in which information, command, and the necessary are welded into a contradictory and effective whole. Now belief and action are demanded: the One has disappeared.

Neither teaching nor religion are partial forces, like science and law; both represent the wholeness of life. But in the teaching all opposites of the wholeness are elevated into the One as the seven colours of the spectrum fuse into white light. In religion these are joined in community like the seven colours in the rainbow. The magic that borders science and law but cannot touch the teaching assumes control of religion. Its binding power unites the contending elements into an iridescent, magic vortex that rules the ages.

Between the teaching and religion, leading from the one to the other, stand parable and myth. These attach themselves to the central human life in which the teaching has found its purest fulfilment: the parable as the word of this man himself, the myth as the impact of this life on the consciousness of the age. The parable, accordingly, still appears to stand wholly on the side of the teaching, myth already wholly on the side of religion. None the less, each carries mediation in itself. This must be understood through the essence of the teaching when it is considered in its relation to man.

The teaching has only *one* subject: the needful. It is realized in genuine life. From the standpoint of man, this realization means nothing other than unity. But that is not, as it might seem, an abstract conception, but the most concrete living. For the unity that is meant is not, in fact, any comprehensive unity of a world or of a body of knowledge, not the established unity of the spirit or of being or of anything that is thought or felt or willed, but the unity of this human life and this human soul that fulfils itself in itself, the unity of your life and your soul, you who are seized by the teaching. Genuine life is united life.

Just as there are two kinds of goodness and two kinds of wisdom, the elemental and the achieved, so also there are two kinds of unity in man, as the consecration of which the teaching can verify and realize itself: the unity of the simple man and the unity of the man who has become unified. But as soon as the central man appears, whose achieved unity has the purity and the ingenuous power of the elemental, he must seek out the simple, his poor brothers in spirit, so that their deep unity, which preserves in its bosom all their sins and follies, may sanctify itself beyond sin and folly. And he speaks to them in the language that they can hear: in parable. And when he dies, the memory of his life becomes a parable itself. But a life that has become parable is called myth.

The parable is the insertion of the absolute into the world of events. The myth is the insertion of the world of things into the absolute.

So long as the teaching speaks only to those who have become unified, it cannot dispense with parable. For naked unity is dumb. Only out of things, events, and relations can it attain to speech; there is no human speech beyond these. As soon as the teaching comes to the things, it comes as parable. So long, however, as the teaching speaks only to those who have become unified, the parable is only a glass through which one beholds the light framed in a border of colours. But as soon as the teaching begins to address the simple through its central men, the parable becomes a prism. Thus the fulfilment leads across to the dissolution, and in the parable of the master there already rests in seed all the intoxication of ritual and the madness of dogma.

Again, the *life*, too, of the central man is not seen as reflected in a mirror, but as refracted in a prism: it is mythicized. *Mythus* does not mean that one brings the stars down to earth and allows them to tread it in human shape; rather in it the bliss-bestowing human shape is elevated to heaven, and moon and sun, Orion and the Pleiades, serve only to adorn it. Myth is not an affair of yonder and of old, but a function of today and of all times, of this city where I write and of all places of men. This is an eternal function of the soul: the insertion of what is experienced into the world process that is perceived as now more driving, now more thoughtful, but even in the dullest still in some way perceived—its insertion into the magic of existence. The stronger the tension and intensity of the experience, the greater the experienced shape, the experienced event, so much the more compelling the myth-forming power. Where the highest shape, the hero and saviour, the sublimest event, the life that he has lived, and the mightiest tension, the profound emotion of the simple, meet, the myth arises which compels all the future. Thus the way of dissolution proceeds; for the myth of the saviour already contains in germ the faith in the insignificant miracle and the misuse of the truth of salvation and redemption.

The dissolution takes place in religion, and is consummated in that perpetuated act of violence that calls itself religion yet holds religiousness in chains. Ever again there awakens in the souls of the religious the ardour for freedom—for the teaching; ever again reformation—restoration—renewal of the teaching—is ventured; ever again this venture must miscarry, ever again the fervent movement must issue not in the teaching but in a mixture of science and law, the so-called purified religion. For the teaching cannot be restored, cannot be renewed. Eternally the same, still it must eternally begin anew. This is the course taken by the history of the highest manifestation of the Eastern spirit.

2

That the teaching perpetually begins anew is in no way to be understood as meaning that it has one content that takes different forms, as those believe who investigate and compare the various teachings to find what is common to them. The opposition of content and form appears here as a dialectical one that does not clarify history but rather confuses it, just as it does not clarify but confuses the apperception of art. The Logos of the Johannine Gospel, the symbol of primal existence taken significantly from the world of speech, is erected as a sign of truth against the encroachment of this dialectic. "The Word" is "in the beginning" because it is the unity that is dialectically dissected. Just for this reason the word is the mediator: because it presents to the products of this dissection, e.g. to divinity and humanity, or otherwise regarded, to "God the Father" and to "the Holy Ghost," the bond that unites them, the original unity that, divided and become flesh, once again reconciles the elements. "The Word" is thereby the companion of every genuine human word, which also is not a content that has taken on a form, but a unity that has been dissected into content and form—a dissection that does not clarify but confuses the history of the human word and the history of each single human word, and whose claim, therefore, cannot reach beyond the province of conceptual classification. The same holds with the teaching.

The teaching proclaims that it is the unity as the necessary. But this is no wise a content that assumes different forms. When we dissect each teaching into content and form, we obtain as the "content" not the unity, but the talk about the kingdom of heaven and the adoption by God, or the talk about the release from suffering and the holy path, or the talk about Tao and non-action. This cannot be otherwise; for the unity was even more than the content of Jesus or Buddha or Lao-tzu, more than they strove to express; it was their meaning and ground. It was more than the content of their word, it was the life of this word and this word itself in its unity. Therefore the fundamental relation with which we are here concerned is not that of content and form but, as is yet to be shown, that of the teaching and the parable.

Some have tried yet again to make unity into a content, into a "common" content, but making the unity of genuine life into the unity of God or of the spirit or of being, common to the teachings—somewhat after the analogy of modern monism which decrees a "unity of being" constituted in one way or another. But it is definitely not essential to the teaching to concern itself about the essence of God. With the Buddha this is, indeed, fully clear; but in the Upanishads, too, the significance of the teaching of the Atman does not lie in the fact that a statement is made thereby about the unity of being, but that what one calls being is nothing other than the unity of the self and that the unified one thereby encounters the world as being, as unity, as his self. Even so, primitive Christianity is not concerned with the unity of God but with the likeness of the unified man to God; here, too, the existent divine is only there, so to speak, for the sake of the necessary. And the same holds with the teaching of the Tao, where all that is said of the "path" of the world points to the path of the perfected man, and receives from it its verification and fulfilment.

It must be difficult, of course, for a modern Westerner to realize this fully, especially for those schooled in philosophy to whom the necessary is, perhaps, being seen *sub specie aeterni,* and unity, perhaps, a synthetic act of knowledge. The teaching concerns itself with being even as little as it concerns itself with the ought. It is concerned only with the reality of genuine life, which is primary and cannot be subsumed. It is inaccessible, therefore, through the distinction between subject and object by which, perhaps, one no longer finds the unity in the object but instead removes it into the subject. This distinction is either not present for the man of the teaching, or he regards it only as an abstract formula for that manifold dialectical opposition on whose surpassing the teaching is built.

3

The way of the teaching is, accordingly, not that of the development of knowledge but that of pure fulfilment in human life. That is to be perceived with greater or lesser clarity in the three manifestations of the teaching that have come down to us with sufficient documentation.

These three manifestations are the Chinese teaching of the Tao, the Indian teaching of liberation, the Jewish and early Christian teaching of the Kingdom of God. The documentation of even these manifestations is insufficient to enable us to survey the whole of their way. Thus we know of the developing Jewish and early Christian teaching something of the living community that bore it—from the Rechabites (Jeremiah 35) to the Essenes, to whom ancient tradition, despite all exaggerations, probably refers correctly—but very little of the words of this, so-to-speak, underground Judaism that we can only thirstily surmise or infer from late sources. In the writings of the Tao-teaching, on the other hand, sayings of the "Old Ones" are handed down to us that conceal the long pre-existence of the teaching, and this is also corroborated through statements of its opponents; but of the life forms in which it was transmitted we have entirely inadequate information. Not even the Indian literature, despite its incomparable vastness, offers a complete view of the links.

Yet the material suffices to show how the teaching takes form independently of science and law and how it fulfils itself in the central man, who conquers science and law without a battle, simply through his teaching and his life. Thus Buddha overcame the Vedic science through the elevation of the "view" that does not concern the perfected man into the "path," and the Brahmanical law through the elevation of the castes into the order. And Lao-tzu overcame the official wisdom through the teaching of "non-being," the official virtue through "non-action."

And we can also see from these manifestations that the central man brings no new element to the teaching, but rather fulfils it. "I am not come to destroy but to fulfil." Lao-tzu also says of himself that he has only to fulfil the unrecognized of earlier times, the faint notion of the One that is contained in the word of the people. He once quotes the saying, "Those who do deeds of violence do not reach their natural death," and adds to it, "What the others teach, I also teach: I shall make out of it a father-ground of the teaching." This corresponds to the saying of the Sermon on the Mount, "But I say unto you"; for violence, to Lao-tzu, is already in itself dead, lifeless because it is Tao-less. To fulfil means here as there to raise something that has been handed down out of the conditioned into the unconditioned.

The central man brings to the teaching no new element, rather he fulfils it; he raises it out of the unrecognized into the recognized and out of the conditioned into the unconditioned.

This unconditionality of the fulfilling man, which sets the world of the conditioned against him, and this his power of fulfilment manifest themselves in his life. For him, in incomparably higher measure than for the great ruler, the great artist, and the great philosopher, all that is scattered, fleeting, and fragmentary grows together into unity; this unity is his life. The ruler has his organization of peoples, the artist has his work, the philosopher has his system of ideas; the fulfilling man has only his life. His words are elements of this life, each an executor and originator, each inspired by destiny and caught up by destiny, the multitude of voices transformed through this human body into a conclusive harmony, the weak movement of many dead joined in him into might, he who is the crossroads of the teaching, of fulfilment and dissolution, salvation and degeneration. There are, therefore, logia that no doubt can touch, and that, striding through the generations without being written down, preserve themselves unmixed, by the strength of their stamp of destiny and the elementary uniqueness of their fulfilling speech. For the fulfilling man, who is assembled out of everything and yet comes out of nothing, is the most unique of men. Though all seeking desires him and all self-communion foresees him, he is recognized by few when he appears, and these few are probably not at all those who foresaw and desired him: so great is his uniqueness—so unoriginal, so unpretentious, so wholly the final genuineness of mankind.

This is most apparent with Jesus, whose witness was perfected through death, the sole absolute that man has to offer. Next to him stands Buddha. Lao-tzu's life holds out least, because his life was just that of his teaching, a hidden life. In the scanty report of the historian all that is necessary is said concerning it; of his life: "His teaching was the concealment of self: what he strove for was to be nameless"; and of his death: "No one knows where he died: Lao-tzu was a hidden wise man."

4

Like his life, his teaching also is the most hidden, for it is the most lacking in parable.

Naked unity is dumb. As soon as the unity becomes teaching out of the ground and goal of a separated man, submerged in wordless wonder, as soon as the word stirs in this man—in the hour of stillness, before the break of day, where there is yet no Thou other than the I, and the lonely talk in the dark traverses the abyss across and back—the unity is already touched by parable. Man utters his words as the *Logos* utters men: his words no longer proceed from pure unity—the manifold, the parable, is already therein. But as the multiplicity of men, so long as they are children, is still tied to the unity, and parable only rests on them as the smile on their lips, so in the hour of stillness the speech of the separated man is only touched at first by the parable as by a smile. And as, when men awaken and themselves beget children, their multiplicity detaches itself from the unity, and the parable flows in them as the blood in their veins, so the parable flows like blood through the speech of the fulfilling man when he goes out to meet his fellows.

But as between the time of childhood and manhood stands youth, the tragedy that is reconciled unperceived, so between solitude and sermon there stands the time of transition which, to be sure, is not reconciled unperceived, but comes to a decision. Buddha calls it the time of temptation. He says to the tempter: "I shall not go into Nirvana, O evil one, before this, my irreproachable way of life, shall have thrived and come to flower, disseminated far, found by many, richly unfolded, so that it is beautifully manifested by men." In this period the parable is no longer the smile, not yet the blood; it still rests upon the spirit already in the spirit—like a dream. Like youth, the transition stands in a dream. Therefore the word of the solitude is the cry and the word of the sermon is the narrative; but the word of the transition is the image.

There is a life, however, in which the transition does not lead from solitude to sermon, but leads from the solitude of the question to the solitude of the fullness, from the solitude of the abyss to the solitude of the sea. That is the hidden life.

I believe that this man is tempted as the others are. Like the others, he does not enter Nirvana, but neither does he go to men: he enters the concealment. The concealment will bear his children. "He who knows his brightness and veils himself in his darkness"—thus Lao-tzu describes it.

What is the sermon to this man? "Heaven does not speak and yet knows how to find answer." What is manhood to him? "He who lives his manhood yet holds to his womanhood, he is the river-bed of all the world."

This man does not talk to himself and he does not talk to men; but into the concealment. Although he is not himself on the way to men, his word is still necessarily on the way to parable; he is not in transition, but his word remains the word of transition: the image. His speech is not a complete speech of parable like that of Buddha or Jesus, but a speech of images. It resembles a youth who has not yet become detached from the unity like a man, but is no longer tied to the unity like a child. But that

would be a youth such as we glimpse, say, in the poems of Hölderlin—
who does not have the striving beyond the self of dream and of tragedy;
but only the visionary fullness of youth, turned into the unconditional
and the eternal where the dream has become mantic and tragedy mystery.

Concealment is the history of Lao-tzu's speech. No matter how mythicized the Sermon of Benares and the Sermon on the Mount may be, that
a great truth lies at the base of each myth is unmistakable. In Lao-tzu's
life there is nothing corresponding. In his words, in his writings, one
marks throughout that his utterances are not at all what we call speech,
but only like the soughing of the sea out of its fullness when it is swept by
a light wind. In the scanty reports of the historian, this too is communicated or represented. Lao-tzu enters his final concealment; he leaves the
country in which he dwelt. He reaches the boundary station. The chief
of the boundary station says to him, "I see that you are entering into the
concealment. Would you yet write a book for me before you go?" There-
upon Lao-tzu wrote a book in two sections, that is the *Book of the Tao
and of Virtue* in a little over five thousand words. Then he departed. And
immediately afterwards the report concludes with the words that I have
cited earlier, "No one knows where he finished his life." Information or
symbol, all the same: this is the truth about Lao-tzu's speech. "Those
who know it do not say it; those who say it do not know it," it is stated in
his book. His speech is just like the soughing of the sea out of its fullness.

The teaching of Lao-tzu is full of images but without parables, provided that we are thinking of the complete parable that develops from
the image to narrative. Thus he committed it to the ages. Centuries
passed over it, then the teaching came to one who—like all great poets,
certainly gathering into himself much folk lore—composed its parable.
This man is called Chuang-tzu.

The parable of the Tao-teaching, therefore, is not, like that in the
teaching of Jesus and of Buddha, the direct word of fulfilment spoken by
the central man. It is, rather, the poetry of one to whom the teaching was
delivered when it had already reached its fulfilment.

The manifestation of the Tao-teaching is split into the first word,
which stands closer to the naked unity than any other word of the human world, and the second word, in which the unity wears a richer and
more delicate drapery than in any other word of the teaching, and can
properly be compared only to the great poems of mankind.

Only the two together give us the completed shape of the teaching in
its purest fulfilment; as it proclaims Tao, "the path," the ground and
meaning of the unified life, as the ground and meaning of all.

5

Chuang-tzu lived in the second half of the fourth and the first half of the third centuries before Christ, hence about two hundred and fifty years after Lao-tzu.[1] But while Paul, that other apostle who did not know his master in the flesh, dissolved his teaching of the unity of the genuine life and perverted it into an eternal antagonism between spirit and nature—that one could not overcome but only escape—Chuang-tzu was a faithful messenger of the teaching: its messenger to the world. That he composed its parable is not to be understood as if he had "explained" it through things or "applied" it to things. Rather, the parable bears the unity of the teaching into all the world so that, as it before enclosed it in itself, the All now appears full of it, and no thing is so insignificant that the teaching refuses to fill it. He who does not zealously spread the teaching, but reveals it in its essence, bestows on each the possibility of also discovering and animating the teaching in himself.

Such an apostleship is silent and solitary, as the master-hood that it serves was silent and solitary. It no longer lives in the concealment, yet it is not bound to men by any duty nor by any aim. History imparts to us almost nothing else concerning Chuang-tzu's life than this, that he was poor and the offices that were offered him were declined with the words, "I shall never accept an office. Thus I shall remain free to follow myself." The same attitude appears in the reports of his life scattered in his books, clearly penned by the hand of a disciple. And nothing else is signified by the report of his death. He forbade that a funeral should be given him, "With earth and heaven for my coffin and grave, with the sun and the moon for my two round holy images, with the stars for my burial jewellery, with all creation for my funeral procession—is not all ready to hand? What could you still add to it?"

It is not surprising that the conditioned world rose against him. His age, which stood under the domination of the Confucian wisdom of the moral ordering of life according to duty and aim, called Chuang-tzu a good-for-nothing. In parables, such as that of the useless tree, he gave his answer to the age. Men do not know the use of the useless. What they call the aimless is the aim of the Tao.

He opposed public opinion, which was the law of his age not in reference to any particular content but in its basic spirit. He who flatters his princes or his parents, he said, he who agrees with them blindly and praises them without merit, is called by the crowd unfilial and faithless. But the man who flatters the crowd is not criticized, he who blindly agrees with it, praises it without cause, he who adjusts his attitude and his expression so as to win favour. Chuang-tzu knew the vanity of the crowd and declared it; he knew that only he wins it who subjugates it. "One man steals a purse and is punished. Another steals a state and becomes a prince." And he also knew that the teaching of the Tao could never subjugate the crowd. For the teaching brings nothing to men; rather, it says to each one that he will have unity if he discovers it in himself and brings it to life. So it is with men: "All strive to comprehend what they do not yet know, none strives to comprehend what he knows." What is great is inaccessible to the crowd because it is simple. Great music, said Chuang-tzu, is not appreciated, but over street songs the populace rejoice. Noble words are not heard while common words predominate; two little earthen bells drown out the peal of the great bell. "Thus the world goes astray; I know the right path, but how can I conduct men to it?"

Thus his apostleship spent itself in parable that was not zealous, but rested in itself, visible and yet hidden. The world, says Chuang-tzu, stands opposed to the path, and the path stands opposed to the world; the path cannot recognize the world, and the world cannot recognize the path—"Therefore the virtue of the wise is hidden, even when they do not dwell in the mountains and in the forest; hidden even when they hide nothing." Thus the apostleship of Chuang-tzu found its issue in that in which the masterhood of Lao-tzu had run its course: in the concealment.

6

"Tao" means the way, the path; but since it also has the meaning of "speech," the term is at times rendered by "logos." For Lao-tzu and his disciples, wherever it is developed figuratively, the first of these meanings is implied. Yet its connotation is related to that of the Heracleitian logos. Both transpose a dynamic principle of human life into the transcendent, though basically they mean nothing other than human life itself, which is the bearer of all transcendence. I shall here set forth this meaning for the Tao.[2]

In the West, Tao has usually been understood as an attempt to explain the world; the explanation of the world that one glimpses therein always coincides in a remarkable way with the current philosophy of the age. Thus Tao first passes for nature, after that reason, and recently it is held to be nothing but energy. In contrast to these interpretations, it must be pointed out that Tao generally means no explanation of the world; it implies that only the whole meaning of being rests in the unity of the genuine life, that it is experienced nowhere else, that it is just this unity which is grasped as the absolute. If one wishes to look away from the unity of the genuine life and seek what underlies it, then nothing is left over but the unknowable, of which nothing further can be said than that it is the unknowable. Unity is the only way to realize it and to experience it in its reality. The unknowable is naturally neither nature nor reason nor energy, but just the unknowable which no image reaches because "the images are in it." But what is experienced is again neither nature nor reason nor energy, but the unity of the path, the unity of the genuine human way that rediscovers the united in the world and in each thing: the path as the unity of the world, as the unity of each thing.

But the unknowableness of the Tao cannot be understood as one speaks of the unknowableness of some principle of a religious or philosophical explanation of the world, in order to say nevertheless something further about it. Even what the word "Tao" expresses does not express the unknowable; "the name that can be named is not the eternal name" (L). If one does not regard Tao as the necessary whose reality is experienced in unified life but as something separate, then one finds nothing to regard: "Tao can have no existence." It cannot be investigated nor demonstrated. Not only can no truth be stated concerning it, but it cannot be a subject of a statement at all. What is said concerning it is neither true nor false. "How can Tao be so obscured that something 'true' or something 'false' appears in it? . . . Tao is obscured because we cannot grasp it." When it appears, therefore, that Tao is more present in one time than in another, this is no reality, but only like the sinking and ascending of the tones in music, "it belongs to the playing." We cannot discover it in any being. If we seek it in heaven and earth, in space and in time, then it is not there; rather, heaven and earth, space and time, are grounded in it alone. And nonetheless "it can be found through seeking" (L): in unified life. There it is not recognized and known, but possessed, lived, and acted.

"Only he who reaches it in silence and fulfils it with his being has it," state the books of Lieh-tzu. And he does not have it as his own but as the meaning of the world. Out of his unity he beholds unity in the world: the unity of the masculine and the feminine elements that do not exist for themselves but only for each other, the unity of the opposites that do not exist for themselves but only through each other, the unity of the things that do not exist for themselves but only with one another. This unity is the Tao in the world. When, in a conversation related by Chuang-tzu, Lao-tzu says to Khung-tzu, "That heaven is high, that the earth is broad, that sun and moon revolve, that the things grow, that is their Tao," this statement is only fully comprehensible through an old verse that Lao-tzu quotes in his book. It runs:

Heaven obtained unity and thereby radiance,
Earth unity and thereby rest and repose,
The spirit unity and thereby understanding,
The brooks unity and thereby full banks,
All beings unity and thereby life,
Prince and king unity in order to give the world
    the right measure.

Thus the unity of each thing determines in itself the manner and nature of this thing; that is, the Tao of the thing, this thing's path and
wholeness. "No thing can beget Tao, and yet each thing has Tao in itself
and begets it ever anew." That means each thing reveals the Tao through
the way of its existence, through its life; for Tao is unity in change, the
unity that verifies itself not only in the manifoldness of things but also in
the successive moments in the life of each thing. The perfect revelation of
Tao, therefore, is not the man who goes his way without alteration, but
the man who combines the maximum of change with the purest unity.

There are two types of life. The one is mere thoughtless living, using
life up until its extinction; the other is the eternal change and its unity in
spirit. He who does not allow himself to be consumed in his life, but
incessantly renews himself and just through that affirms his self in
change—which is not, indeed, a static being but just the way, Tao—he
attains the eternal change and self-affirmation. For, here as always in the
Tao-teaching, consciousness effects being, spirit effects reality. And as in
the connection of the life-moments of a thing, so in the connection of the
life-moments of the world, Tao verifies itself—in the coming and going
of all things, in the unity of their eternal changes. Thus it says in the
Books of Lieh-tzu: "What has no origin and continually engenders is
Tao. From life to life, therefore, although ending, not decaying, that is
eternity . . . what has an origin and continually dies is likewise Tao.
From death to death, therefore, although never ending, yet decaying,
that also is eternity." Tao is unloosing, it is transition to new shape, it is a
moment of sleep and contemplation between two world lives. All is becoming and change in the "great house" of eternity. As in the existence
of things, separation and gathering, change and unity succeed each
other, so in the existence of the world life and death follow each other,
together verifying Tao as the unity in change. This eternal Tao, which is
the denial of all illusory being, is also called non-being. Birth is not beginning, death is not an end, existence in space and time is without limit
and cessation, birth and death are only entrance and exit through "the
invisible gate of heaven that is called non-being. This is the dwelling-
place of the perfected man."

Here, too, the perfected man, the unified one, is described as he who directly experiences Tao. He beholds the unity in the world. But that is not to be understood as if the world were a closed thing outside of him whose unity he penetrates. Rather the unity of the world is only the reflection of his unity; for the world is nothing alien, but one with the unified man. "Heaven and earth and I came together into existence, and I and all things are one." But since the unity of the world only exists for the perfected man, it is, in truth, his unity that sets unity in the world. That also proceeds from the nature of the Tao as it appears in things. Tao is the path of things, their manner, their peculiar order, their unity; but as such it exists in things only potentially; it first becomes active in its contact with others: "If there were metal and stone without Tao, there would be no sound. They have the power of sound, but it does not come out of them if they are not struck. Thus it is with all things."

Consciousness, however, never characterizes a receiving but a giving: "Tao is conveyed but not received." As the Tao of things only becomes living and manifest through their contact with other things, so the Tao of the world only becomes living and manifest through its unconscious contact with the conscious being of the unified man. This is expressed by Chuang-tzu through the statement that the perfected man reconciles and brings into accord the two primal elements of nature, the positive and the negative, yang and yin, which the primal unity of being tore asunder. And in the "Book of Purity and Rest," a late Taoist tract that appears in this point to rest on a tradition all too narrowly comprehended, it says, "When man persists in purity and rest, heaven and earth return"; that is, to unity, to undivided existence, to Tao. In the late, degenerated literature, the unified man is still understood as the giving. We may say: the unified man is for the Tao-teaching the creating man; for all creating, from the point of view of this teaching, means nothing other than to call forth the Tao of the world, the Tao of things, to make the latent unity living and manifest.

We shall try to sum it up:

Tao in itself is the unrecognizable, the unknowable. "The true Tao does not explain itself." It cannot be represented: it cannot be thought, it has no image, no word, no measure. "The right measure of the Tao is its self" (L).

Tao appears in the becoming of the world as the original undivided state, as the primal existence from which all elements sprang, as "mother of all beings" (L), as the "spirit of the valley" that bears everything. "The spirit of the valley is deathless; it is called the deep feminine. The deep feminine portal is called the roots of heaven and of earth" (L).

Tao appears in the being of the world as the constant undividedness:

as the united transformation of the world, as its order. "It has its movement and its truth, but it has neither action nor shape." It is "eternally without action and yet without non-action" (L). It "perseveres and does not change" (L).

Tao appears in things as the personal undividedness: as each thing's particular manner and power. There is nothing in which the whole Tao is not present as this thing's self. Here, too, Tao is eternally without action and yet without non-action. The self of things has its life in the way in which things answer things.

Tao appears in men as purposeful undividedness: as the unifying force that overcomes all straying away from the ground of life, as the completing force that heals all that is sundered and broken, as the atoning force that delivers from all division. "He who is in sin, Tao can atone for him" (L).

As purposeful undividedness Tao has its own fulfilment as its goal. It wills to realize itself. In men Tao can become pure unity as it cannot in the realm of things. He in whom Tao becomes pure unity is the perfected man. In him Tao no longer appears but is.

The perfected man is self-enclosed, secure, united out of Tao, unifying the world, a creator, "God's companion": the companion of all-creating eternity. The perfected man possesses eternity. Only the perfected man possesses eternity. The spirit wanders through things until it blooms to eternity in the perfected man.

It is this that is signified by the word of Lao-tzu: "Ascend the height of renunciation, embrace the abyss of rest. The numberless beings all arise. Therein I recognize their return. When the being unfolds itself, in the unfolding each returns to his root. To have returned to the root means to rest. To rest means to have fulfilled one's destiny. To have fulfilled one's destiny means to be eternal."

Tao realizes itself in the genuine life of the perfected man. In his pure unity it grows out of appearance to direct reality. The unknowable and the unified human life, the first and the last, touch one another. In the perfected man Tao returns to itself from its world wandering through the manifestation. It becomes fulfilment.

7

But what is the unified human life in its relation to things? How does the perfected man live in the world? What shape does knowledge assume in him, the coming of things to man? What shape action, the coming of man to the things?

The teaching of the Tao answers this question with a vigorous denial of all that men call knowledge and action.

What men call knowledge rests on the sundering of the senses and the powers of the mind. What they call action rests on the sundering of intentions and deeds. Each sense receives something different, each mental power elaborates it differently, they all stagger through one another in infinity: that is what men call knowledge. Each purpose tugs at the structure, each act interferes with the order, they all are entangled in infinity: that is what men call action.

What is called knowledge by men is no knowledge. In order to demonstrate this, Chuang-tzu assembles almost all the reasons that the human mind has ever devised for putting itself in question.

There is no perception, since things incessantly change.

There is no knowledge in space because only relative and not absolute extension is accessible to us. All greatness exists only in relation—"under heaven there is nothing that is greater than the point of a blade of grass." We cannot swing out of our own measure. The cricket does not understand the flight of the giant bird.

There is no knowledge in time because duration exists for us only relatively. "No being attains a higher age than a child that dies in the cradle." We cannot swing out of our own measure. A morning mushroom knows not the alternation of day and night, a butterfly chrysalis knows not the alternation of spring and fall.

There is no certainty of life; for we have no criterion by which we could decide what is the real and determining life, waking or dream. Each state holds itself to be the real.

There is no certainty of values; for we have no measure of right by which we could decide what is beautiful and what is ugly, what is good and what is evil. Each being calls itself good and its opposite evil.

There is no truth in concepts, for all speech is inadequate.

All this signified only one thing for Chuang-tzu: that what men call knowledge is no knowledge. In separation there is no knowledge. Only the undivided man knows; for only in him in whom there is no division is there no separation from the world, and only he who is not separated from the world can know it. Not in the dialectic of subject and object, but only in the unity with the all is knowledge possible. Unity is knowledge.

This knowledge is not put in question by anything, for it embraces the whole. It overcomes relation in the unconditionality of the all-embracing. It receives each pair of opposites as a polarity without wishing to eliminate their oppositeness, and it includes all polarities in its unity; it "reconciles in its light the yes with the no."

This knowledge is without passion and seeking. It rests in itself. "It is not by going out of the door that one knows the world; it is not by gazing through the window that one sees the way of heaven" (L). It is without the mania for knowledge. It has things, it does not know them. It does not take place through senses and mental powers, but through the wholeness of the being. It lets the senses continue, but only like children at play; for all that they bring to it is only a varicoloured, glittering, uncertain reflection of its own truth. It lets the mental powers continue, but only as dancers who make its music into images, unfaithful and unsteady and rich in shapes, after the manner of dancers. The "organ playing of heaven," the playing of unity on the manifoldness of our nature ("as the wind plays on the openings of the trees"), becomes here the organ-playing of the soul.

This knowledge is not knowing but being. Because it possesses things in its unity, it never stands over against them; and when it regards them, it regards them from the inside out, each thing from itself outward; but not from its appearance, rather from the essence of this thing, from the unity of this thing that it possesses in its own unity. This knowledge is each thing that it regards, and thus it lifts each thing that it regards out of appearance into being.

This knowledge embraces all things in its being; that is, in its love. It is the all-embracing love that overcomes all opposites.

This knowledge is the deed. The deed is the eternal measure of right, the eternal criterion, the absolute, the speechless, the unchangeable. The knowledge of the perfected man is not in his thinking but in his action.

What is called action by men is no action.

It is not an effecting of the whole being but single intentions groping their way in the web of the Tao, the interference of single actions in the manner and order of things. It is entangled in aims.

In so far as they approve of it, men call it virtue. What is called virtue by men is no virtue. It exhausts itself in "love of mankind" and "righteousness."

What men call love of mankind and righteousness has nothing in common with the love of the perfected man.

It is perverted because it comes forward as an ought, as the subject of a command. But love cannot be commanded. Commanded love works only evil and harm; it stands in contradiction to the natural goodness of the human heart; it troubles its purity and disturbs its immediacy. Therefore, those who preach thus pass their days in complaining about the wickedness of the world. They injure the wholeness and truthfulness of things and awaken doubt and division. Intentional love of mankind and intentional righteousness are not grounded in the nature of man; they are superfluous and burdensome like surplus fingers or other protuberances. Therefore, Lao-tzu says to Khung-tzu, "As horseflies keep one awake the whole night, so this talk of love of mankind and righteousness plagues me. Strive to bring the world back to its original simplicity."

But in still another sense "love of mankind and righteousness" have nothing in common with the love of the perfected man. They rest upon a man's standing opposite the other men and then treating them "lovingly" and "justly." But the love of the perfected man, for which each man can strive, rests upon unity with all things. Therefore Lao-tzu says to Khung-tzu, "For the perfected men of ancient times, love of mankind was only a station and righteousness only an inn on the way to the kingdom of the undivided, where they nourish themselves in the fields of equanimity and dwell in the gardens of duty-lessness."

As the true knowledge, seen from the standpoint of human speech, is called by Lao-tzu "not-knowing" ("He who is illumined in Tao is like full night"), so the true action, the action of the perfected man, is called by him "non-action." "The perfected man performs the non-action" (L). "The rest of the wise man is not what the world calls rest: it is the work of his inner deed."

This action, the "non-action," is an effecting of the whole being. To interfere with the life of things means to harm both them and oneself. But to rest means to effect, to purify one's own soul means to purify the world, to collect oneself means to be helpful, to surrender oneself to Tao means to renew creation. He who imposes himself has the small, manifest might; he who does not impose himself has the great, secret might. He who "does nothing" effects. He who is in complete harmony is surrounded by the receiving love of the world. "He is unmoved like a corpse whereas his dragon-power reveals itself all around; he is in deep silence, whereas his thunder voice resounds; and the powers of heaven answer each movement of his will, and under the flexible influence of his non-action all things ripen and flourish."

This action, the "non-action," is an effecting out of gathered unity. In ever new parable Chuang-tzu says that each does right who gathers himself to unity in his act. The will of him who is concentrated into one becomes pure power, pure effecting; for when there is no division in the willing person, there is no longer any division between him and what is willed—being; what is willed becomes being. The nobility of a being lies in its ability to concentrate itself into one. For the sake of this unity Lao-tzu says, "He who has the fullness of virtue in himself is like a newborn child." The unified man is like a child that screams the whole day and is not hoarse, out of the harmony of his forces, keeps his fists shut the whole day out of concentrated virtue, stares the whole day at *one* thing out of undivided attention, that moves, rests, relieves himself without knowing it, and lives beyond all distress in a heavenly light.

This action, the "non-action," stands in harmony with the nature and destiny of all things, with Tao. "The perfected man, like heaven and earth, has no love of mankind." He does not stand opposite the creature but embraces it. Therefore his love is wholly free and unlimited, does not depend upon the conduct of men and knows no choice; it is the *unconditioned* love. "Good men—I treat them well, men who are not good—I also treat them well: virtue is good. True men—I deal with them truly, men who are not true—I also deal with them truly: virtue is true" (L). And because he has no "love of mankind," the perfected man does not interfere in the life of beings, he does not impose himself on them, but he "helps all beings to their freedom" (L): through his unity he leads them, too, to unity, he liberates their nature and their destiny, he releases Tao in them.

As natural virtue, the virtue of each thing, consists of its "non-being," in that it rests in its limits, in its primary condition, so the highest virtue, the virtue of the perfected man, consists of its "non-action," in his effecting out of undivided, opposite-less, enclosed unity. "He closes his exits, fastens his doors, he breaks his edges, scatters abroad his fullness, makes mild his brilliance, becomes one with his dust. That means deep self-unification" (L).

8

Unity alone is true power. Therefore the unified man is the true ruler.

The relation of the ruler to his kingdom is the highest proclamation of the Tao in the life together of beings.

The kingdom, the community of beings, is not something artificial and arbitrary, but something inborn and self-determining. "The kingdom is a spiritual instrument and cannot be made. He who makes it destroys it" (L).

Therefore what is called ruling by man is no ruling but a destroying. He who interferes with the natural life of the kingdom, he who wants to lead, master, and determine it from the outside, he annihilates it, he loses it. He who guards and unfolds the natural life of the kingdom, he who does not impose upon it command and compulsion, but submerges himself in it, listens to its secret message, and brings it to light and to

work, he rules it in truth. He performs the non-action; he does not interfere, but guards and unfolds what wills to become. In the need and drive
of the kingdom the will of the Tao reveals itself to him. He joins his own
will to it so that he may become an instrument of the Tao, and all things
change of themselves. He knows no violence, and yet all beings follow
the gesture of his hand. He uses neither reward nor punishment, and yet
what he wants to happen happens. "I am without action," speaks the
perfected man, "and the people change of themselves; I love rest, and the
people become righteous of themselves; I am without industry, and
the people become rich of themselves; I am without desires, and the
people become simple of themselves" (L).

To rule means to become a part of the natural order of appearances.
But only he can do that who has found unity, and out of it beheld the
unity of each thing in itself and the unity of things with one another. He
who becomes free of the distinctions and joins himself to the infinite, he
who restores both the things and himself to the primal existence, he who
liberates and brings to unity both himself and the world, he who re-
deems both from the slavery of violence and bustle—he rules the world.

The kingdom has degenerated; it has declined to the act of violence of
government. It must be liberated from it. That is the goal of the true
ruler.

What is the act of violence of government? The compulsion of false
might. "The more prohibitions and restraints the kingdom has, so much
the more impoverished the people; the more arms the people have, so
much the more will the land be disquieted; the more artificiality and
cunning the people have, so much the more monstrous things arise; the
more laws and ordinances are proclaimed, so much the more robbers
and thieves are there" (L). The government is the parasite that takes
away from the people its life strength. "The people are hungry because
the government consumes too many taxes. Therefore they are hungry.
The people are hard to rule because the government is all too interfering.
Therefore they are hard to rule. The people are heedless of death because
they long in vain for fullness of life. Therefore they are heedless of death"
(L). The true ruler liberates the people from the violent acts of government because in place of might he allows the "non-action" to govern. He
exercises his transforming influence on all beings, and yet they know
nothing of it, for he influences them in agreement with their primal nature. He causes men and things to be cheerful of themselves. He takes all
their suffering on himself. "To bear the country's need and pain, that is
to be the kingdom's king" (L).

In the degenerated kingdom no one is granted the privilege of con-
ducting his affairs according to his own insight, but each stands under

the dominion of the multitude. The true ruler liberates the individual from this dominion; he makes the crowd no longer a crowd, and allows everyone freely to administer his own affairs and the community the common affairs. But he does all this in the manner of non-action, and the people does not notice that it has a ruler. It says, "We have become so of ourselves."

The true ruler stands as the perfected man beyond love of mankind and righteousness. Certainly the wise prince is to be praised who gives to each his own and is just; still more highly to be praised is the virtuous one who stands in community with all and practises love; but the only one who can fulfil on earth the kingdom, the spiritual vessel, is the spiritual prince who creates perfection: unity with heaven and earth, freedom from all ties that conflict with the Tao, deliverance of things to their primal nature, to their virtue.

The true ruler is Tao's executor on earth. Therefore it says, "Tao is great, heaven is great, the earth is great, the king also is great" (L).

9

I have not considered the Tao-teaching in its "development" but in its unity. The teaching does not develop, it cannot develop after it has found its fulfilment in the central human life. Instead it becomes a rule, like the teaching of the Buddha, if the apostle who receives it (never directly) from the hands of the fulfilling man is an organizer like Asoka; or it becomes dialectic, like the teaching of Jesus, if this man is a man of action like Paul; or it becomes poetry, like the teaching of the Tao, if the propagator is a poet like Chuang-tzu. Chuang-tzu was a poet. He did not "develop"[3] the teaching as it had been given in the words of Lao-tzu, but he shapes it into poetry and into philosophy; for he was a poet of ideas, like Plato.

Chuang-tzu shows many resemblances to Greek philosophers in other respects. He has been compared with Heracleitus; and, in fact, there are words of Heracleitus that could not be associated with any other philosophy with the same justification as with the Tao-teaching: words such as that of the unknowable logos that yet works in all, of the unity that is at once nameless and named, of its manifestation as the eternal order in the world, of the eternal transformation from totality to unity and from unity to totality, of the harmony of opposites, of the relation between waking and dream in the existence of the individual, of that between life and death in the existence of the world. Further, Chuang-tzu may perhaps be compared with the total shape of Greek philosophy that transferred the teaching from the sphere of genuine life into the sphere of the explanation of the world, into an ideological structure, thereby, to be sure, creating something wholly individual and powerful in itself.

It is tempting to compare Chuang-tzu also with Western poets, for which purpose even isolated motifs offer themselves in a strange correspondence. One might proceed from outward to ever more inward affinities: one would begin by placing the story of the skull next to Hamlet's speech in the churchyard, then juxtapose Chuang-tzu's story of silence and the narrative in *The Little Flowers of St. Francis* of Brother Aegidus' meeting with Louis of France, in order, finally, to rediscover in the conversation of eternal dying Goethe's holy longing of "Die and become" ("*Stirb und werde*") in more austere, more thought-like counterpart. But all this can only be a transition to an acceptance in which one no longer attempts to enregister Chuang-tzu in a category, but receives him in his whole real existence without comparison and co-ordination; him, that is, his work—the parable.

Notes

The Teaching of the Tao

1. I cannot agree with the late dating of Lao-tzu that is recently gaining ground.

2. Citations without special marking are taken from Chuang-tzu, those with (L) from Lao-tzu.

3. The teaching that I have presented last, that of the kingdom, is already well established in Lao-tzu, even in the stamp of the words.

8

Pioneering—"Halutziuth"[1]

An Experiment That Did Not Fail*

The era of advanced Capitalism has broken down the structure of society. The society which preceded it was composed of different societies; it was complex, and pluralistic in structure. This is what gave it its peculiar social vitality and enabled it to resist the totalitarian tendencies inherent in the pre-revolutionary centralistic State, though many elements were very much weakened in their autonomous life. This resistance was broken by the policy of the French Revolution, which was directed against the special rights of all free associations. Thereafter centralism in its new, capitalistic form succeeded where the old had failed: in atomizing society. Exercising control over the machines and, with their help, over the whole society, Capitalism wants to deal only with individuals; and the modern State aids and abets it by progressively dispossessing groups of their autonomy. The militant organizations which the proletariat erected against Capitalism—Trades Unions in the economic sphere and the Party in the political—are unable in the nature of things to counteract this process of dissolution, since they have no access to the life of society itself and its foundations: production and consumption. Even the transfer of capital to the State is powerless to modify the social structure, even when the State establishes a network of compulsory associations, which, having no autonomous life, are unfitted to become the cells of a new socialist society.

From this point of view the heart and soul of the Co-operative Movement is to be found in the trend of a society towards structural renewal, the re-acquisition, in new tectonic forms, of the internal social relationships, the establishment of a new *consociatio consociationum*. It is (as I have shown [earlier in *Paths in Utopia*]) a fundamental error to view this trend as romantic or utopian merely because in its early stages it had romantic reminiscences and utopian fantasies. At bottom it is thoroughly topical and constructive; that is to say, it aims at changes which, in the given circumstances and with the means at its disposal, are fea-

*Epilogue reprinted from *Paths in Utopia* (Boston: Beacon, 1958), pp. 139–49.

190

sible. And, psychologically speaking, it is based on one of the eternal human needs, even though this need has often been forcibly suppressed or rendered insensible: the need of man to feel his own house as a room in some greater, all-embracing structure in which he is at home, to feel that the other inhabitants of it with whom he lives and works are all acknowledging and confirming his individual existence. An association based on community of views and aspirations alone cannot satisfy this need; the only thing that can do that is an association which makes for communal living. But here the co-operative organization of production or consumption proves, each in its own way, inadequate, because both touch the individual only at a certain point and do not mould his actual life. On account of their merely partial or functional character all such organizations are equally unfitted to act as cells of a new society. Both these partial forms have undergone vigorous development, but the Consumer Co-operatives only in highly bureaucratic forms and the Producer Co-operatives in highly specialized forms: they are less able to embrace the whole life of society to-day than ever. The consciousness of this fact is leading to the synthetic form: the Full Co-operative. By far the most powerful effort in this direction is the Village Commune, where communal living is based on the amalgamation of production and consumption, production being understood not exclusively as agriculture alone but as the organic union of agriculture with industry and with the handicrafts as well.

The repeated attempts that have been made during the last 150 years, both in Europe and America, to found village settlements of this kind, whether communistic or co-operative in the narrower sense, have mostly met with failure.[1] I would apply the word "failure" not merely to those settlements, or attempts at settlements, which after a more or less short-lived existence either disintegrated completely or took on a Capitalist complexion, thus going over to the enemy camp; I would also apply it to those that maintained themselves in isolation. For the real, the truly structural task of the new Village Communes begins with their *federation*, that is, their union under the same principle that operates in their internal structure. Hardly anywhere has it come to this. Even where, as with the Dukhobors in Canada, a sort of federative union exists, the federation itself continues to be isolated and exerts no attractive and educative influence on society as a whole, with the result that the task never gets beyond its beginnings and, consequently, there can be no talk of success in the socialist sense. It is remarkable that Kropotkin saw in these two elements—isolation of the settlements from one another and isolation from the rest of society—the efficient causes of their failure even as ordinarily understood.

The socialistic task can only be accomplished to the degree that the new Village Commune, combining the various forms of production and uniting production and consumption, exerts a structural influence on the amorphous urban society. The influence will only make itself felt to the full if, and to the extent that, further technological developments facilitate and actually require the decentralization of industry; but even now a pervasive force is latent in the modern communal village, and it may spread to the towns. It must be emphasized again that the tendency we are dealing with is constructive and topical: it would be romantic and utopian to want to destroy the towns, as once it was romantic and utopian to want to destroy the machines, but it is constructive and topical to try to transform the town organically in the closest possible alliance with technological developments and to turn it into an aggregate composed of smaller units. Indeed, many countries to-day show significant beginnings in this respect.

As I see history and the present, there is only one all-out effort to create a Full Co-operative which justifies our speaking of success in the socialistic sense, and that is the Jewish Village Commune in its various forms, as found in Palestine. No doubt it, too, is up against grave problems in the sphere of internal relationships, federation, and influence on society at large, but it alone has proved its vitality in all three spheres. Nowhere else in the history of communal settlements is there this tireless groping for the form of community-life best suited to this particular human group, nowhere else this continual trying and trying again, this going to it and getting down to it, this critical awareness, this sprouting of new branches from the same stem and out of the same formative impulse. And nowhere else is there this alertness to one's own problems, this constant facing up to them, this tough will to come to terms with them, and this indefatigable struggle—albeit seldom expressed in words— to overcome them. Here, and here alone, do we find in the emergent community organs of self-knowledge whose very sensitiveness has constantly reduced its members to despair—but this is a despair that destroys wishful thinking only to raise up in its stead a greater hope which is no longer emotionalism but sheer work. Thus on the soberest survey and on the soberest reflection one can say that, in this one spot in a world of partial failures, we can recognize a non-failure—and, such as it is, a signal non-failure.

What are the reasons for this? We could not get to know the peculiar character of this co-operative colonization better than by following up these reasons.

One element in these reasons has been repeatedly pointed out: that the Jewish Village Commune in Palestine owes its existence not to a doctrine but to a situation, to the needs, the stress, the demands of the situation. In establishing the "Kvuza" or Village Commune the primary thing was not ideology but work. This is certainly correct, but with one limitation. True, the point was to solve certain problems of work and construction which the Palestinian reality forced on the settlers, by collaborating; what a loose conglomeration of individuals could not, in the nature of things, hope to overcome, or even try to overcome, things being what they were, the collective could try to do and actually succeeded in doing. But what is called the "ideology"—I personally prefer the old but untarnished word "Ideal"—was not just something to be added afterwards, that would justify the accomplished facts. In the spirit of the members of the first Palestinian Communes ideal motives joined hands with the dictates of the hour; and in the motives there was a curious mixture of memories of the Russian *Artel,* impressions left over from reading the so-called "utopian" Socialists, and the half-unconscious after-effects of the Bible's teachings about social justice. The important thing is that this ideal motive remained loose and pliable in almost every respect. There were various dreams about the future: people saw before them a new, more comprehensive form of the family, they saw themselves as the advance guard of the Workers' Movement, as the direct instrument for the realization of Socialism, as the prototype of the new society; they had as their goal the creation of a new man and a new world. But nothing of this ever hardened into a cut-and-dried programme. These men did not, as everywhere else in the history of co-operative settlements, bring a plan with them, a plan which the concrete situation could only fill out, not modify; the ideal gave an impetus but no dogma, it stimulated but did not dictate.

More important, however, is that, behind the Palestinian situation that set the tasks of work and reconstruction, there was the historical situation of a people visited by a great external crisis and responding to it with a great inner change. Further, this historical situation threw up an élite—the "Chaluzim" or pioneers—drawn from all classes of the people and thus beyond class. The form of life that befitted this élite was the Village Commune, by which I mean not a single note but the whole scale, ranging from the social structure of "mutual aid" to the Commune itself. This form was the best fitted to fulfil the tasks of the central Chaluzim, and at the same time the one in which the social ideal could materially influence the national idea. As the historical conditions have shown, it was impossible for this élite and the form of life it favoured to become static or isolated; all its tasks, everything it did, its whole pioneering spirit made it the centre of attraction and a central influence. The Pioneer spirit ("Chaluziuth") is, in every part of it, related to the growth of a new and transformed national community; the moment it grew self-sufficient it would have lost its soul. The Village Commune, as the nucleus of the evolving society, had to exert a powerful pull on the people dedicated to this evolution, and it had not merely to educate its friends and associates for genuine communal living, but also to exercise a formative structural effect on the social periphery. The dynamics of history determined the dynamic character of the relations between Village Commune and society.

This character suffered a considerable setback when the tempo of the crisis in the outer world became so rapid, and its symptoms so drastic, that the inner change could not keep pace with them. To the extent that Palestine had been turned from the one and only land of the "Aliyah"—ascent—into a country of immigrants, a quasi-Chaluziuth came into being alongside the genuine Chaluziuth. The pull exerted by the Commune did not abate, but its educative powers were not adapted to the influx of very different human material, and this material sometimes succeeded in influencing the tone of the community. At the same time the Commune's relations with society at large underwent a change. As the structure of the latter altered, it withdrew more and more from the transforming influence of the focal cells, indeed, it began in its turn to exert an influence on them—not always noticeable at first, but unmistakable to-day—by seizing on certain essential elements in them and assimilating them to itself.

In the life of peoples, and particularly peoples who find themselves in the midst of some historical crisis, it is of crucial importance whether genuine élites (which means élites that do not usurp but are called to their central function) arise, whether these élites remain loyal to their duty to society, establishing a relationship to it rather than to themselves, and finally, whether they have the power to replenish and renew themselves in a manner conformable with their task. The historical destiny of the Jewish settlements in Palestine brought the élite of the Chaluzim to birth, and it found its social nuclear form in the Village Commune. Another wave of this same destiny has washed up, together with the quasi-Chaluzim, a problem for the real Chaluzim élite. It has caused a problem that was always latent to come to the surface. They have not yet succeeded in mastering it and yet must master it before they can reach the next stage of their task. The inner tension between those who take the *whole* responsibility for the community on their shoulders and those who somehow evade it can be resolved only at a very deep level.

The point where the problem emerges is neither the individual's relationship to the idea nor his relationship to the community nor yet to work; on all these points even the quasi-Chaluzim gird up their loins and do by and large what is expected of them. The point where the problem emerges, where people are apt to slip, is in their relationship to their fellows. By this I do not mean the question, much discussed in its day, of the intimacy that exists in the small and the loss of this intimacy in the big Kvuza; I mean something that has nothing whatever to do with the size of the Commune. It is not a matter of intimacy at all; this appears when it must, and if it is lacking, that's all there is to it. The question is rather one of openness. A real community need not consist of people who are perpetually together; but it must consist of people who, precisely because they are comrades, have mutual access to one another and are ready for one another. A real community is one which in every point of its being possesses, potentially at least, the whole character of community. The internal questions of a community are thus in reality questions relating to its own genuineness, hence to its inner strength and stability. The men who created the Jewish Communes in Palestine instinctively knew this; but the instinct no longer seems to be as common and alert as it was. Yet it is in this most important field that we find that remorselessly clear-sighted collective self-observation and self-criticism to which I have already drawn attention. But to understand and value it aright we must see it together with the amazingly positive relationship —amounting to a regular faith—which these men have to the inmost being of their Commune. The two things are two sides of the same spiritual world and neither can be understood without the other.

In order to make the causes of the non-failure of these Jewish communal settlements sufficiently vivid, in Palestine, I began with the non-doctrinaire character of their origins. This character also determined their development in all essentials. New forms and new intermediate forms were constantly branching off—in complete freedom. Each one grew out of the particular social and spiritual needs as these came to light—in complete freedom, and each one acquired, even in the initial stages, its own ideology—in complete freedom, each struggling to propagate itself and spread and establish its proper sphere—all in complete freedom. The champions of the various forms each had his say, the pros and cons of each individual form were frankly and fiercely debated—always, however, on the plane which everybody accepted as obvious: the common cause and common task, where each form recognized the relative justice of all the other forms in their special functions. All this is unique in the history of co-operative settlements. What is more: nowhere, as far as I see, in the history of the Socialist movement were men so deeply involved in the process of differentiation and yet so intent on preserving the principle of integration.

The various forms and intermediate forms that arose in this way at different times and in different situations represented different kinds of social structure. The people who built them were generally aware of this as also of the particular social and spiritual needs that actuated them. They were not aware to the same extent that the different forms corresponded to different human types and that just as new forms branched off from the original Kvuza, so new types branched off from the original Chaluz type, each with its special mode of being and each demanding its particular sort of realization. More often than not it was economic and suchlike external factors that led certain people to break away from one form and attach themselves to another. But in the main it happened that each type looked for the social realization of its peculiarities in this particular form and, on the whole, found it there. And not only was each form based on a definite type, it moulded and keeps on moulding this type. It was and is intent on developing it; the constitution, organization and educational system of each form are—no matter how consciously or unconsciously—dedicated to this end. Thus something has been produced which is essentially different from all the social experiments that have ever been made: not a laboratory where everybody works for himself, alone with his problems and plans, but an experimental station where, on common soil, different colonies or "cultures" are tested out according to different methods for a common purpose.

Yet here, too, a problem emerged, no longer within the individual group but in the relation of the groups to one another; nor did it come from without, it came from within—in fact, from the very heart of the principle of freedom.

Even in its first undifferentiated form a tendency towards federation was innate in the Kvuza, to merge the Kvuzoth in some higher social unit; and a very important tendency it was, since it showed that the Kvuza implicitly understood that it was the cell of a newly structured society. With the splitting off and proliferation of the various forms, from the semi-individualistic form which jealously guarded personal independence in its domestic economy, way of life, children's education, etc., to the pure Communistic form, the single unit was supplanted by a series of units in each of which a definite form of colony and a more or less definite human type constituted itself on a federal basis. The fundamental assumption was that the local groups would combine on the same principle of solidarity and mutual help as reigned within the individual group. But the trend towards a larger unit is far from having atrophied in the process. On the contrary, at least in the Kibbuz or Collectivist Movement, it asserts itself with great force and clarity; it recognizes the federative Kibbuzim—units where the local groups have pooled their various aspirations—as a provisional structure; indeed, a thoughtful leader of their movement calls them a substitute for a Commune of Communes. Apart from the fact, however, that individual forms, especially, for instance, the "Moshavim" or semi-individualistic Labour Settlements—though these do not fall short of any of the other forms in the matter of communal economic control and mutual help—are already too far removed from the basic form to be included in a unitary plan, in the Kibbuz Movement itself subsidiary organizations stand in the way of the trend towards unification which wants to embrace and absorb them. Each has developed its own special character and consolidated it in the unit, and it is natural that each should incline to view unification as an extension of its own influence. But something else has been added that has led to an enormous intensification of this attitude on the part of the single units: political development. Twenty years ago a leader of one of the big units could say emphatically: "We are a community and not a Party." This has radically changed in the meantime, and the conditions for unification have been aggravated accordingly. The lamentable fact has emerged that the all-important attitude of neighbourly relationship has not been adequately developed, although not a few cases are on record of a flourishing and rich village giving generous help to a young and poor neighbour which belonged to another unit. In these circumstances the great struggle that has broken out on the question of unification, particularly in the last decade, is the more remarkable. Nobody who is a Socialist at heart can read the great document of this struggle, the Hebrew compilation entitled *The Kibbuz and the Kvuza*, edited by the late labour leader Berl Kaznelson, without being lost in admiration of the high-minded passion with which these two camps battled with one another for genuine unity. The union will probably not be attained save as the outcome of a situation that makes it absolutely necessary. But that the men of the Jewish Communes have laboured so strenuously with one another and against one another for the emergence of a *communitas communitatum*, that is to say, for a structurally new society—this will not be forgotten in the history of mankind's struggle for self-renewal.

I have said that I see in this bold Jewish undertaking a "signal non-failure." I cannot say: a signal success. To become that, much has still to be done. Yet it is in this way, in this kind of tempo, with such setbacks, disappointments, and new ventures, that the real changes are accomplished in this our mortal world.

But can one speak of this non-failure as "signal"? I have pointed out the peculiar nature of the premises and conditions that led to it. And what one of its own representatives has said of the Kvuza, that it is a typically Palestinian product, is true of all these forms.

Still, if an experiment conducted under certain conditions has proved successful up to a point, we can set about varying it under other, less favourable, conditions.

There can hardly be any doubt that we must regard the last war as the end of the prelude to a world crisis. This crisis will probably break out—after a sombre "interlude" that cannot last very long—first among some of the nations of the West, who will be able to restore their shattered economy in appearance only. They will see themselves faced with the immediate need for radical socialization, above all the expropriation of the land. It will then be of absolutely decisive importance *who* is the real subject of an economy so transformed, and who is the owner of the social means of production. Is it to be the central authority in a highly centralized State, or the social units of urban and rural workers, living and producing on a communal basis, and their representative bodies? In the latter case the remodelled organs of the State will discharge the functions of adjustment and administration only. On these issues will largely depend the growth of a new society and a new civilization. The essential point is to decide on the fundamentals: a re-structuring of society as a League of Leagues, and a reduction of the State to its proper function, which is to maintain unity; or a devouring of an amorphous society by the omnipotent State; Socialist Pluralism or so-called Socialist Unitarianism. The right proportion, tested anew every day according to changing conditions, between group-freedom and collective order; or absolute order imposed indefinitely for the sake of an era of freedom alleged to follow "of its own accord." So long as Russia has not undergone an essential inner change—and to-day we have no means of knowing when and how that will come to pass—we must designate one of the two poles of Socialism between which our choice lies by the formidable name of "Moscow." The other, I would make bold to call "Jerusalem."

Notes

Chapter Title

1. We have used the usual modern spelling rather than "Chaluziuth," which Buber uses—Ed.'s Note.

An Experiment That Did Not Fail

1. Of course, I am not dealing here with the otherwise successful "socio-economic or-ganizations, used by governmental or semi-governmental agencies to improve rural condi-tions" (Infield, *Co-operative Communities at Work*, p. 63).

IV

THE DYNAMICS OF
SOCIAL RETROGRESSION

In this last part, several excerpts continue some of Buber's analyses on utopia—especially in its relation to the political realm.

These excerpts point out quite clearly that, contrary to many of the pure utopians, who negated the political, Buber saw it as an essential, autonomous component of social life, which if kept within proper limits—limits that change according to circumstances—constitutes a positive force in the process of social creativity.

9

The Interrelations between the Social
and the Political Dimensions
of Human Experience

Society and the State*

In Bertrand Russell's book on *Power,* which appeared late in 1938—the author calls it a "new social analysis"—power is defined as "the fundamental concept in social science, in the same sense in which energy is the fundamental concept in physics." This bold concept on the part of a distinguished logician, which reminds us of Nietzsche's doctrine that he attacked so vigorously, is a typical example of the confusion between the social principle and the political principle even in our time, one hundred years after the rise of scientific sociology. It has long been recognized that all social structures have a certain measure of power, authority, and dominion, without which they could not exist; in none of the non-political structures, however, is this the essential element. But it is inherent in all social structures that men either find themselves already linked with one another in an association based on a common need or a common interest, or that they band themselves together for such a purpose, whether in an existing or a newly-formed society. The primary element must not be superseded by the secondary element—association by subordination, fellowship by domination or, schematically speaking, the horizontal structure by the vertical. The American political scientist, MacIver, has rightly said that "to identify the social with the political is to be guilty of the grossest of all confusions, which completely bars any understanding of either society or the state."

The defective differentiation between the social and the political principles, upon which the more or less problematical co-operation of all human group-existence rests, goes back to very ancient times. A classic example of mistaking the one principle for the other, though, to be sure,

---

*Reprinted from *Pointing the Way: Collected Essays,* trans. and ed. Maurice Friedman (New York: Harper and Bros., 1957), pp. 161–76.

of a very different kind, is the well-known chapter in the *Politeia*, where Plato begins by tracing the origin of the *polis* directly from the primeval social fact of division of labour, and then, almost imperceptibly, goes on to include among the essential occupations that of the rulers, so that we suddenly find the population split up into two pre-eminently political sections: those who give orders and those who obey them; rulers and ruled; those who possess the instruments of coercion and those who are subject to them—all this under the harmless guise of the mere division of labour. We should take careful note of what Plato does here. He has his Socrates set his interlocutors the task of "seeing with their mind's eye a *polis* in the making." The readers of this dialogue naturally thought in terms of the contemporary Athens as it had emerged from the reforms of Kleisthenes—in other words, in terms of a society of free citizens who were hardly aware of the difference between the rulers and the ruled because of the constant interchange between the former and the latter within the citizenry, whereby the constituents of today became the representatives of tomorrow; and because, furthermore, the fact that the officials could be elected and dismissed obviated any feeling that an irksome bureaucracy might arise. This community, in which a firm foundation of slavery made it theoretically possible for every citizen to participate in the business of the Council while engaged in his private concerns, could, indeed, be deduced from an evolution of the division of labour—an evolution in which the vocation of politics was not specialized. However, the class—or rather the caste of the guardians—which Plato introduces into this discussion comes not within the scope of the historical *polis* but of that of his Utopia, where this caste, which has been represented to us as one vocation among others, actually stands in a political relationship to the rest of the community: that of a ruling society over against a society of the ruled. The term "society" and not a mere "group" is used here advisedly inasmuch as, in liberating its members from private property and private marriage, Plato raises it above the general community and constitutes it as a separate society.

This confusion of the social principle with the political is typical of by far the greater part of the thinking of ancient times. There is no tendency whatever towards an ideological distinction between political and non-political social structures in most of the ancient empires, obviously because the latter were allowed no independent existence or development of any kind. The one exception in this respect is ancient China, where two civilizations existed side by side: the State-urban civilization, which was centred in the royal court and based on the army, the bureaucracy and the litterati; and the rural civilization, which was based solely on the village community. The former was a political-historical civilization in every respect, while the latter was absolutely unhistorical, being determined solely by the unchanging natural rhythm of the seasons and of the human generations, that is to say, a social civilization in the strictest sense of the term. It was the latter civilization, relatively self-sufficient and enclosed within itself, that served as the foundation for Lao-tse's doctrine. That doctrine interposed between the individual and the state (the single States which together constituted the empire) two purely social structures, namely the home and the community. In the Confucian system, which was rooted in the urban civilization, there remained, however, only one of these two social structures—the home, the family, which, contrary to its status in the village, was in its urban form completely integrated into the State.

A similar ideological development took place in classical antiquity, but from very different causes. There—at all events in the *polis* where, in the main, discursive thought was evolved, that is to say, in that of Athens—the well-developed social principle had penetrated so deeply into political life and merged with it so completely that while, on the one hand, the Demos was almost like a social gathering, on the other the family receded into the background of social life, and corporate existence, however firmly entrenched, nowhere attained genuine autonomy. In this connection, as we have already seen in Plato's thinking, no strictly ideological distinction was drawn between the State and the unions, which were not part of the State: The State, the *polis,* so completely coincided with society, or the community, the *koinonia,* that asocial persons, the *dyskoinoetoi,* were regarded as the antithesis of the friends of the State, the *philopolides,* as though it were not possible for a man to be social and yet not political in his thinking. It was only with the decline of the *polis,* when it was fast disintegrating from within and servitude loomed on the historical horizon without, that the thinking finally drew a distinction between the two principles. Two hundred years after Lao-tse, Aristotle interposed the family and the community—by which term he, too, meant primarily the rural community—between the State and the individual; and to the community were joined various kinds of associations. But of the social category, that of the *koinonia,* he had only the most general notion, so that he could describe the State as a certain kind of *koinonia* though, indeed, one transcending and comprehending all the others, while all the others are regarded as mere preliminary stages to this society on the one hand, and mere means towards the ends of the State on the other. Thus, even here, no genuine categorical distinction between the social and the political principle can be drawn; and even though Aristotle in one passage calls a man a *zoon koinonikon* and in another a *zoon politikon,* both terms mean the same thing. And though

Aristotle explicitly tells us that man was not created solely for the political community but also for the home, he sees in the *polis* the consummation of the *koinonia,* in which—and in which alone—men's coexistence in a community has any purpose and significance. In fact, the *polis* is called the *koinonia* of all the particular *koinonias* within which all families and communities and societies and associations of all kinds band themselves together. Aristotle's idea of the State is identical here with ours of society, that is to say, a unit comprehending all the different associations within a specific national entity. Such an idea of the State bars any approach to a strict and consistent differentiation and separation between the social and the political principles. Incidentally, it is noteworthy that of all the unions which Aristotle recognizes as special forms of the *koinonia,* he attaches significance to the family alone and, unlike Plato, recognizes it as the primeval cell in the process of the division of labour. In his view, the family alone is the foundation of the State, and he does not attach any permanent importance to the rural community, since it is destined to be absorbed in the *polis,* while he considers the associations important only because they have a place within the State. The restrictive process of thought, which was evolved from Lao-tse down to Confucius and from which all social structures that might successfully have resisted absorption by the centralizing State are excluded, here comes to full flower in the thinking of a single philosopher.

The post-Aristotelian thought of ancient times did not remedy this defect in the ideological approach to the principles in question. Even the apparently more precise Latin idea which, for the "collectivity" (*koinonia*) substituted "society" (*societas*), did not serve the purpose. True, in those days there was no such thing as a society of citizens in the modern sense of an all-inclusive society existing side by side with the State and *vis-à-vis* the State; but sociality did exist in all its forms, which manifested itself in all the large and small associations; and the same principle of co-operation predominated in all of them, a principle which enters into all kinds of alliances with the political principle, but nevertheless possesses a specific reality of its own which strives for recognition. Even the *stoa,* which went farthest in this direction, did not explicitly recognize the social principle. In the last days of the *stoa* Marcus Aurelius did, indeed, give the Aristotelian definition a social stamp by saying that "We are born to co-operate"; but what was not achieved was just that which must be required of any ideological specification if it is to achieve the character of genuine apperception, namely, the search for, description and interpretation of those elements of reality which correspond to the newly-acquired specific idea. The new concept of society loses concreteness because it is deprived of its limitations; this occurs in the most sublime manner in that the ideal of universal humanism is formulated without any indication being given as to how it is to be realized. Whether the Stoic speaks in the new terms of a society of the human race (*societas generis humani*) or in the old terms of a megalopolis, it amounts to the same thing: a high-souled idea emerges to confront reality but cannot find a womb from which to propagate a living creature because it has been stripped of corporeality. Plato's State which, though directed against the *polis,* was nevertheless derived from it, actually was a structure, though it existed only in thought. Zenon's slogan— "Only one way of life and only one political régime"—as proclaimed a century later, was only a fine sentiment; and finally so little remained of it that Cicero could envisage the Roman Empire as the fulfilment of cosmopolitanism. Incidentally, there is no practicable universalism— universalism that is realizable, though with the utmost effort—except that adumbrated by the prophets of Israel, who proposed not to abolish national societies together with their forms of organization, but rather to heal and perfect them, and thereby to pave the way for their amalgamation.

Medieval Christianity adopted the fundamental concept of the Stoic universalism in a Christianized form, in that at one time it designated the unified humanity to be striven for as a *res publica generis humani,* a world State, and at another as an *ecclesia universalis,* a universal church. Nevertheless, the social principle as such is expressed now and then in this connection in a purer form than was ever conceived by the Stoics. Thus, for example, William of Occam, the great fourteenth-century thinker whose theory of intuition gave the *quietus* to scholasticism, said: "The whole human race is one people; the collectivity of all mortal men is a single community of those who wish for communion with one another." Every particular association is recognized by him as a part of this community. In general, however, medieval thought did not go beyond Aristotle's amalgamation of the social with the political. The flourishing corporations of the period were, indeed, taken into account in the legal ideology; but no sociological recognition of the non-political associations as such was evolved. On the contrary: there was a growing tendency to include them, in theory, within the State and, in practice, to subject all of them to it; or, as the legal historian Gierke put it: "Exclusive representation of all community life by the State."

It was only in the late Renaissance that thinking reached the point of a vigorous stand in defence of the rights of the non-political unions in relation to the State. The most vigorous expression of this point of view is to be found in the book entitled *Politics* by the German jurist

Althusius (1603). Even there these bodies do not stand between the individual and the all-inclusive society—this special concept is still lacking—but between the individual and the State as in Aristotle's concept. Hence no difference in kind is recognized between the associations and the State, except that each and every one of the farmers enjoys relative autonomy, while the State possesses exclusive sovereignty. Nevertheless, the State is faced by an "insurmountable barrier" (as Gierke phrases it) in relation to the unions; in other words, the State may not infringe upon the special rights of these social unions. Society is not yet, indeed, conceived as such in this view, but it is constituted in its idea; it is not society, but the State under its name, which appears as the "immortal and eternal society," as Grotius formulated it, or under its own name as a "composite society," in the words of Althusius—the association of associations. But the very fact that all of them are viewed as being linked with one another was in itself something definitely new in sociological thought. This new idea was suppressed for two hundred years by the idea of the unlimited power of the State, which took on a more logically consistent form than ever before.[1]

In Hobbes' system of thought the intermediate formations are missing as a matter of principle, since he recognizes no stages precedent to the establishment of the State, in which the unorganized individuals unite for fear that otherwise they will destroy one another. Such a unification, which is achieved by means of the subjection of the wills of all the individuals to the will of a single person or a single assembly, is designated by Hobbes in his book *De Cive* as *civitas sive societas civilis*. Here, for the first time as far as I am aware, we have in the writings of a modern thinker the widely disseminated idea of the "civil society," which we find again late in the seventeenth century in Locke's essays, in the eighteenth century in Adam Smith's *Lectures on Justice* and in Ferguson's *Essay on the History of Civil Society,* and which recurs, in the nineteenth century, in the philosophy of Hegel and the sociology of Lorenz von Stein, as the antithesis to the State. In Hobbes' view, civil society is entirely identical with the State. Hobbes, too, is cognizant of the social principle—in the form of free contracts between individuals for the recognition and preservation of the rights of ownership; he is aware of its existence, and tolerates it in the above sense because he regards the political "Leviathan" as still incomplete. But the German sociologist Tönnies doubtless apprehends Hobbes' ultimate meaning when he interprets his views in the following terms: "The State would carry out its idea to perfection if it controlled all the activities of its citizens, if all wills were directed in harmony with a single supreme will. So long as this has not come to pass, society still exists within the State." In other words, when the State finally becomes complete, it will annihilate the last vestige of society. Such a complete State has been approximated in a considerable degree in our own time by that known as the totalitarian type.

The age of Hobbes saw the rise of the Third Estate, which attempted to supersede the double society of the Middle Ages by a unitary society which did not, however, extend beyond its own bounds and which evoked a liberal attitude on the part of the State towards the individual, but an increasingly illiberal attitude on its part towards associations. The State was prepared to tolerate only a pulverized, structureless society, just as modern industrial capitalism at first tolerated only individuals without the right of association. A little over a century after the appearance of the "Leviathan," the physiocrat Turgot declared in the *Encyclopaedia* (in an article entitled "Fondations"): "The citizens have rights, rights sacred for the actual body of society (by which he meant nothing else but the State); they have an existence independent of it; they are its essential elements . . . but the particular bodies do not exist in their own right and for their own sake. They have been constituted solely for the sake of society, and they must cease to exist as soon as their usefulness is at an end." Turgot does not, however, include among his "particular bodies" all the free associations, some of which he lauds in the course of that same article. Yet only five years later Rousseau wrote the contrary in his *Contrat Social* where, in his fundamental concept, the *volonté générale*, the social and political principles are again confused in the most dubious manner, though he was well able to distinguish between the social contract and the establishment of a State in a legal manner: "So that the common will may be manifested, there must be no partial associations within the State." In other words, there may not exist within the State any society which is constituted of various large and small associations; that is to say, a society with a truly social structure, in which the diversified spontaneous contacts of individuals for common purposes of co-operation and co-existence, i.e. the vital essence of society, are represented. But if "partial societies" already exist, Rousseau goes on to say, "their number should be increased and inequalities prevented." In other words, if it proves impossible to suppress the formation of free associations, their scope should be restricted by creating other associations determined entirely by the purposes and planning of the State; moreover, care must be taken that the free societies should never become stronger than the unfree ones.

In general, the French Revolution could content itself with carrying out the first of these two precepts, especially since it had abolished the right of association (an attempt in that direction had already been made under Louis XVI) because an "absolutely free State should not tolerate corporations in its midst" (resolution of the Constitutional Assembly, August 1791). On the other hand, both of Rousseau's methods were applied jointly in a large measure during the Russian Revolution.

Only after a fully-fledged bourgeoisie had sprung from the loins of the French Revolution did it become possible to attempt to set the State and Society, as such, over against one another. The first two attempts in this direction were far apart in every respect.

The first of the two attempts was suggested by Saint-Simon. The more or less chimerical plans for reforms of this highly ingenious dilettante were based, in essence, on an accurate and important distinction between two modes of leadership, namely, social leadership, or Administration, and political leadership, or Government. Saint-Simon did not adequately define these types of leadership, but we shall convey his meaning correctly if we say that administrative powers are limited by the technical requirements implicit in the specific conditions and functions of the leadership, while governmental powers are limited, at any given time, solely by the relation between the power of government and that of other factors. Society—by which Saint-Simon means the subject of economic and cultural production—administers, in so far as it is organized; but the State governs. Saint-Simon's proposal to divide the conduct of the State—that is to say, to entrust the conduct of the national affairs to a select group of men, capable and well versed in the sphere of social production, thereby giving it an administrative character, while leaving to the political authorities only the responsibility for the defence and security of the country—this proposal need not concern us here. But it is worth-while quoting what Saint-Simon said in this connection: "The nation went into the revolution to be governed less; but it achieved nothing except to be governed more than ever."

The other fundamental division between the social and the political principle, that of Hegel, is antithetical to Saint-Simon's in its evaluation of the two. But its very purpose is different. Unlike Saint-Simon, Hegel compares not two forms of leadership with one another, but civil society in general with the State in general. The two factors are not, however, placed in polar opposition: society stands between the family and the State, between a relative whole and unity and an absolute whole and unity, as an incomplete and disunited multiformity, between form and form as something formless, an offspring of the modern world, an aggregation of individuals in which each is an end in himself and concerned with nothing else whatsoever; and all of them work together only because each uses the others as a means towards his own ends; and the groups and classes composed of individuals obsessed with their own ends get into conflicts which society, by its very nature, is unable to resolve: such power inheres in the State alone, because it prevails over the "waves of passion" by means of the "Reason that illumines them." The State is the "moderator of social misery" because its substance is not a private matter like that of society, but generality and unity, while its foundation is "the force of Reason manifesting itself as will." Such is the result of the most unequivocal distinction ever made between the two principles—a glorification of the State that reminds us of Hobbes. Hegel's critical portrait of society lacks everything that is still to be found in our own age, such as social consciousness, solidarity, mutual aid, loyal comradeship, spirited enthusiasms for a common enterprise; there is no trace whatever of creative social spontaneity which, though it is not concentrated like the power of the State, nevertheless exists in numerous single collective phenomena and, within the social sphere, very quietly counterbalances the conflicting forces. On the other hand, a State is seen here which we know, not from world history, but only from Hegel's system. He tells us, indeed, that in pondering the idea of the State we must not have any particular State in mind, but that "the idea, this true God, must be considered for itself." A given historical State exists, so says Hegel, "in the world, hence in the sphere of arbitrariness, accident and error." And just as a cripple is a living man for all that, "the affirmative, life, exists" in spite of the defect; and it is this "affirmative" which is the essential thing here. But if we apply this to society as well, the whole picture will be completely changed.

With Saint-Simon and Hegel we find ourselves on the threshold of modern sociology. But the society known to this sociology has become something different, namely, the society of the modern class struggle. Two men at that time undertook, each after his own fashion, to create a synthesis between Hegel and Saint-Simon. One was Lorenz von Stein, the founder of scientific sociology, and the other Karl Marx, the father of scientific socialism. The thinking of both men was so deeply rooted in the new situation that, on the crucial issue of the relationship between the social and the political principle, they were unable to take over the heritage either of Saint-Simon or of Hegel. Stein, who was a disciple of Saint-Simon's, could not share his belief that control of the State should be taken over by the leaders of social production because he regarded society only as the main arena of human conflict. He tried to hold fast to Hegel's views concerning the overmastering and unifying function of the perfect State, but did not really succeed. Marx, who adopted Hegel's mode of thought, objected to such a function on the part of the State because, as a "superstructure," the latter was necessarily a tool in the hands of the ruling class of society, and he strove to set up in its stead a State that would pave the way for a classless society by means of a dictatorship of the lowest social order, which would then be absorbed into the classless society. Stein, who held that "the movement of opposition between the State and society was the content of the whole inner history of all the peoples," attributes supremacy to the State in terms of philosophical abstraction; but in dealing with the concrete reality he affirms society, which is shaken through and through by conflicts; his concern is with that society. Hence the science of social reality begins with Stein (and not with Comte, as some think, because the latter lags behind his master Saint-Simon in distinguishing between the social and the political principle). Marx, who evinced no particular interest in the State in his theoretical thinking, could suggest nothing but a highly centralized all-embracing and all-disposing revolutionary State which leaves no room for the social principle and so thoroughly absorbs the free society that only in a messianic vision can it be merged in it. That is why a socialist movement began with Marx in which the social principle is found only as an ultimate aim, but not in the practical scheme.

Even nowadays, in the midst of wide-ranging and extremely detailed social knowledge and planning, sociology is faced ever and again with the problem of the relationship between the social and the political principle. This relationship must not be confused with that between Society and the State because, as Tarde rightly says, there is no form of social activity which cannot, on some side or at some moment, become political; we must realize that social forms, on the one hand, and State institutions, on the other, are crystallizations of the two principles. But it is most essential that we recognize the structural difference between the two spheres in regard to the relationship between unity and multiformity.

The society of a nation is composed not of individuals but of societies, and not, as Comte thought, of families alone but of societies, groups, circles, unions, co-operative bodies, and communities varying very widely in type, form, scope, and dynamics. Society (with a capital S) is not only their collectivity and setting, but also their substance and essence; they are contained within it, but it is also within them all, and none of them, in their innermost being, can withdraw from it. In so far as the mere proximity of the societies tends to change into union, in so far as all kinds of leagues and alliances develop among them—in the social-federative sphere, that is to say—Society achieves its object. Just as Society keeps individuals together in their way of life by force of habit and custom and holds them close to one another and, by public opinion, in the sense of continuity, keeps them together in their way of thinking, so it influences the contacts and the mutual relations between the societies. Society cannot, however, quell the conflicts between the different groups; it is powerless to unite the divergent and clashing groups; it can develop what they have in common, but cannot force it upon them. The State alone can do that. The means which it employs for this purpose are not social but definitely political. But all the facilities at the disposal of the State, whether punitive or propagandistic, would not enable even a State not dominated by a single social group (that is to say, by one relatively independent of social divarications) to control the areas of conflict if it were not for the fundamental political fact of general instability. The fact that every people feels itself threatened by the others gives the State its definitive unifying power; it depends upon the instinct of self-preservation of society itself; the latent external crisis enables it when necessary to get the upper hand in internal crises. A permanent state of true, positive, and creative peace between the peoples would greatly diminish the supremacy of the political principle over the social. This does not, however, in the least signify that in that event the power to control the internal situation of conflict would necessarily be lessened thereby. Rather is it to be assumed that if, instead of the prevailing anarchical relationships among the nations, there were co-operation in the control of raw materials, agreement on methods of manufacture of such materials, and regulation of the world market, Society would be in a position, for the first time, to constitute itself as such.

Administration in the sphere of the social principle is equivalent to Government in that of the political principle. In the sphere of the former, as of the latter, it is essential that experts demonstrate how the wishes and decisions of the union or the association are to be carried into effect; and it is also essential that those appointed to carry out the experts' instructions should follow those instructions, with everyone doing his share. By Administration we mean a capacity for making dispositions which is limited by the available technical facilities and recognized in theory and practice within those limits; when it oversteps its limits, it seals its own doom. By Government we understand a non-technical, but "constitutionally" limited body; this signifies that, in the event of certain changes in the situation, the limits are extended and even, at times, wiped out altogether. All forms of government have this in common: each possesses more power than is required by the given conditions; in fact, this excess in the capacity for making dispositions is actually what we understand by political power. The measure of this excess, which cannot of course be computed precisely, represents the exact difference between Administration and Government. I call it the "political surplus." Its justification derives from the external and internal instability, from the latent state of crisis between the nations and within every nation, which may at any moment become an active crisis requiring more immediate and far-reaching measures and strict compliance with such measures. Special powers must be accorded to the government even in States under a parliamentary régime when a crisis arises; yet in such States also it is in the nature of the case that the "political surplus" should be indeterminate. The political principle is always stronger in relation to the social principle than the given conditions require. The result is a continuous diminution in social spontaneity.

Yet the social vitality of a nation, and its cultural unity and independence as well, depend very largely upon the degree of social spontaneity to be found there. The question has therefore been repeatedly raised as to how social spontaneity can be strengthened by freeing it as much as possible from the pressure of the political principle. It has been suggested that decentralization of political power, in particular, would be most desirable. As a matter of fact, the larger the measure of autonomy granted to the local and regional and also to the functional societies, the more room is left for the free unfolding of the social energies. Obviously, the question cannot be formulated as a choice between "Centralization" and "Decentralization." We must ask rather: "What are the spheres in which a larger measure of decentralization of the capacity to make dispositions would be admissible?" The demarcation would naturally have to be revised and improved continually to conform to the changing conditions.

Apart from this change in the *apportionment of power,* it is also in the interest of a self-constituting society to strive towards a continuous change in the *nature* of power, to the end that Government should, as much as possible, turn into Administration. Let us put it in this way: Efforts must be renewed again and again to determine in what spheres it is possible to alter the ratio between governmental and administrative control in favour of the latter. Saint-Simon's requirement, that a society productive in the economic and cultural spheres should have a larger share in shaping public life, cannot be fulfilled, as has been suggested in our own days, by having the administrators seize the government (which would certainly not lead to any improvement), but by transforming Government into Administration as far as the general and particular conditions permit.

Will Society ever revolt against the "political surplus" and the accumulation of power? If such a thing were ever possible, only a society which had itself overcome its own internal conflicts would ever venture to embark upon such a revolution; and that is hardly to be expected so long as Society is what it is. But there is a way for Society—meaning at the moment the men who appreciate the incomparable value of the social principle—to prepare the ground for improving the relations between itself and the political principle. That way is Education, the education of a generation with a truly social outlook and a truly social will. Education is the great implement which is more or less under the control of Society; Society does not, however, know how to utilize it. Social education is the exact reverse of political propaganda. Such propaganda, whether spread by a government or by a party, seeks to "suggest" a ready-made will to the members of the society, i.e., to implant in their minds the notion that such a will derives from their own, their innermost being. Social education, on the other hand, seeks to arouse and to develop in the minds of its pupils the spontaneity of fellowship which is innate in all unravaged human souls and which harmonizes very well with the development of personal existence and personal thought. This can be accomplished only by the complete overthrow of the political trend which nowadays dominates education throughout the world. True education for citizenship in a State is education for the effectuation of Society.

The Demand of the Spirit and Historical Reality*

Modern sociology as an independent science was originally critical and demanding. The man to whose influence its founding can be traced is Henri de Saint-Simon. Although no sociologist and in general no scientist, he may, none the less, be described as the father of modern sociology. Saint-Simon was a social critic and demander who perceived the inner contradiction of the age and designated scientific knowledge of social conditions as the decisive step towards its overcoming. Not incorrectly did one of his contemporaries call his fundamental concept an ideocracy—he discerned in the knowing and planning spirit the dictator of things to come.

Both Auguste Comte and Lorenz von Stein—the men who under his influence undertook in very different ways to found the new science—held fast to the intention of overcoming the crisis of the human race. When Comte turned against his teacher he characterized his programme, nevertheless, as *une régénération sociale fondée sur une rénovation mentale;* his own programme was just this. Already in his youth he saw the "profound moral and political anarchy" that threatened society with dissolution, and demanded a spiritual establishment of a new so-

---

*Inaugural lecture, The Hebrew University, Jerusalem, 1938, reprinted from *Pointing the Way: Collected Essays,* trans. and ed. Maurice Friedman (New York: Harper and Bros., 1957), pp. 177–91.

cial structure. New institutions could not bring salvation if a new spiritual attitude were not prepared beforehand to prevent the degeneration and perversion of the institutions. "I consider all discussions about institutions pure farce," wrote Comte in a letter in 1824, "so long as the spiritual reorganization of society is not realized or at least strongly furthered."

Comte, to be sure, did not compose a sociology in the scientific sense; what he calls such in his work is only general reflections about the historical workings of different spiritual principles on the social situation and the political condition. Stein was the first to attempt a genuine philosophical comprehension and clarification of basic social concepts. But he, too, wanted to know in order to change. The scientific conception of society as a reality to be distinguished from the state—indeed in many ways to be opposed to it, "The existence of an independent society"— was evident to him from the serious *disturbances* that carry the social life of our age towards a state of things "that we could describe as the dissolution of the community and its organism." This "the powerful deed of science" shall prevent. The present situation and its origin must be known for the sake of the new order: "we think of the future when we talk of this present, and it is useless to hide it—*when* it is talked about, it is just for the sake of that future that it is talked about." Stein sees the necessary knowledge as having already arisen. "At all points," he wrote in the book *The Socialism and Communism of Present-Day France* (that appeared in 1842, at the same time therefore as the concluding volume of Comte's major work), "human knowing begins to receive a new, powerful shape."

Modern sociology originates, therefore, in the meeting of the spirit with the crisis of human society, which the spirit accepts as its own crisis and which it undertakes to overcome through a spiritual turning and transformation. Sociology is just this insight into the nature of the crisis, its causes, and the problems set by it, the beginning of this turning and transformation.

An American sociologist of our time, Edward Ross, holds that a sociologist is "a man who wishes to change something." That says too little and it says too much. One may better describe the sociologist as one who wishes to know what is to be changed. But this is a question of knowing a world *in crisis,* and the knowing spirit knows that it stands with the world in the crisis. Not as if this spirit were merely a piece of social reality. Rather it is its partner, destined to learn from it what is and to show it in return what should be—the crisis embraces them both together. In the new sociological vision the scientist must acquire to know what is to be known, he obtains at the same time a new life relationship in which he is bound with reality without being submerged in it. He obtains a new dialogical relation that purifies him.

In his book *Critique of Sociology* a younger sociologist, Siegfried Landshut, has grasped the character of modern sociology much more profoundly than Ross. "It only understands itself rightly today," he says, "when it comprehends itself as the contradiction of historical-social reality that has come to word." In it is expressed "that 'Copernican revolution' of public consciousness through which the decisive expectations and claims of the life of personal individuals prepare a way to the *organizations and institutions* of life with one another." Here an error is joined with an important insight: from being the partner of reality who must, of course, remain wholly turned to it in order to perceive its question aright, the spirit is made into its spokesman in whom it "comes to word." But where the spirit becomes the mere voice of reality, it forgets that that altered direction of its expectations, the direction towards organizations and institutions, becomes false in becoming exclusive. Only when it remains the partner of reality does it remain aware of its office of working for the transformation of the spirit, for its own transformation without which the altered institutions must decline to emptiness, to unfruitfulness, to ruin. *Une rénovation mentale,* such as Saint-Simon had in mind, is certainly not sufficient; the spirit of which I speak is not one of the potentialities or functions of man but his concentrated *totality.* Man must change himself in the same measure as the institutions are changed in order that these changes may have their expected effect. If the new house that man hopes to erect is not to become his burial chamber, the essence of living together must undergo a change at the same time as the organization of living. If the representative of the spirit of the new sociological view has merely succeeded in politicizing sociologically, then that is lost which he and he alone can give to reality—he is lost himself. He must also *educate* sociologically, he must educate men in living together; he must educate man so he can live with man.

One will perhaps object that both, the political and the educational influence, overstep the proper limits of sociology. This protest has an historical foundation. From the philosophizing about social subjects that Comte and Stein pursued, as Hobbes and Condorcet pursued it before them, an independent science detached itself in the second half of the nineteenth century and the beginning of the twentieth that retained the name of sociology and set as its goal the description and analysis of social phenomena. From its character as an "objective" science it frequently deduced the duty to be "value-free," as Max Weber and other German sociologists called it; that is, to present and to explain facts and connections without expressing any value-judgment in so doing. But when one of these sociologists, Ferdinand Tönnies, opened the first German congress of sociology in 1910, he began his address with the statement, "Sociology is first of all a philosophical discipline," and remarked further that one could call theoretical sociology social philosophy also. He asserted thereby that the observation of the social sphere as a whole, the determination of the categories ruling within it, the knowledge of its relations to the other spheres of life, and the understanding of the *meaning* of social existence and happenings are and remain a philosophical task. But there is no philosophy unless the philosophizing man is ready, whenever the urgent question approaches, not to hold back the decision whether a thought is right or wrong, whether an action is good or bad and so on. The philosopher must be ready on the basis of known truth, to the extent of his knowledge, to make these decisions and implement them without reserve and to release them thereby as a working force in the world. Philosophical treatment of social conditions, events, and structures, accordingly, includes valuation; it includes criticism and demand—not as something customary, but as something difficult and responsible that one does not shrink from doing if it comes to that.

But can there be an independent valuation of the subjects that concern the relations of classes to one another, the relations of peoples and states? Can the social philosopher keep his knowledge *pure,* and the decisions that he makes on the basis of it? Yet true social thinking comes to a person only when he really lives with men, when he remains no stranger to its structures and does not know even its mass movements from the outside alone. Without genuine social binding there is no genuine social experience, and without genuine social experience there is no genuine sociological thinking.

None the less, all knowledge is an *ascetic* act. At the moment of knowledge the knower must bring something paradoxical to pass; certainly he must enter into the knowledge with his whole being, he must also bring unabridged into his knowing the experiences his social ties have presented him with. But he must free himself from the influence of these ties through the concentration of spiritual power. No one becomes a sociological thinker if his dream and his passion have never mingled with the dream and passion of a human community; but in the moment of thinking itself, as far as it stands in his power, he must exist only as person, the person open to the subject of thought. If this relation is maintained, he need not unduly trouble himself with the question of how far his knowledge was determined against his will by his membership in a group. In the relationship of a man to the truth that he has discovered, freedom and obligation, vision and blindness, are always merged. Our concern is only this—to will with all the power of our spirit to achieve the free vision. On the basis of the knowledge thus won, the sociological thinker may value and decide, censure and demand, when the urgent question approaches, without violating the law of his science. Only so can the spirit preserve itself in the crisis that embraces it and historical reality together. The spirit asserts the demand that reality, the heart of sick reality, demands of it—of it as of its partner, not as its spokesman. The representative of the spirit speaks his word to a generation of the spirit that must be educated, and he speaks it to a world that must be changed.

But what weight has his word, what effectiveness is allotted to him?

The ideocratic certainty of Saint-Simon did not hold its own for long. Since then with ever greater proximity we have become acquainted with that which massively opposes and resists the spirit; this is usually but misleadingly called "history." What is meant is that world which in the last hundred years liberated itself anew and ever more completely from all spiritual control, resolved on actual conquest and exercise of power. The demand for the "value-freedom" of sociology has resulted in a resignation that may be formulated in these words: The spirit is still effective indeed, but only in so far as it places itself under the sway of powerful groups, under the dictates of what rules in history, that is, of power—we wish, therefore, to define its limits as a sphere where spirit is not to act but *only* to know, and within this sphere to guarantee still its independence.

Since then the resignation of Europe to "history" has progressed much farther. The tempo of its advance in America is a slower one, due probably to the fact that America has not become so intimately acquainted with "history." The great historian Jacob Burckhardt, as is well known, once said that power is in itself evil. Power in this sense means power for itself; that is, when it wills itself, when it resists the spirit, when power takes possession of those who use it, penetrates them, permeates them with the drive for power for itself. Since Hegel, power has learned to offer a grandiose justification of its resistance to the spirit: true spirit, so we are told, manifests itself in history, in its struggles for power and its power-decisions. He who serves power, therefore, is proclaimed as the true representative of the spirit, and he who opposes it with criticism and demand has obviously fallen into the impudent madness of believing there is something that is superior to history. Power employs this justification even when the criticism and demand of the spirit have stood at its origin; then that spirit is said to be the right one, whereby the spirit that steps athwart it with criticism and demand is unmasked as a false and unauthorized intruder.

Faced with this situation and its problematic, the social thinker who

understands his office must ever again pose the question: How can the
spirit influence the transformation of social reality?

Plato was about seventy-five years old when the assassination of the
prince Dion, master of Syracuse, his friend and disciple, put an end to
the enterprise of founding a republic in accordance with the concepts of
the philosopher. At this time Plato wrote his famous letter to his friends
in Sicily, in which he rendered an account of his lifelong ambition to
change the structure of the state (which for him included the structure of
society), of his attempts to translate this purpose into reality, and of his
failure in these attempts. He wrote that, having observed that all states
were poorly governed, he had adopted the opinion that man would not
be free from this evil until one of two things happened: either philosophers be charged with the function of government, or the potentates
who ruled states lived and acted in harmony with the precepts of philosophy. Plato had formulated this thesis, though somewhat differently,
about twenty years earlier in a central passage of his *Republic*. The
central position given the passage indicates that in the final analysis he
believed that individuals, above all, leaders, were of more importance
than particular institutions—such institutions as the book deals with.
According to Plato, there are two ways of obtaining the right persons to
be leaders: either the philosopher himself must come to power, or those
who rule must be educated to conduct their lives as philosophers.

In his memorable tractate *Towards Perpetual Peace,* Kant opposed
Plato's thesis without mentioning him by name. The rebuttal is part of a
section which appeared only in the second edition, and which Kant designated as a "secret article" of his outline of international law. He wrote:
"Because the wielding of power inevitably corrupts the free judgment of
reason, it is not to be expected that kings should philosophize or philosophers be kings, nor even to be desired. But one thing is indispensable
to both in order to illuminate their affairs, and that is that kings or
kingly nations, i.e., nations which govern themselves on the basis of laws
of equality, should not dispense with or silence the class of philosophers,
but let them express themselves in public." Previously Kant emphasized
that this was not meant to suggest that the state should prefer its power
to be represented by the principles of the philosopher rather than the
dicta of the jurist, but merely that the philosopher should be heard. This
line of thought clearly indicates not only a resignation of but also a disappointment in the spirit itself, for Kant had been forced to relinquish
faith in the spirit's ability to achieve power and, at the same time, to remain pure. We may safely assume that Kant's disillusionment is moti-
vated by his knowledge of the course of Church history, which in the two

thousand years and more between Plato and Kant came actually to be the history of spirit's power.

Plato believed both in the spirit and in power, and he also believed in the spirit's call to the assumption of power. What power he saw was decadent, but he thought it could be regenerated and purified by the spirit. The young Plato's own epochal and grave encounter with "history" took place when the city-state of Athens condemned and executed his teacher Socrates for disobeying authority and obeying the Voice. Yet, among all those who concerned themselves with the state, Socrates alone knew how to educate the young for a true life dedicated to the community; like the seer Tiresias in Hades, he was the only spiritually alive man amid a swarm of hovering shades. Plato regarded himself as Socrates' heir and deputy. He knew himself called to renew the sacred law and to found the just state. And he knew that for this reason he had a right to power. But while the spirit is ready to accept power from the hands of God or man, it is not willing to seize it. In the *Republic,* Socrates is asked whether the philosophic man, as Socrates describes him, would be apt to concern himself with affairs of state. To this question Socrates replies that the philosophic man in his own state would certainly concern himself with such matters, but this state which he conceives and which is suitable to him would have to be a state other than his native one, "unless there is some divine intervention." Even prior to this passage, he speaks of the man who is blessed with spirit confronting a furious mob, confronting it without confederates who could help maintain justice, feeling as if he were surrounded by wild beasts. Such a man, he goes on to say, will henceforth keep silence, attend to his own business, become a spectator, and live out his life without doing any wrong to the end of his days. But when Socrates' listeners interpose that such a man will thus have accomplished a great work by the time he dies, he contradicts them, "But not the greatest, since he has not found the state which befits him."

That is the gist of Plato's resignation. He was called to Syracuse and went there repeatedly, even though he suffered one disappointment after another. He went because he was called and because the divine voice might possibly be speaking in the voice of man. According to Dion there was a possibility that then, if ever, the hope to link philosophers and rulers to each other might there be fulfilled. Plato decided to "try." He reports he was ashamed not to go to Syracuse, lest he should seem to be nothing but "words." "Manifest," is the word he once used to Dion; we must manifest ourselves by truly being what we profess in words. He had used the word "must," not "want to." He went and failed, returned home, went once more and still another time, and failed again. At the third failure, he was almost seventy. Not until then did the man Plato had educated come into power. But before he was able to master the chaos, he was murdered by one who had been his fellow-student at Plato's academy.

Plato held that mankind could recover from its ills only if either the philosophers, "who now are termed useless," became kings or the kings became philosophers. He himself hoped first for the one and then for the other of these alternatives to occur as the result of "divine intervention." But he himself was not elevated to a *basileus* in Greece, and the prince whom he had educated to be a philosopher did not master the chaos in Sicily. It might possibly be said that the peace which Timoleon of Corinth established in Sicily after the death of this prince was achieved under the touch of Plato's spirit, and that Alexander, who later united all of Greece under his rule, certainly had not in vain studied philosophy with Plato's most renowned disciple. But neither in the one case nor in the other was Plato's ideal of the state actually realized. Plato did not re-generate the decadent Athenian democracy, and he did not found the republic he had projected.

But does this glorious failure prove that the spirit is always helpless in the face of history?

Plato is the most sublime instance of that spirit whose intercourse with reality proceeds from its own possession of truth. According to Plato, that soul is perfect which remembers its vision of perfection. Before its life on earth, the soul had beheld the idea of the good. In the world of ideas, it had beheld the shape of pure justice, and now, with the spirit's growth, the soul recollects what it had formerly beheld. The soul is not content to know this idea and to teach it to others. The soul yearns to infuse the idea of justice with the breath of life and establish it in the human world in the living form of a just state. The spirit is in possession of truth; it offers truth to reality; truth becomes reality through the spirit. That is the fundamental basis of Plato's doctrine. But this doctrine was not carried out. The spirit did not succeed in giving reality the truth it strove to impress it with. Was reality alone responsible? Was not the spirit itself responsible as well? Was not its very relationship to the truth responsible? These are questions which necessarily occur in connection with Plato's failure.

But the spirit can fail in another and very different way.

"In the year that King Uzziah died" (Isa. 6.1) Isaiah had a vision of the heavenly sanctuary in which the Lord chose him as his prophet. The entire incident points to the fact that King Uzziah was still alive. The king had long been suffering from leprosy. It is well known that in Biblical times leprosy was regarded not as a mere physical ailment but as the physical symptom of a disturbance in man's relationship to God. Rumour had it that the king had been afflicted because he had presumed to perform in the sanctuary of Jerusalem sacral functions which exceeded his rights as a political lieutenant of God (2 Chr. 26.16–21). Moreover, Isaiah felt in Uzziah's leprosy more than a personal affliction; it symbolized the uncleanliness of the entire people, and Isaiah's own uncleanliness as well. They all had "unclean lips" (Isa. 6.5). Like lepers, they must all cover "their upper lip" (Lev. 13.45) lest by breath or word their uncleanliness go forth and pollute the world. All of them have been disobedient and faithless to the true King, the King whose glory Isaiah's eyes now behold in his heavenly sanctuary. Here God is called *ha-Melekh;* this is the first time in the Scriptures that he is designated so plainly as the King of Israel. *He* is the King. The leper the people call "king" is only a faithless lieutenant. Now the true King sends Isaiah with a message to the entire people, at the same time telling him that his message will fail; he will fail, for the message will be misunderstood, misinterpreted and misused, and thus confirm the people—save for a small "remnant"—in their faithlessness, and harden their hearts. At the very outset of his mission, Isaiah, the carrier of the spirit, is told that he must fail. He will not suffer disappointment like Plato, for in his case failure is an integral part of the way he must take.

Isaiah does not share Plato's belief that the spirit is a possession of man. The man of spirit—such is the tradition from time immemorial—is one whom the spirit invades and seizes, whom the spirit uses as its garment, not one who contains the spirit. Spirit is an event, something which happens to man. The storm of the spirit sweeps man where it will, then storms on into the world.

Neither does Isaiah share Plato's notion that power is man's possession. Power is vouchsafed man to enable him to discharge his duties as God's lieutenant. If he abuses this power, the power destroys him, and in place of the spirit which came to prepare him for the use of power (I Sam. 16.14), an "evil spirit" comes upon him. The man in power is responsible to one who interrogates him in silence, and to whom he is answerable, or all is over with him.

Isaiah does not hold that spiritual man has the prerogative of power. He knows himself to be a man of spirit and to be without power. Being a prophet means being powerless, powerlessly confronting the powerful and reminding them of their responsibility, as Isaiah reminded Ahaz "in the highway of the fuller's field" (Isa. 7.3). To stand powerless before the power he calls to account is part of the prophet's destiny. He does not himself seek for power; the special sociological significance of his office is based on that very fact.

Plato believed that his soul was perfect. Isaiah did not, regarding and acknowledging himself unclean. He felt the uncleanliness which tainted his breath and his words being burned from his lips so that those lips might speak the message of God.

Isaiah beheld the throne and the majesty of Him who entrusted him with the message. He did not see the just state which Plato beheld in his mind's eye as something recollected. Isaiah knew and said that men are commanded to be just to one another. He knew and said that the unjust are destroyed by their own injustice. And he knew and said that there would come a dominion of justice and that a just man would rule as the faithful lieutenant of God. But he knew nothing and said nothing of the inner structure of that dominion. He had no idea; he had only a message. He had no institution to establish; he had only a proclamation, a proclamation in the nature of criticism and demand.

His criticism and demand are directed towards making the people and their prince recognize the reality of an invisible sovereignty. When Isaiah uses the word *ha-Melekh* it is not in the sense of a theological metaphor but in that of a political constitutional concept. But this sovereignty of God which he propounded is the opposite of the sovereignty of priests, which is commonly termed theocracy and which has very properly been described as "the most unfree form of society," for it is "unfree through the abuse of the Highest knowable to man."[1] None but the powerless can speak the true King's will with regard to the state, and remind both the people and the government of their *common* responsibility towards this will. The powerless man can do so because he breaks through the illusions of current history and recognizes potential crises.

That is why his criticism and demand are directed towards society, towards the life men live together. A people which seriously calls God Himself its King must become a true people, a community where all members are ruled by honesty without compulsion, kindness without hypocrisy, and the brotherliness of those who are passionately devoted to their divine leader. When social inequality, distinction between the free and the unfree, splits the community and creates chasms between its members, there can be no true people, there can be no "God's people." So criticism and demand are directed towards every individual whom other individuals depend upon, towards everyone who has a hand in shaping the destinies of others; that means directed towards every one of us. When Isaiah speaks of justice, he is not thinking of institutions but of you and me, because without you and me the most glorious institution becomes a lie.

Finally, the criticism and demand apply to Israel's relationship to other nations. Israel is warned not to engage in the making of treaties, not to rely on this or that so-called world power, but to "keep calm" (Isa. 7.4; 30.15), to make itself a true people, faithful to its divine King. Then they will have nothing to be afraid of. "The head of Damascus," Isaiah told Ahaz in the highway of the fuller's field, "is Rezin, and the head of Samaria, Pekah," meaning "but you know who is the Head of Jerusalem—if you want to know." But "If you will not trust, you will not be confirmed" (Isa. 7.9).

There has been much talk in this connection of "utopian" politics which would relate Isaiah's failure to that of Plato, who wrote the utopian *Republic*. What Isaiah said to Ahaz is accepted as a sublimely "religious" but a politically valueless utterance, implying one which lends itself to solemn quotation but one inapplicable to reality. Yet the only political chance for a small people hemmed in between world powers is the metapolitical chance Isaiah pointed to. He proclaimed a truth which could not, indeed, be tested by history up to that time, but only because no one ever thought of testing it. Nations can be led to peace only by a people which has made peace a reality within itself. The realization of the spirit has a magnetic effect on mankind which despairs of the spirit. That is the meaning Isaiah's teachings have for us. When the mountain of the Lord's house is "established" on the reality of true community life, then, and only then, the nations will "flow" towards it (Isa. 2.2), there to learn peace in place of war.

Isaiah too failed, as was predicted when he was called to give God's message. People and king opposed him, and even the king's successor, who attached himself to Isaiah, was found wanting in the decisive hour, when he flirted with the idea of allying with the Babylonian rebel against Assyria. But this failure is quite different from Plato's. Our very existence testifies to this difference. We live by that encounter in the highway of the fuller's field, we live by virtue of the fact that there were people who were deadly serious about this *ha-Melekh* in relation to all their social and political reality. They are the cause of our survival until this new chance to translate the spirit into the reality we have a presentiment of. We may yet experience an era of history which refutes "history." The prophet fails in the hour of history, but not in so far as the future of his people is concerned. The prophetic spirit does not succeed in giving the reality of its hour what it wills to give it. But it instils the vision in the people for all time to come. It lives within the people from then on as a longing to realize the truth.

The prophetic spirit does not believe, like the Platonic, that it possesses a universal and timeless ideal truth. The Hebrew prophet invariably receives only a message for a particular situation. But for this very reason his word still speaks after thousands of years to manifold situations in the history of peoples. He sets no universally valid image of perfection, no pantopia or utopia, before men; he has no choice, therefore, between his fatherland and another land that "suits him" better; for realization he is directed to the *topos*, to this place, to this people, it being the people that must *begin*. But he lacks, too, unlike the Platonic spirit, the possibility of withdrawing into the attitude of a calm spectator when he feels himself surrounded by wild beasts. He must speak his message. That message will be misunderstood, misjudged, misused; it will strengthen and "harden" the people still further in their untruth. But its sting will rankle within them for all time.

The social thinker is not a prophet but a philosopher. He does not have a message, he has a teaching. But for the transformation of the social reality he intends what is decisive. This is no Platonic task, no erection of a universally valid image of perfection; it is the prophetic task of criticism and demand within the present situation. Where an urgent question impinges, he cannot, of course, express criticism and demand as a message, but he can certainly express them on the basis of his knowledge.

Must not this social thinker fail, none the less, like his greater predecessors? Even Kant's "secret article" has not yet come into force: that the kings and the peoples should *listen to* the philosophers.

Up to now the crisis of the human race has made men only still deafer to the spirit. But that condition will surely change in the course of the crisis, only in a late phase, to be sure, when men despair of power and its autonomous decisions, when power for power's sake grows bewildered and longs for direction.

The spirit is hardly called, as Saint-Simon thought, to be the dictator of things to come. But it can be the preparer and counsellor. It can educate men for what is to come. And when a change is accomplished, the spirit must keep watch so that the altered institutions may not fall into corruption and do violence to the life struggling upward.

Amid the confusion and obliteration of basic social concepts, human knowledge of society must today, in many respects, begin anew with a new conceptual clarification, with a cleansing of the type. Perhaps just this silent, difficult work will help society to a new shape, as Lorenz von Stein proclaimed a century ago. Knowledge, he said, will become "powerful"; we would say rather: knowledge will become effective.

For Jerusalem, however, still more than this is to be said. There are situations in the lives of peoples in which the people becomes, as it were, plastic, and the impossible becomes possible. Perhaps such an hour is near. We think of this "perhaps" when we perform our service. We would also perform it, of course, if this possibility did not exist. For, resigned or unresigned, the spirit works.

The Validity and Limitation of the Political Principle*

It is characteristic of the great imperishable sayings of religious teaching that they are bound to situations. Their place is never beyond human intercourse. They arise as spoken response to some occasions. A group is assembled, whether one that had previously joined the speaker or one that has gathered around him at the moment. To the members of that group the word is directed, perhaps to summon them in a given situation or to answer a question raised just then in connection with a situation. Demanding or demanded, the message of the particular man is addressed to their special circumstances; it concerns itself with the present moment and aims to affect it.

But once this word has spread abroad and has entered thereby into the memory and tradition of other generations, each generation fashions out of that word the counsel and encouragement, the exhortation and comfort, it has need of in the new conditions of its existence. The original saying proves to be able to bestow manifold gifts far beyond its initial intention, gifts for manifold situations in historical and personal life; indeed, we may even say it contains these gifts. Such a message is directed to a particular group, but it is also directed to the human world—not to a vague and universal world, but to the concrete, the actual, historically-burdened and historically-inflamed world. The interpretation will be true to the saying only when it unites to its intention at the hour in which it was spoken the intention unfolded throughout all the hours of its working and, in a special way, the intention of this hour when the interpretation is made. History not only expands, it also deepens the significance of the saying, for what is successively derived from it penetrates farther into its ground.

Jesus' saying concerning the tribute money, on the basis of which I shall proceed in order to discuss the value and limitation of the political principle as it concerns our historical hour, is a message of this kind. Interpreters of this saying have repeatedly and rightly pointed out that Jesus deduced from the image of Caesar on the coin the duty not to re-

---

*Reprinted from *Pointing the Way: Collected Essays*, trans. and ed. Maurice Friedman (New York: Harper and Bros., 1957), pp. 208–19.

fuse tax to the earthly ruler. On the other hand, it seems to me an error to understand the duty, as has been done, as lying in the fact that the payment has been described as a restitution. Neither a financial expert nor a normal human being conceives the money that he inherits or earns to be a gift of the state out of its treasury. The relation of the state that coins money to the economic society that employs money, at whose disposal the state places the medium of exchange, is, in fact, a wholly different one. And what is far more important: the giving to God that is enjoined in the latter part of the saying can only by a strained interpretation be explained as a giving back; indeed, this construction would warp the meaning of the saying. The only legitimate interpretation, as has been maintained in this connection,[1] is one that follows the clue of the sense of the Greek word: "to render what one has to give in the fulfilment of a duty or expectation."

But there already begins that necessary striving I have spoken of: to draw close to the original ground of the message that no longer pertains to one time but to all times. What, we ask, does it mean that time after time man can and should give something to God, as time after time he can and should give something to the earthly power ruling over him; and further what does it mean that the subject of that gift is designated as "what is God's"—or in the translation closer to the original (which is to be assumed when translating the Greek text into Aramaic), "that which belongs to God" or "is due" Him, on the same plane with that which belongs to or is due Caesar. That one should "give," that one is obliged to render to Caesar, the superior power, the state, what the state legitimately demands of its citizens—namely, what is due to the state on the ground of the reciprocal relationship, a relationship of reciprocal, limited claim—is clear enough. But how can that which he is obliged to give to God be placed on the same level? Is the reciprocal relationship between God and man which each human creature enters into by his existence also one of a reciprocal, limited claim? Does man, then, have any claim at all on God? When he actually turns to God—that is, when he prays in truth and reality—he can hardly persist in a claim for a moment. But if God has a claim on man, how can it be limited? If one begins to measure from the side of Caesar what a man has to "give," shall the remainder, or the actual part of the remainder, fall to the share of God? In this wise it has clearly been understood by those who have explained the saying as meaning that one ought to comply with the worldly power so long as it demands nothing that stands in contradiction to the reverence due God in the form of creed and service, hence nothing such as sacrificing to the Roman emperor as a godlike being. But thereby the sphere of the divine, the sphere in the life of man pledged to God, is inevitably reduced to cult and confession. In other words, instead of being the Lord of existence, God is made into the God of religion.

If, on the other hand, we begin measuring from the side of God and try first, without regard for other claims, to ascertain what is due God without reserve, then we encounter in the depths of man's experience of himself a dark but elemental knowledge that man owes himself, the totality of his existence, to God. From this primal knowledge the central act of the cult, the sacrifice, apparently derives: man understands his offering as a symbolic substitute permitted him in place of himself. Thus the body of the sacrificial animal (as we find again and again, from a Phoenician formula to one of Indian Islam) represents his own body. Later we encounter in the language of that revelation in whose tradition Jesus grew up and to which he fundamentally referred himself, the awesome command he himself cited as the first of all: man shall love God "with all his might." If one takes the primacy of this commandment as seriously as Jesus took it, then one must exclude at the outset the acknowledgment of any special sphere to which one has to "give" anything at all in independence of his relationship with God.

Unless we seek to allay the disquietude aroused in us by the saying about the tribute money through summarily relegating it, as some theologians have done, to the "enigmatic sayings," we are obliged to abandon the current interpretation according to which the statement is concerned with a division between different provinces of the same sphere. Building upon the experiences of all the generations that have encountered the sayings of Jesus in their hours of historical decision, and also on the dearly purchased self-understanding of our own generation, we must turn to another explanation. I can indicate it in modern terms alone, since, as far as I know, this explanation has not been previously dealt with. But its basic, non-conceptual content must be numbered among the presuppositions that, though unexpressed, need no expression, since every central figure has them in common with the inner circle of his hearers.

The human person, ontologically regarded, constitutes not a single sphere, but a union of two spheres. By this I in no way imply the duality of body and soul, allotting to one the kingdom of Caesar and to the other the kingdom of God; such a dualism would be in clear conflict with the teaching of Jesus. Rather, proceeding from that word of Deuteronomy, "with all thy soul and with all thy might," I mean the sphere of wholeness and that of separation or division. When, and in so far as, man becomes whole, he becomes God's and gives to God; he gives to God just this wholeness. The realization of wholeness afforded man in any earthly matter is ultimately, and beyond any name that one can give it, connected with this. His human life, imprinted with mortality, cannot run its course in wholeness; it is bound to separation, to division. But he may and should elicit from the former direction for the latter. What is legitimately done in the sphere of separation receives its legitimacy from the sphere of wholeness. In the sermon of Deuteronomy the commandment to love is followed soon after by a noteworthy dual statement. First it is said that God loves the stranger who is a guest among you, and then it bids, "You shall love the stranger." Our duty to love the stranger in the sphere of separation follows, if we love God in the sphere of wholeness, from God's love for him, the exposed man.

Thus giving to the state, giving that which is due it in the sphere of separation, is authorized by the sphere of wholeness in which we give to God what is due Him: ourselves. The same insight can be phrased in other categories: those of the direct and the indirect relationship. The being directed to God in his wholeness stands in direct relation to Him; all direct relationship has its ground of being therein, and all indirect relationship can receive measure and direction only from there. Give to God your immediacy, the saying about tribute money says to us, and from so doing you will learn ever anew what of your mediacy you shall give to Caesar.

Since the time when certain opponents of Jesus—called "the Pharisees" by the Evangelists, in starkly oversimplified fashion—asked him whether the Judaic man is obliged by God to pay taxes or may exercise passive resistance, generations of world history have met the saying of Jesus with questions born of their particular situations, and these situations have become ever more difficult and contradictory. The question now is not one of foreign rule but of one's own; not one of a government sustained by force but of a government whose legitimacy is willingly acknowledged. The question does not pertain to acts governed by law; it no longer merely concerns carrying out what is ordered. The question in increasing measure is one of man himself. It is not, however, the state in its empirical manifestation that first raised the claim that has put man in question. It is rather the political thinker who elevated the state above the multiplicity of its empirical forms of manifestation into the absolute.

The decisive stretch of this way leads from Hobbes, the hostile son of the English Revolution, to Hegel, the hostile son of the French. Hobbes, to be sure, subjects the interpretation of the word of God to the civil power, but he holds fast to the unconditional superiority of the God who transcends it. Thus there can still persist here, even if only in a secondary and dependent fashion *de facto,* what is God's. For Hegel, who sees in the fact "that the state is" the "walking of God in the world" in which the idea, as the "real God," "consciously realizes" itself, for Hegel, who understands the national spirit as "the divine that knows and wills itself," there is no longer anything that can be distinguished from what is Caesar's. If man has "his being only therein" in what he owes the state, if he has "his entire value" "only through the state," then logically he himself is the tribute he owes to "Caesar." In place of the empirical state, which was not or was not yet able to raise this claim (in its totalitarian form, of course, the state has already since then come quite close to it), it has been raised in the still-unconcluded age of Hegel by the political principle. This principle no longer confronts the individual and places a demand on him, like its predecessor; it permeates his soul and conquers his will.

By "the political principle" I designate that so-to-speak practical axiom that predominates in the opinion and attitude of a very great part of the modern world. Formulated in a sentence, it means roughly that public régimes are the legitimate determinants of human existence. Chief emphasis lies naturally on the adjective "legitimate." The principle does not simply take cognizance of the fact that in the era of the so-called world wars the fate of those involved therein is elementarily and ever-increasingly dependent upon what happens between the states or, more concretely, between their representatives. It aims rather to establish that this is rightfully the case, since the political environment constitutes the essential condition of man, and it does not exist for his sake but he for it. Man, accordingly, is essentially Caesar's. So far as this practical axiom prevails, the saying concerning the tribute money is virtually nullified. Whether the remainder that is left after the abstraction of the essential can still be booked to the account of "God"—where this word has largely either been stricken from the current vocabulary or employed only metaphorically or conventionally—is hardly of importance.

In a human world so constituted, to discuss the value and limitation of the political principle in the spirit of the saying about tribute money means to criticize at the decisive point the would-be *absoluta,* the archons of the hour.

It is not the case, indeed, that in our age the absolute character of any kind of being is simply contested. The relativizing of the highest values that marks this age has halted before the political principle. More than that, within the practical pragmatism that is the basic form of this relativizing, the initial individualistic phase, in which the ethical, noetic, and religious values are tested by their utility for the life of the individual and are only sanctioned according to this utility, is succeeded by a second, collectivistic phase. Here truth is no longer understood and dealt with as what is advantageous to me, but to "us." This "we" is ostensibly that of the collectivity, perhaps of the "people"; in fact, however, it is the advantage of those who are currently ruling. In the interest of the maintenance and expansion of their power, these rulers seek in manifold ways to preserve in the people a belief in the existence of a truth which they themselves no longer share. The individualistic doctrine of relativism which we perceive in its most grandiose form in Stirner and Nietzsche is supplanted—in an order the reverse of the sequence in the history of the sophists—partly by the collectivistic relativism of Marxism, partly by the various species of existentialism, which are in some points singularly close to Marxism. Among these the German variety of existentialism, an ontological affirmation of history, appears to me especially significant. I can touch here only on what directly concerns our problem, in which connection I may note that not only Marx but also Heidegger descends essentially from Hegel.

Marx's so-called "inversion" of the Hegelian world image is at the same time a reduction, since, following the great Vico, of all that exists, in nature and spirit, he allots to our knowledge only that in whose occurrence we men have historically participated; he combines with this reduction a still more intensive historicization of being than is found in Hegel. Apparently the historical economic process alone is accorded absoluteness—although, of course, only an historically existent one—and the state belongs only to its "superstructure" and as such is relativized. But since the political order appears here as the bearer of the future change of all things and the highly centralized political concentration of power as the indispensable preparation for it, the unlimited state is postulated as the unconditional determining force until, according to the eschatological myth of the withering away of the state, the miraculous leap from the realm of necessity to that of freedom can be made.

The existentialism of Heidegger is also rooted in Hegel's thought, but in a deeper, indeed the deepest possible, level. For Hegel world history is the absolute process in which the spirit attains to consciousness of itself; so for Heidegger historical existence is the illumination of being itself; in neither is there room for a suprahistorical reality that sees history and judges it. For both philosophers the historical allows itself to be sanctioned in the last resort by its own thought concerning history; here as there, accordingly, reflection on man's boldest concept, that of eternity set in judgment above the whole course of history and thereby above each historical age, is not admitted. Time is not embraced by the timeless, and the ages do not shudder before One who does not dwell in time but only appears in it. The knowledge has vanished that time can in no wise be conceived as a finally existing reality, independent and self-contained, and that absurdity lies in wait for every attempt to reflect on it in this way no matter whether time be contemplated as finite or as infinite. If historical time and history are absolutized, it can easily occur that in the midst of present historical events the time-bound thinker ascribes to the state's current drive to power the character of an absolute and in this sense the determination of the future. After that, the goblin called success, convulsively grinning, may occupy for a while the divine seat of authority.

But how does it happen at all that the state can everywhere be absolutized when it exists in fact only in the plural, as "the states," each of them being continually reminded of its relativity through the existence of the others?

Hegel could conceive of the state as absolute precisely because history for him was absolute, and the state that had become representative in any historical epoch signified, in his mind, the current actuality of the being of the state. In Heidegger one may still read something of the same notion between the lines. But in the concreteness of lived life a strange singularizing has been accomplished here; it would call to mind the myths of primitive tribes, in which the creation of the world is related as the creation of the tiny territory of the tribe, were these myths not concerned with something essentially different from the state, with something, in distinction to it, corporeal and pregnant with mystery, the fatherland. Hegel has not noticed this vast difference; thus he can write, "While the state, the fatherland, makes up the community of existence . . ." Jacob Grimm has come closer to perceiving the true nature of the matter.

On the other hand, all relative valuation of the state rests for the most part just on the fact of plurality, since the defence against the outside world generally asserts itself far more emphatically than a defence against inside perils. Enemy communities are, in general, far more clearly discernible than hostile elements within. The state, of course, only reluctantly leaves the measure of its value to be determined within the limits of actual differences of interest; not infrequently it fosters a perspective which allows differences of interest to appear as radical opposition. The accumulated power of mastery thrives on drawing profit from a—so to speak—latent exceptional condition. Vast sectors of the economy are inclined, understandably, to help perpetuate this tendency. Thus in times like ours the cold war tends to become the normal historical condition. Already at the beginning of our historical period we saw teachers of the law appear who, obedient to this trait of the times, defined the concept of the political so that everything disposed itself within it according to the criterion "friend-enemy," in which the concept of enemy includes "the possibility of physical killing." The practice of states has conveniently followed their advice. Many states decree the division of mankind into friends who deserve to live and enemies who deserve to die, and the political principle sees to it that what is decreed penetrates the hearts and reins of men.

Note carefully that I do not speak of the conduct of war itself, where personal decisions are, to some extent, taken away beforehand and in the abyss of events killing becomes kindred with being killed. I refer only to that realm of life in which free decision becomes unexpectedly unfree.

The clearest example of this condition is furnished by that certainly most remarkable structure within the public organization that we call the party. Among the members of the political party are people of the most scrupulous integrity in their private lives. Yet when their party has specified who the (in this case internal) "enemy" is, these same people will day after day, with peaceful and untroubled conscience, lie, slander, betray, steal, torment, torture, murder. In the factories of party doctrine, good conscience is being dependably fashioned and refashioned.

I have no warrant whatever to declare that under all circumstances the interest of the group is to be sacrificed to the moral demand, more particularly as the cruel conflicts of duties and their unreserved decision on the basis of the situation seem to me to belong to the essential existence of a genuine personal ethos. But the evident absence of this inner conflict, the lack of its wounds and scars, is to me uncanny. I am not undertaking to set material limits to the validity of the political principle. That, rather, is just what must take place in reality time after time, soul after soul, situation after situation, I mean only to say that this occurrence has obviously become an exceptional one.

That one cannot serve God and Mammon is an entirely true saying, for Mammon embraces the soul and leaves nothing of it free. On the other hand, I believe that it is possible to serve God and the group to which one belongs if one is courageously intent on serving God in the sphere of the group as much as one can. As much as one can at the time; "*quantum satis*" means in the language of lived truth not "either-or," but "as-much-as-one-can." If the political organization of existence does not infringe on my wholeness and immediacy, it may demand of me that I do justice to it at any particular time as far as, in a given inner conflict, I believe I am able to answer for. At any particular time; for here there is no once-for-all: in each situation that demands decision the demarcation line between service and service must be drawn anew—not necessarily with fear, but necessarily with that trembling of the soul that precedes every genuine decision.

Another note must still be added. When men of integrity join a party, they do so out of a conviction that the party strives for a goal of the same general character as their own, and that this goal is to be reached solely through an energetic alliance of the like-minded. An actual party, however, consists both of genuinely convinced members and of only ostensibly convinced men who have entered it for all kinds of motives, usually out of an inextricable tangle of motives. It may easily happen, of course, that those of pretended convictions predominate. Be that as it may, it is incumbent on those of genuine conviction to resist the dominance of the fictitious faction within the party without crippling the party's energy. A thorny business this is; but without it one cannot serve God in the party, one cannot render Him in the sphere of political organization what is His, God's. What is at stake here is shown most clearly when means are proposed whose nature contradicts the nature of the goal. Here, too, one is obliged not to proceed on principle, but only to advance ever again in the responsibility of the line of demarcation and to answer for it; not in order to keep one's soul clean of blood—that would be a vain and wretched enterprise—but in order to guard against means being chosen that will lead away from the cherished goal to another goal essentially similar to those means; for the end never sanctifies the means, but the means can certainly thwart the end.

There is, it seems to me, a front—only seldom perceived by those who compose it—that cuts across all the fronts of the hour, both the external and the internal. There they stand, ranged side by side, the men of real conviction who are found in all groups, all parties, all peoples, yet who know little or nothing of one another from group to group, from party to party, from people to people. As different as the goals are in one place and in another, it is still *one* front, for they are all engaged in the one fight for human truth. But human truth is nothing other than the faithfulness of man to the one truth that he cannot possess, that he can only serve, his fidelity to the truth of God. Remaining true to the truth as much as he can, he strives to his goal. The goals are different, very different, but if each way has been trod in truth, the lines leading to these goals intersect, extended beyond them, in the truth of God. Those who stand on the crossfront, those who know nothing of one another, have to do with one another.

We live at a juncture in which the problem of a common human destiny has become so obstinate that the experienced administrators of the political principle are, for the most part, only able to go through the motions of matching its demands. They offer counsel but know none. They struggle against one another, and every soul struggles against itself. They need a language to understand one another, and have no language except the current political jargon fit only for declamations. For sheer power they are impotent, for sheer tricks they are incapable of acting decisively. Perhaps in the hour when the catastrophe sends in advance its final warning, those who stand on the crossfront will have to come to the rescue. They who have in common the language of human truth must then unite to attempt in common at last to give to God what is God's, or, what here means the same thing, since when mankind has lost its way it stands before God, to give to man what is man's in order to rescue him from being devoured by the political principle.

Lenin and the Renewal of Society*

Just as the principle of the renewal of society from within, by a regeneration of its cell-tissue, found no fixed place derivable from the idea itself in Marx's doctrine, so there was no place for it in the most tremendous attempt of our time to realize this doctrine through the admirable but highly problematical application of conscious human will. In both cases this negative fact can, as we have seen [earlier in *Paths in Utopia*], be justified as regards the pre-revolutionary era by saying that under the reign of capitalism no social regeneration whatsoever, even if only fragmentary, could be accomplished; but as regards the post-revolutionary era it is stated in both cases that it would be "utopian" to outline the appropriate forms of this regeneration. "Utopia," Engels writes in 1872, "arises when, 'from the existing conditions,' people undertake to prescribe the form wherein this, that or the other contradiction in existing society will be resolved." "In Marx," says Lenin, "you will find no trace of Utopianism in the sense of inventing the 'new' society and constructing it out of fantasies." But useless as such fantasy-pictures indeed are, it is also of vital importance to let the idea to which one clings dictate the direction towards which one may actively strive. The socialist idea points of necessity, even in Marx and Lenin, to the organic construction of a new society out of little societies inwardly bound together by common life and common work, and their associations. But neither in Marx nor Lenin does the idea give rise to any clear and consistent frame of reference for action. In both cases the decentralist element of re-structure is displaced by the centralist element of revolutionary politics.

In both cases the operative law is that strictly centralist action is necessary to the success of the revolution, and obviously there is no small truth in this; what is wanting is the constant drawing of lines of demar-

*Reprinted from *Paths in Utopia* (Boston: Beacon, 1958), pp. 99–128.

cation between the demands of this action and—without prejudicing it—the possible implementation of a decentralized society; between what the execution of the idea demands and what the idea itself demands; between the claims of revolutionary politics and the rights of an emergent socialist life. The decision always falls—in the theory and directives of the movement with Marx, in the practice of revolution and the reordering of the State and economics with Lenin—essentially in favour of politics, that is, in favour of centralization. A good deal of this can certainly be attributed to the situation itself, to the difficulties which the Socialist movement had to face and the quite special difficulties faced by the Soviet régime; but over and above that a certain conception and a certain tendency subsequently came to the fore which we may find in Marx and Engels and which thereafter devolved upon Lenin and Stalin: the conception of one absolute centre of doctrine and action from which the only valid theses and the only authoritative decrees can issue, this centre being virtually a dictatorship masked by the "dictatorship of the proletariat"—in other words: the tendency to perpetuate centralist revolutionary politics at the cost of the decentralist needs of a nascent socialist community. It was easy for Lenin to give way to this tendency because of the situation itself, which clearly pointed to the fact that the Revolution had not yet reached its end. The contradiction between Marx's demand for the supersession of the political by the social principle on the one hand and the incontestible persistence of it on the other is disguised and justified by the alleged incompleteness of the revolution; but this does not, of course, take into account the circumstance that for Marx socialism was to slough off its political skin the moment *"its organizing activity begins."* Here there lurks a problem which in its turn is masked by nothing less than the materialistic interpretation of history: according to this view, politics is merely the exemplification and expression of the class-struggle, and with the abolition of the class-state the ground will consequently be cut from under the political principle. The life-and-death struggle of the sole valid doctrine and sole programme of action against all other versions of socialism cannot pass itself off as unpolitical; it must, therefore, brand every other kind of socialism as bogus, as a vestige of bourgeois ideologies; for so long as any other version of socialism exists the Revolution cannot yet be at an end, obviously, and the political principle cannot yet have been superseded by the social, although the organizing activity has already begun. Political power "in the improper sense" can indeed become far more comprehensive, ruthless and "totalitarian" in its centralist pretensions than political power "in its proper sense" ever was. This is not to say that Lenin was a centralist pure and simple: in certain respects he was less so than Marx and in this he was closer to Engels; but in his thought and will the revolutionary-political motif dominated as with Marx and Engels and suppressed the vital social motif which requires decentralized community-living, with the result that this only made itself felt episodically. The upshot of all this was that there was no trace in the new State-order of any agency aiming at the liquidation of State centralism and accumulation of power. How such a liquidation was ever to take place by degrees in the absence of such an agency is inconceivable. Lenin once remarked, in 1918: "What Socialism will be we just don't know. When has any State begun to wither away?" And in history there is indeed no example, however small, to which one could refer. To achieve this for the first time in the world's history one would have needed to set about it with a tremendously vital and idealistic store of decentralizing energy. No such thing happened. That under these circumstances a voluntary renunciation of accumulated power and a voluntary liquidation of centralization would ever take place has not unjustly been characterized (by a Socialist) as a belief in miracles.

The doctrine of the "withering away" of the State after the social revolution was elaborated by Engels from Marx's for the most part very tentative adumbrations. It would not be unprofitable to bring his chief utterances on this subject together in chronological sequence. In 1874 he declared that the State, "as a result of the social revolution of the future, would vanish" because all public functions would simply be changed from political into administrative ones. In 1877 he said more precisely that the proletariat, by converting the means of production into State property, would abolish the State as State and that, moreover, this same seizure of the means of production would "at once be its last independent act as a State," that it would then "fall asleep" or "wither away of itself." In 1882 there follows the eschatological interpretation of this "at once": there would be the "leap of humanity out of the realm of necessity into the realm of freedom"; nothing could be more outspoken than this. Now, however, a remarkable retreat ensues. After Marx's death we hear no more of this "at once" from Engels' lips. When he announces in 1884 that the whole machinery of State will be relegated to the Museum of Antiquities, the date of this singular proceeding is no longer the moment when the means of production have been nationalized, but evidently a much later moment, and evidently the proceedings will be long-drawn, for the authority which undertakes that relegation to the Museum is now "society, which will organize production anew on the basis of the free and equal association of the producers"—a task only inaugurated, naturally, by the unique act of nationalization. This accords with the formula in the Communist Manifesto about "the course of development," a formula which Engels recalls here, save that there the formula speaks of the concentration of production "in the hands of associated individuals" as being the result of a development in whose train public power would lose its political character. In 1891 Engels retreats still further, so far indeed that no additional retreat is necessary or even possible. The proletariat, he says, victorious in the struggle for mastery, will not be able to avoid "at once paring down the worst aspects of the State, until a new generation grown up in new, free social conditions is capable of putting aside the whole paraphernalia of State." Engels says this in his Foreword to the new edition of Marx's *Civil War in France,* in which the latter had written twenty years previously that the working-class "will have to go through long struggles, a whole series of historical processes which will completely transform men and circumstances alike." In his Foreword Engels transposes this conception to the post-revolutionary period. But by so doing the cogency of that "at once" is enormously weakened. Not only is it no longer the case that the proletariat will abolish the State as State with the nationalization of the means of production, but also it will, to begin with and right up to the coming of age of the "new generation," merely "pare down" the worst aspects of the State. And yet in that same book Marx had said of the Constitution of the Paris Commune that, had the Commune triumphed, it would have given back to the social body all the powers which hitherto "the parasitic excrescence of the State" had eaten up; consequently he had laid the main stress on the change brought about by the workings of the Commune—hence on the "at once." But now Engels in his Foreword retreats far beyond this. No doubt certain historical experiences were to blame; but that Engels let himself be influenced by them so profoundly is due to the fact that neither with him nor with Marx was there any uniform and consistent ideal aiming at the restructuring of society or at preparations for the abolition of the State, or any strong and steadfast will for decentralizating action. It was a divided spiritual inheritance into which Lenin entered: socialist revolutionary politics without socialist vitality.

As is well known, Lenin tried to overcome the problematical nature of Engels' doctrine by pointing out with great emphasis that "the abolition" referred to the bourgeois State but that "the withering away" referred to the "remains of the proletarian State system after the Socialist revolution." Further, that since the State as (in Engels' definition) a "special repressive power" was necessary at first for the suppression of the bourgeoisie, it was also essential as the dictatorship of the proletariat, as the centralized organ of its power. That Lenin hit off Marx's (and Engels') intention is indisputable; he rightly quotes the passage in which

Marx, in 1852, had characterized this dictatorship as being the transition to a classless society. But for the Marx of 1871 with his enthusiasm for the Commune it was certain that a decentralization would simultaneously be preparing itself in the midst of the centralism necessary for revolutionary action; and when Engels called the nationalization of the means of production an abolition of the State "as State," he meant the all-important process that would be worked out to the full immediately after the completion of the revolutionary act.

Lenin praises Marx for having "not yet, in 1852, put the concrete question as to what should be set up in place of the State machinery after it had been abolished." Lenin goes on to say that it was only the Paris Commune that taught Marx this. But the Paris Commune was the realization of the thoughts of people who had put this question very concretely indeed. Lenin also praises Marx for having "held strictly to the factual basis of historical experience." But the historical experience of the Commune became possible only because in the hearts of passionate revolutionaries there lived the picture of a decentralized, very much "de-Stated" society, which picture they undertook to translate into reality. The spiritual fathers of the Commune had just that ideal aiming at decentralization which Marx and Engels did not have, and the leaders of the Revolution of 1871 tried, albeit with inadequate powers, to begin the realization of that ideal in the midst of the revolution.

As to the problem of action Lenin starts off with a purely dialectical formula: "So long as there is a State there is no freedom. Once there is freedom there will be no more State." Such dialectics obscures the essential task, which is to test day by day what the maximum of freedom is that can and may be realized to-day; to test how much "State" is still necessary to-day, and always to draw the practical conclusions. In all probability there will never—so long as man is what he is—be "freedom" pure and simple, and there will be "State," i.e. compulsion, for just so long; the important thing, however, is the day to day question: no more State than is indispensable, no less freedom than is allowable. And freedom, socially speaking, means above all freedom for community, a community free and independent of State compulsion.

"It is clear," says Lenin, "that there can be no talk of a definite time when the withering away of the State will begin." But it is not at all clear. When Engels declares that, with the seizure of the means of production, the State will in fact become representative of society as a whole and will thereby make itself superfluous, it follows that this is the time when the withering away must begin. If it does not begin then it proves that the withering tendency is not an integral and determining part of the revolutionary action. But in that case a withering away or even a shrinking of the State cannot be expected of the Revolution and its aftermath. Power abdicates only under the stress of counter-power.

"The most pressing and topical question for politics to-day," states Lenin in September, 1917, "is the transformation of all citizens into workers and employees of one big 'syndicate,' namely, the State as a whole." "The whole of society," he continues, "will turn into one office and one factory with equal work and equal pay." But this reminds us, does it not, of what Engels said of the tyrannical character of the automatic mechanism of a big factory, that over its portal should stand written: *Lasciate ogni autonomia, voi ch'entrate.* To be sure, Lenin sees this factory discipline only as "a necessary stage in the radical purging of society"; he thinks that it will pass as soon as "everybody has learnt to manage society's production by himself," for from this moment the need for any government whatever will begin to disappear. The possibility that the capacity for managing production is unequally distributed and that equal training may not be able to make up for this natural deficiency never seems to have entered Lenin's head. The thing that would meet the human situation much more would be the de-politicization of all the functions of management as far as practicable; that is, to deprive these functions of all possibility of degenerating into power-accretions. The point is not that there should be only managers and no managed any more—that is more utopian than any Utopia—but that management should remain management and not become rulership, or more precisely, that it should not appropriate to itself more rulership than the conditions at any time make absolutely necessary (to decide which cannot, of course, be left to the rulers themselves).

Lenin wanted, it is true, one far-reaching change to take place "immediately": immediately after they had wrested political power the workers were to "smash the old apparatus of bureaucracy, raze it to its foundations, leave not one stone upon another," and replace it by a new apparatus composed of these same workers. Time and again Lenin reiterates the word "immediately." Just as the Paris Commune had done, so now such measures shall "immediately" be taken as are necessary to prevent the new apparatus from degenerating into a new bureaucracy, chief among them being the ability to elect and dismiss officials and, in Marx's language, to hold them "strictly answerable." This fundamental transformation is not, in contra-distinction to all the others, to be left to the process of "development," it is supposed to be implicit in the revolutionary action itself as one of its most momentous and decisive acts. A "new, immeasurably higher and incomparably more democratic type of State-apparatus" is to be created "immediately."

On this point, therefore, Lenin held an immediate change in the social structure to be necessary. He realized that in its absence, despite all the formidable interventions, the new institutions, the new laws and new power-relationships, at the heart of the body politic everything would remain as of old. That is why, although he was no adherent of any general decentralist tendency, he was such an emphatic advocate of this demand for immediate change which, as far as the Paris Commune was concerned, had been an organic part of the decentralist order of society and which can only be fulfilled in a society pressing towards the realization of this order. As an isolated demand it has not been fulfilled in Soviet Russia. Lenin himself is reported to have said with bitterness at a later phase: "We have become a bureaucratic Utopia."

And yet a beginning had been made with structural transformation, not indeed on Lenin's initiative, although he recognized its importance if not all its potential structural qualities—a peculiarly Russian beginning akin to the proposals of the Paris Commune and one that had tremendous possibilities—namely the Soviets. The history of the Soviet régime so far, whatever else it is, has been the history of the destruction of these possibilities.

The first Soviets were born of the 1905 Revolution primarily as "a militant organization for the attainment of certain objectives," as Lenin said at the time; first of all as agencies for strikes, then as representative bodies for the general control of the revolutionary action. They arose spontaneously, as the institutions of the Commune did, not as the outcome of any principles but as the unprepared fruit of a given situation. Lenin emphasized to the anarchists that a Workers' Council was not a parliament and not an organ of self-administration. Ten years later he stated that Workers' Councils and similar institutions must be regarded "as organs of revolt" which could only be of lasting value "in connexion with the revolt." Only in March, 1917, after the Sovietic pattern had been, in Trotsky's words, "almost automatically reborn" in Russia and after the first reports of the victory of the revolution had reached Lenin in Switzerland, did he recognize in the St. Petersburg Soviet "the germ-cell of a workers' government" and in the Councils as a whole the fruit of the experiences of the Paris Commune. By this he still meant, of course, first and foremost "the organization of the revolution," that is to say, of the "second real revolution" or "organized striking-force against the counter-revolution," just as Marx saw in the institutions of the Commune above all the organs of revolutionary action; nevertheless Lenin described the Councils, which he held to be of the same nature as the Commune, as already constituting "the State we need," that is, the State "which the proletariat needs" or which is "the foundation we must continue to build on." What he demanded immediately after his arrival in

Russia was, in opposition to the opinion prevailing in the Workers' Council itself, "a republic of Workers', Landworkers' and Peasants' Deputy Councils throughout the country, from top to bottom." In this sense the Soviet that then existed was, in his view, "a step towards Socialism," just as the Paris Commune had been for Marx—but of course only a political, a revolutionary-political step as that also had been for Marx: an institution, namely, in which revolutionary thinking could crystallize, the "revolutionary dictatorship, that is, a power supported from below by the direct initiative of the masses and not by the law, which was dispensed by a centralized State-power"; in other words, "direct usurpation." The devolution of power on the Soviets still meant for Lenin not only no real decentralization but not even the incentive to the formation of anything of the kind, since the political function of the Soviets was not an integral part of a plan for a comprehensive, organic order that should include society as well as its economy. Lenin accepted the Councils as a programme for action but not as a structural idea.

The utterance Lenin made the day after his arrival, at a meeting of the Bolshevist members of the All-Russian Conference of Councils, is characteristic: "We have all clung to the Councils, but we have not grasped them." The Councils, therefore, already had an objective historical significance for him, quite independent of the significance they had for themselves and for their own members. For the Mensheviks and the social revolutionaries the Councils were what they had been for the former in 1905 and what they in fact more or less were at the time of Lenin's arrival in Russia: organs for the control of Government, guarantees of democracy. For Lenin and his adherents among the Bolsheviks they were very much more—they were the Government itself, the "only possible form of revolutionary Government"; they were, indeed, the new emergent State—but no more than that. That the decentralist form of this State *in statu nascendi* did not disturb Lenin is due to the fact that the only thing to make active appearance in the Councils Movement at this purely dynamic phase of the Revolution was the undivided will to revolution.

The model of the Paris Commune was vitally important for Lenin both because Marx had exemplified through it—and through it alone— the essential features of a new State-order and because Lenin's mind, like that of all the leading Russian revolutionaries, had been lastingly influenced by the revolutionary tradition of France as being the "classic" of its kind. The influence of the great French revolution, the habitual measuring of their own revolution by it and the constant comparison of equivalent stages, etc., were themselves sufficient to exercise a negative effect, particularly as regards the bias towards centralism. But Lenin did

not apply the model afforded by the Commune to any general understanding of history. The fact that (as Arthur Rosenberg rightly stresses in
connexion with Kropotkin and Landauer) whenever, in history, the masses
endeavoured to overthrow a feudal or a centralist power-apparatus it
always ended in these same Commune-like experiments was either unknown to him or did not interest him; still less did he grapple with the
fact (although he once spoke of the Soviets being "in their social and
political character" identical with the State of the Commune) that in all
those experiments *social* decentralization was linked up with political
decentralization, if in differing degrees. For him, the only decisive lesson
of history was the conviction that hitherto humanity had not brought
forth a higher and better type of government than the Councils. Therefore the Councils had to "take *the whole* of life into their own hands."

Naturally Lenin did not fail to realize that the Councils were in essence
a decentralist organization. "All Russia," he says in April, 1917, "is already overspread by a network of local organs of self-administration."
The specific revolutionary measures—abolition of the police, abolition
of the standing army, the arming of the whole population—could also
be put into effect by local self-government; and that is the whole point.
But that these organs could and should come together as a lasting
organism based on local and functional decentralization after the ac-
complishment of this task is not so much as hinted at by a single word,
apparently not even by a thought. The setting up and strengthening
of self-administration has no ultimate purpose or object other than
a revolutionary-political one: to make a self-administration a reality
means "to drive the Revolution forwards." Admittedly in this connexion a social note is also struck, if only in passing: the village Commune
—which, it is said, means "complete self-administration" and "the absence of all tutelage from above"—would suit the peasantry very well
(that "nine-tenths of the peasantry would be agreeable to it" was, be it
noted by the way, a fundamental error). But the reason for this follows at
once: "We must be centralists; yet there will be moments when the task
will shift to the provinces; we must leave the maximum of initiative to
individual localities. . . . Only our party can give the watchwords which
will really drive the Revolution forwards." At first glance it does not
seem clear how this obligatory centralism can be compatible with the
complete self-administration mentioned above; on closer inspection,
however, we remark that this compatibility rests on the fact that the
guiding point of view is, purely and simply, the revolutionary-political
one or even the revolutionary-strategic one: in this case, too, self-
administration is only a component of the programme of action and not
the practical conclusion drawn from a structural idea. This more than

anything else enables us to understand why the programmatic demand for "the absence of all tutelage from above" (a demand not envisaged for any post-revolutionary development, but as something to be secured in the midst of the revolution and destined to drive it forwards) turned so rapidly into its exact opposite. Instead of the watchword, "We must be centralists, yet there will be moments . . . ," a genuinely socialist attitude would have put it the other way round: "We must be decentralists, federalists, autonomists, yet there will be moments when our main task will shift to a central authority because revolutionary action requires it; only we must take care not to let these requirements swamp its objective and temporal frame of reference."

For a clearer understanding of the antagonism between centralism and the above-mentioned "moments" we must realize that in the provinces, as Lenin himself emphasized, "communes are being formed at a great rate, particularly in the proletarian centres," so that the revolution was progressing "in the form of local communes." The "watchwords" corresponded to these facts. A watchword corresponding to this description of the situation, such as "Local Communes, complete regional autonomy, independence, no police, no officials, sovereignty of the armed masses of workers and peasants"—such a watchword, appeal as it might to the experience of the Paris Commune, was and remained a revolutionary-political one; that is, it could not, of its own nature, point beyond the revolution to a decentralized social structure; centralism continued to be its fixed basis. We cannot help being profoundly impressed when we read, in the same draft (of May, 1917), from which I have quoted just now, of Lenin's demand that the provinces should be taken as a model and communes formed of the suburbs and metropolitan areas; but once again no other *raison d'être* is granted them except to drive the Revolution forwards and to lay down a broader basis for "the passing of the total power of the State to the Councils." ("We are now in the minority, the masses do not believe us as yet," says Lenin at about the same time.) Lenin is without a doubt one of the greatest revolutionary strategists of all time; but the strategy of revolution became for him, as the politics of revolution became for Marx, the supreme law not only of action but of thinking as well. We might say that precisely this was the cause of his success; it is certain at any rate that this fact—together with a tendency to centralism rooted very deeply in him as in Marx—was to blame for it if this success did not ultimately contribute to the success of Socialism.

Nevertheless these words should not be construed to imply that I would charge the Lenin of 1917 with not intending to permit the nascent power of the Soviets to continue beyond the revolution. That would be nonsensical; for did he not expressly say at the time, in his significant *Report on the Political Situation,* of the State that would arise when the Councils took the power into their own hands (a State that "would no longer be a State in the accepted sense"), that although such a Power had never yet maintained itself in the world for any length of time, "the whole Workers' Movement all over the world was going in that direction"? What I complain of in Lenin is rather his failure to understand that a fundamental centralism is incompatible with the existence of such a Power beyond the Revolution's immediate sphere of action. It is noteworthy that Lenin says in the same Report that the latter was a State-form "which represents the first steps towards Socialism and is unavoidable in the first phases of socialist society." These words indicate, I think, that it was conceived of as being only a stepping-stone to a higher, "socialist" centralism; and doubtless in the field of economics so vitally important for any final remodelling of society Lenin saw strict centralism as the goal. At that very meeting he emphasized that "the French Revolution passed through a period of municipal revolution when it settled down to local self-administration," and that the Russian revolution was going through a similar phase. It is difficult not to think of the extreme centralism that followed this period of the French Revolution.

Viewed from yet another angle Lenin's doctrine of 1917 leads us to the same result. "Private ownership of ground and of land must be abolished," he says. "That is the task that stands before us, because the majority of the people are for it. That is why we need the Councils. This measure cannot possibly be carried through with the old State officials." Such is the substance of the answer which Lenin gives in his political Report to the question: "Why do we want power to pass into the hands of the Workers' and Soldiers' Deputy Councils?" Here the Marxist respect for "circumstances" is carried to doubtful lengths: private ownership of land is to be abolished not to build up Socialism but simply and solely because the majority of the people want it; and the Councils are necessary not to serve as cells of the new society but to execute the measures demanded by the majority. I would like to assume that we would do well not to take this argument of Lenin's too literally.

But only now does Lenin's theory of the Councils enter the decisive phase. The months in which he was preparing, from Finland, the Bolshevist "special action," "the Second Revolution," were at the same time those in which he based his thought as to the function of the Councils primarily and in principle on Marx's idea of the Commune (in his well-known *State and Revolution*), and then expanded it in practice, with reference to the action he had prepared (in his most important political essay *Will the Bolshevists Maintain Power?*). The bulk of the former was written in September at the time of the attempted counter-revolution and its suppression—an attempt whose only effect was to rouse the fighting spirit of the masses and bring them closer to the radical Party—the second in the middle of October, when the majority of the St. Petersburg and Moscow Soviets opted for this party and, as a direct result of this, the call "All Power to the Soviets!," from being a revolutionary-political demand, became the slogan of the impending attack.

Fired by these events, Lenin glorified in his essay the significance of the Councils for the development of the revolution as never before. In connexion with the statement made by the Menshevik leader Martov that the Councils had been "called into being in the first days of the revolution by the mighty outburst of genuine creative folk-power," Lenin says: "Had the creative folk-power of the revolutionary classes [this latter term goes beyond Martov's words and gives them a Bolshevist twist] not produced the Councils, the proletarian revolution in Russia would have been a hopeless affair." Here the conception of the Councils as an instrument for "driving the revolution forwards" struck its most powerful historical note.

In this essay Lenin lists for the first time the various elements which in his view give the Councils their fundamental importance. The sequence in which he cites these elements is characteristic of his outlook.

Firstly, the "new State apparatus," by substituting the Red Guard for the standing Army, invests the people themselves with armed power.

Secondly, it establishes an indissolubly close and "easily controlled" bond between the leaders and the masses.

Thirdly, by means of the principle of eligibility and dismissibility, it puts an end to bureaucracy.

Fourthly, by the very fact that it establishes contact with the various professions (later Lenin puts it more precisely: professions and productive units) it facilitates the weightiest reforms.

Fifthly, it organizes the Avant-garde, which shall raise up and educate the masses.

Sixthly, by means of the tie between the Legislature and the Executive it unites the advantages of Parliamentarianism with those of non-parliamentary Democracy.

The first place is given to revolutionary power-politics; the second to the organization of reforms; the third to the form of the State. The question of the possible importance of the Councils for a reshaping of the social structure is not even asked.

In Lenin's view, however, it only became possible for the Councils to master the tasks set them because the Bolsheviks had seized control in and through the Councils and filled the new form with a concrete content of action, whereas formerly they had been "reduced by the Social Revolutionaries and the Mensheviks to chatter-boxes," more, to "a body rotting on its feet." "The Councils," Lenin continues, "can only really develop, only display their talents and capabilities to the full, after the seizure of supreme power, for otherwise they have nothing to do, otherwise they are either simple germ-cells (and one cannot be a germ-cell for too long) or a plaything." This sentence is remarkable for more than one reason. The simile of the germ-cells necessarily forces the question on us as to whether in Lenin's opinion the Councils might not, by growth and association, ripen sufficiently to become the cells of a renewed social organism; but evidently that is not Lenin's opinion. And then the expression "plaything" turns up again a few days later in a curious connection, in Lenin's theses for a Conference in St. Petersburg, where we read: "The whole experience of the two revolutions of 1905 and 1917 confirms that the Workers' and Soldiers' Deputy Councils are only real as organs of revolt, as organs of revolutionary force. Outside these tasks the Councils are a mere plaything." This makes it unmistakably plain what the important thing really is for Lenin. He had, to be sure, to lay stress on the question of the hour; but the exclusiveness with which he does so, brooking no thought whatever of the Councils eventually becoming independent and permanent entities, speaks a language that cannot be misunderstood. In addition those phrases of 1915 ("organs of revolt" and "only in connexion with the revolt") recur almost word for word; whatever Lenin may have learnt and thought about the Councils during those two years in which he became essentially the historical Lenin, they still remained for him the means to a revolutionary end. That the Councils might not merely exist for the sake of the revolution, but that—and this in a far more profound and primary sense—the revolution might exist for the sake of the Councils, was something that simply never occurred to him. From this point of view— by which I mean not Lenin as a person but the sort of mentality that found an arch-exemplar in him—it is easy to understand why the Councils petered out both as a reality and as an idea.

That Lenin's slogan "All power to the Soviets!" was meant in nothing but a revolutionary-political sense is forced upon us even more strikingly when we come to the following exclamation in that essay: "And yet the 240,000 members of the Bolshevik Party are supposed to be incapable of governing Russia in the interests of the poor and against those of the rich!" So that "All power to the Soviets!" means little more at bottom than "All power to the Party through the Soviets!"—and there is nothing that points beyond this revolutionary-political, indeed party-political aspect to something different, socialistic and structural. Soon afterwards Lenin asserts that the Bolsheviks are "centralists by conviction, by the nature of the programme and the whole tactics of their party"; hence centralism is expressly characterized as being not merely tactical but a matter of principle. The proletarian State, we are told, is to be centralist. The Councils, therefore, have to subordinate themselves to a "strong Government"—what remains then of their autonomous reality? It is true that they, too, are conceded a "special centralism": no Bolshevist has anything to say against their "concentration into branches of production," their centralization. But obviously Lenin had no inkling that such "concentrations" bear a socialist, socially formative character only when they arise spontaneously, from below upwards, when they are not concentrations at all but associations, not a centralist process but a federalist one.

In Lenin's summons "To the People" ten days after the seizure of power we read: "From now on your Councils are organs of State-power, fully authorized to make all decisions." The tasks that were assigned soon afterwards to the Councils referred essentially to control. This was due very largely to the situation itself, but the frame of reference was far too small; the positive counterbalance was missing. Such petty powers were not enough to enable the Councils "to display their talents and capabilities to the full." We hear Lenin repeating in March, 1918, at the Party Congress his ideas about the new type of State "without bureaucracy, without police, without a standing Army," but he adds: "In Russia hardly more than a beginning has been made, and a bad beginning at that." It would be a grave error to think that only the inadequate execution of an adequate design was to blame: the design itself lacked the substance of life. "In our Soviets," he says by way of explanation, "there is still much that is crude, incomplete"; but the really dire and disastrous thing about it was that the leaders, who were not merely political but spiritual leaders as well, never directed the Soviets towards development and completion. "The men who created the Commune," Lenin goes on, "did not understand it." This is reminiscent of his utterance the day after his arrival in Russia: "We have clung to the Councils, but have not grasped them." The truth is that he did not "understand" them even now for what they really were—and did not wish to understand them.

In the same speech Lenin declared in answer to Bukharin, who had demanded that an outline of the socialist order be included in the programme, that "We cannot outline Socialism. What Socialism will look like when it takes on its final forms we do not know and cannot say." No doubt this is the Marxist line of thought, but it shows up in the full light of history the limitations of the Marxist outlook in its relation to an

emergent or would-be emergent reality: a failure to recognize potentialities which require, if they are to develop, the stimulus of the idea of
social form. We may not "know" what Socialism will look like, but we
can know what we want it to look like, and this knowing and willing,
this conscious willing itself influences what is to be—and if one is a centralist one's centralism influences what is to be. Always in history there
exist, even if in varying degrees of strength, centralist and decentralist
trends of development side by side; and it is of vital importance in the
long run *for which* of the two the conscious will, together with whatever
power it may have acquired at the time, elects. What is more, there is
scarcely anything harder, or more rare, than for a will invested with
power to free itself from centralism. What more natural or more logical
than that a centralist will should fail to recognize the decentralist potentialities in the forms it makes use of? "The bricks are not yet made," says
Lenin, "with which Socialism will be built." Because of his centralism
he could not know and acknowledge the Councils as such bricks, he
could not help them to become so, nor did they become so.

Soon after the Party Congress Lenin stated in the first draft of the
Theses on the Immediate Tasks of Soviet Authority, in a section not included in the final version: "We are for democratic centralism. . . . The
opponents of centralism are always pointing to autonomy and federation as a means of combating the hazards of centralism. In reality democratic centralism in no way precludes autonomy, rather it postulates the
need for it. In reality even federation [here Lenin only has political
federation in mind] in no way contradicts democratic centralism. In a
really democratic order, and all the more in a State built up on the Soviet
principle, federation is only a step towards a really democratic centralism." It is clear that Lenin has no thought of limiting the centralist principle by the federalist principle; from his revolutionary-political point of
view he only tolerates a federal reality so long as it resolves itself into
centralism. The direction, the whole line of thought is thus unequivo-
cally centralistic. Nor is there any essential difference when we come to
local autonomy: it is expedient to permit this to a certain degree and to
grant it its terms of action; only the line must be drawn at that point
where the real decisions and consequently the central instructions begin. All these popular and social formations only have political, strate-
gic, tactical and provisional validity; not one of them is endowed with a
genuine *raison d'être,* an independent structural value; not one of them
is to be preserved and fostered as a living limb of the community-to-be.

A month after Lenin had dictated his draft the "Left Communists"
pointed out how injurious it was for the seeds of Socialism that the form
which State administration was taking lay in the direction of bureaucra-

tic centralization, elimination of the independence of the local Soviets and repudiation, in fact, of the type of "Commune-State" governing itself from below—the very type, therefore, of which Lenin said in his speech that the Soviet Authority actually was. There can be no more doubt to-day as to who was right in assessing the situation and the trends to come—Lenin or his critics. But Lenin himself knew it well enough towards the end of his life. References to the Paris Commune become fewer and fewer after that speech, until they cease altogether.

A year after the October Revolution, Lenin had stated that "the apparatus of officialdom in Russia was completely shattered," but at the end of 1920 he characterized the Soviet Republic as "a Work-State with bureaucratic excrescences," and that, he said, "was the truth about the transition." The fact that in the years to come the proportion of excrescences to the trunk from which they sprouted increased alarmingly, and the buddings of the state of affairs to which the transition was supposed to lead grew less and less, could not remain hidden from Lenin. At the end of 1922 in the report *Five Years of Russian Revolution and the World Revolution in Perspective* which Lenin made to the Fourth Congress of the Communist International, he says simply: "We have taken over the old State apparatus." He solaces himself with the assurance that in a few years they will succeed in modifying the apparatus from top to bottom. This hope was not fulfilled and could not be fulfilled given Lenin's assumptions: he was thinking in the main of training and attracting new forces, but the problem was one of structure and not of personnel; a bureaucracy does not change when its names are changed, and even the best-trained graduates of the Soviet schools and Workers' Faculties succumb to its atmosphere.

Lenin's main disappointment was the continued existence of the bureaucracy which, if not in its personnel, certainly in its ruthless efficacy, once more proved stronger than the revolutionary principle. He does not seem to have touched the deeper causes of this phenomenon, and that is understandable enough. The October Revolution was a social revolution only in the sense that it effected certain changes in the social order and its stratification, in the social forms and institutions. But a true social revolution must, over and above that, establish the rights of society *vis-à-vis* the State. Although in respect of this task Lenin pointed out that the withering away of the State would be accomplished by way of a development whose duration could not as yet be measured nor its manner imagined, yet, to the extent that this development could be realized right now, he acknowledged the task as determining the leaders' immediate programme of action and called the new State-form whose realization was to be tackled at once the "Commune State."

But the "Commune State" had been characterized clearly enough by Marx as freeing economic society to the greatest possible extent from the shackles of the political principle. "Once the communal order of things," he wrote, "had been introduced in Paris and in the centres of second rank, the old centralized government would have had to give way in the provinces also to the producers' self-government." This shifting of the power of decision from the political to the social principle—which had been worked out and given its ideal basis in France by the social thinking from Saint-Simon to Proudhon—was proclaimed by Lenin as the base-line for the organizing activity of the leaders, but in point of fact it did not become such a base-line. The political principle established itself anew, in changed guise, all-powerful; and the perils actually threatening the revolution gave him a broad justification. Let it remain undisputed that the situation as it was would not have allowed of a radical reduction of the political principle; what, however, would at any rate have been possible was the laying down of a base-line in accordance with which, as changing circumstances allowed, the power-frontiers of the social principle could have been extended. Precisely the opposite happened. The representatives of the political principle, that is, mainly the "professional revolutionaries" who got to the top, jealously watched over the unrestrictedness of their sphere of action. It is true that they augmented their ranks with competent persons recruited from the people and that they filled up the gaps as they arose, but those who were admitted to the directorate bore the stamp of the political principle on their very souls; they became elements of the State substance and ceased to be elements of the social substance, and whoever resisted this change could not make himself heard at the top or soon ceased to want to. The power of the social principle could not and dared not grow. The beginnings of a "producers' self-government" to which the revolution spontaneously gave rise, above all the local Soviets, became, despite the apparent freedom of expression and decision, so enfeebled by the all-pervading Party domination with its innumerable ways visible and invisible of compelling people to conform to the doctrine and will of the Central Authority, that little was left of that "outburst of creative folk-power" which had produced them. The "dictatorship of the proletariat" is *de facto* a dictatorship of the State over society, one that is naturally acclaimed or tolerated by the overwhelming mass of people for the sake of the completed social revolution they still hope to see achieved by this means. The bureaucratism from which Lenin suffered, and suffered precisely because it had been his business to abolish it (the "Commune State" being, for him, nothing less than the debureaucratized State), is merely the necessary concomitant to the sovereignty of the political principle.

It is worth noting that within the Party itself attempts were made again and again to break this sovereignty. The most interesting of them, because it sprang from the industrial workers, seems to my mind to be the "Workers' Opposition" of March, 1921, which proposed that the Central Organs for the administration of the whole national economy of the Republic should be elected by the united trades-associations of producers. This was not a Producers' Government by any means but it was an important step towards it, although lacking any real decentralist character. Lenin rejected this "anarcho-syndicalist deviation" on the ground that a union of producers could be considered by a Marxist only in a classless society composed exclusively of workers as producers, but that in Russia at present there were, apart from remnants of the capitalist epoch, still two classes left—peasants and workers. So long, therefore, as Communism was still aiming at perfection and had not turned all peasants into workers a self-governing economy could not, in Lenin's opinion, be considered. In other words (since the completion of Communism coincides with the complete withering away of the State): a fundamental reduction of the State's internal sphere of power cannot be thought of before the State has breathed its last. This paradox has become the operative maxim for the directorate of the Soviet Régime.

Only from this point of view can Lenin's changing attitude to the Co-operative System be grasped as a whole.

There is no point, however, in picking on the contradictions in a critical spirit. Lenin himself emphasized in 1918, not without reason, that always when a new class enters the historical arena as the leader of society there comes unfailingly a period of experiment and vacillation over the choice of new methods to meet the new objective situation; three years later he even asserted that things had only proved, "as always in the history of revolutions, that the movement runs in a zigzag." He failed to notice that though all this may be true of political revolutions, yet when, for the first time in history on so large a scale, the element of social change is added, humanity as a whole (and this means the people to whom events happen as well as the witnesses of them) longs despite all the experiments and vacillations to be made aware of the one clear earnest of the future: the movement towards community in freedom. In the case of the Russian Revolution whatever else may have appeared to them in the way of portents nothing of this kind ever became visible, and Lenin's changing attitude to the Co-operative system is one proof the more that such a movement does not exist.

In the pre-revolutionary period Lenin regarded the Co-operatives existing in bourgeois society as "miserable palliatives" only and bulwarks
of the petty bourgeois spirit. A month before the October Revolution,
faced with the tremendous economic crisis that was sweeping Russia, he
put forward among the "revolutionary-democratic" measures to be
taken immediately, the compulsory unification of the whole nation into
Consumer Co-operatives. The following January he wrote in the draft of
a decree: "All citizens must belong to a local Consumer Co-operative"
and "the existing Consumer Co-operatives will be nationalized." In
some Party circles this demand was understood and approved as aiming
at the elimination of the Co-operatives, for they saw, as a Bolshevist the-
oretician no doubt rightly expressed it, in the element of *voluntary* membership the essential hallmark of a Co-operative. Lenin did not intend it
to be understood that way. True, the Co-operative as a small island in
capitalist society was, so he said, only "a shop," but the Co-operative
which, after the abolition of private capital, comprises the whole of society "is Socialism," and it is therefore the task of the Soviet authorities
to change all citizens without exception into members of a general State
Co-operative, "a single gigantic Co-operative." He does not see that the
Co-operative principle thereby loses all independent content, indeed its
very existence as a principle, and that nothing remains but a necessarily
centralist-bureaucratic State-institution under a name that has become
meaningless. The realization of this programme was undertaken in the
years immediately following: all Co-operatives were merged under the
leadership of the Consumer Co-operatives, which were turned into
what amounted to State goods-distribution centres. As to immediate
nationalization pure and simple, even two years after he had formulated
the "Tasks of the Soviet Authority" Lenin was still holding back. He de-
nounced those who were outspoken enough to demand a single nexus of
State organizations to replace the Co-operatives. "That would be all
right, but it is impossible," he said, meaning "impossible at present." At
the same time he held fast in principle to the idea of the Co-operative as
such, which, he declared (recalling Marx and his own attitude at the
Copenhagen Congress of the International in 1910, where he had
stressed the possible socializing influence of the Co-operative after the
capitalists had been expropriated), might be a means of building the new
economic order. It was therefore a question, he said, of finding new Co-
operative forms "which correspond to the economic and political conditions of the proletarian dictatorship" and which "facilitate the transition to real socialist centralism." An institution the very essence of
which is the germ and core of social decentralization was in consequence to be made the building element of a new close-meshed State

centralism of "socialist" stamp. Obviously Lenin was not proceeding from theoretical assumptions but from the practical requirements of the hour, which, as the world knows, were extremely grave and necessitated the most strenuous exertions. When Lenin, in a statement reminiscent of the postulates of the "Utopians" and "Anarchists"—but naturally twisting their meaning into its exact opposite—demanded the union of the Producer and Consumer Co-operatives, he did so because of the need to increase the supply of goods: the fitness of this measure being proved by the experience of the last two years. A year later we hear him polemicizing violently against the Co-operatives, which in their old and still unconquered form were a "bulwark of counter-revolutionary opinion." In his famous treatise on *Taxation in Kind* (spring, 1921) he points emphatically to the danger that lurks in the co-operation of small producers: it inevitably strengthens petty bourgeois capitalism. "The freedom and rights of the Co-operatives," he continues, "mean under present conditions in Russia, freedom and rights for capitalism. It would be a stupidity or a crime to close our eyes to this obvious truth." And further: "Under Soviet power Co-operative capitalism, as distinct from private capitalism, creates a variant of State capitalism and is as such advantageous and useful to us at present. . . . We must endeavour to guide the development of capitalism into the channels of Co-operative capitalism." This instructive warning only expressed what, in those years of falsely so-called "War Communism" (in October, 1921, Lenin himself spoke retrospectively of the mistake that had been made by "our having resolved to take in hand the immediate changeover to communist production and distribution") had been the guiding principle in practice.

But in the wake of the unfavourable outcome of extreme centralization and in connexion with the "New Economic policy" just beginning, a regressive tendency was already making itself felt. Shortly before that warning declaration of Lenin's a decree had been promulgated on the re-establishment of the various kinds of Co-operative—Consumer, Agricultural and Industrial—as an economic organization. Two months later there followed a decree with which a beginning was made for the wholesale cancellation of the previously arranged merging of all Co-operatives in the Association of Consumer Co-operatives, the "Zentro-soyus." Towards the end of the same year the president of this Association declared in a speech on the position and tasks of the Co-operatives that it was only natural that the State Co-operative apparatus, functioning in accordance with a fixed plan, should have become "bureaucratic, inelastic and immovable," and he made mention of the voices "that spoke of the necessity of freeing the Co-operative from slavery to the

State," indeed, he even admitted that there were times "when one had to speak of such a freeing." And true enough the people had often come to compare compulsory organization with bondage. Now the authorities "completely and unreservedly" abjured all official interference in the affairs of the Agricultural Co-operatives and contented themselves with the wide possibilities within the system of State Capitalism for "influencing and regulating the Co-operatives by economic pressure," until those that "could not or would not adapt themselves" had been "rubbed out and liquidated." All the same, care was taken that reliable Party members should get into the directorate of the central as well as of the individual Societies and that the necessary "purges" were carried out under the representatives of the Co-operative.

Two years after the appearance of his *Taxation in Kind,* Lenin, in May, 1923, the peak period of the New Economic Development, provided the latter with its theoretical foundation in his great essay on the Co-operative System. "When we went over to the New Economics," he said, "we acted precipitately in one respect, namely, we forgot to think of the Co-operative System." But he no longer contents himself now with approving the Co-operative as a mere element to be built into the State economy of the transition period. All of a sudden the Co-operative is jerked into the very centre of the social new order. Lenin now describes the Co-operative education of the people as "the only task that is left us." The "co-operativization" of Russia has acquired in his eyes a "colossal," a "gigantic," a "limitless" significance. "It is," he says, "not yet the actual building of the socialist society, but it contains everything necessary and sufficient for the building of this society." Yes, he goes even further: the Co-operative has become for him not merely the precondition of social building but the very core of it. "A social order of enlightened Co-operatives," he asserts, "with common ownership of the means of production, based on the class-victory of the proletariat over the bourgeoisie—that is a socialist order of society," and he concludes: "The simple growth of the Co-operative is as important for us as the growth of socialism," yes, "conditional to the complete co-operativization of Russia we would be already standing with both feet on socialist ground." In the planned, all-embracing State Co-operative he sees the fulfilment of the "dreams" of the old Co-operatives "begun with Robert Owen." Here the contradiction between idea and realization reaches its apogee. What those "Utopians," beginning with Robert Owen, were concerned about in their thoughts and plans for association was the voluntary combination of people into small independent units of communal life and work, and the voluntary combination of those into a community of communities. What Lenin describes as the fulfilment of these thoughts and plans is the diametrical opposite of them, is an immense, utterly centralized complex of State production-centres and State distribution-centres, a mechanism of bureaucratically run institutes for production and consumption, each locked into the other like cog-wheels: as for spontaneity, free association, there is no longer any room for them whatever, no longer the possibility of even dreaming of them—with the "fulfilment" of the dream the dream is gone. Such at any rate had been Lenin's conception of the dovetailing of the Co-operative system into the State, and in that otherwise very exhaustive essay of his written eight months before his death he did not deny it. He wanted to give the movement which had then reached its peak and which implied a reduction of centralism in all fields, a definitive theoretical basis; but he denied it—necessarily, given his train of thought—the basis of all bases: the element of freedom.

Some people have thought they could see in this marked turning of Lenin's towards the Co-operatives an approach to the theories of the Russian Populists, for whom such forms of communal association as persisted or renewed themselves within the body of the people were the core and bud of a future order of society, and whom Lenin had fought for so long. But the affinity is only apparent. Even now Lenin was not thinking for a moment of the Co-operative as a spontaneous, independent formation growing dynamically and a law unto itself. What he was now dreaming of—after all his grievous efforts to weld the people into a uniform whole that would follow him with utter devotion, after all his disappointments over "bureaucratic excrescences," with the mark of illness on him and near to death—was to unite two things which cannot be united, the all-overshadowing State and the full-blooded Co-operative, in other words: compulsion and freedom. At all periods of human history the Co-operative and its prototypes have been able really to develop only in the gaps left by the effective power of the State and its prototypes. A State with no gaps inevitably precludes the development of the Co-operative. Lenin's final idea was so to extend the Co-operative in scope and so to unify it in structure that it would only differ from the State functionally but coincide with it materially. That is the squaring of the circle.

Stalin has explained the change in Lenin's attitude to the Co-operatives from 1921 to 1923 by saying that State Capitalism had not gained foothold to the degree desired, and that the Co-operatives with their ten million members had begun to ally themselves very closely with the newly developing socialized industries. This certainly draws attention to Lenin's real motives, but it is not sufficient to explain his unexpected enthusiasm for Co-operatives. Rather, it is obvious that Lenin now perceived in the Co-operative principle a counterbalance to the bureaucracy he found so offensive. But the Co-operative could only have become such a counterbalance in its original free form, not in Lenin's compulsory form, which was dependent on a truly "gigantic" bureaucracy.

As we have said, Lenin's idea of compulsion was not carried out to the full. The regressive movement finally led, in May, 1924, to the restoration of voluntary membership, at first only for full citizens, that is, citizens entitled to vote, but later, early in 1928, in the rural Consumer Co-operatives for others as well, although with some limitation as to their rights. Towards the end of 1923 the Board of the Zentrosoyus stated: "We must confess that this change-over to free membership ought to have been made earlier. We could then have met this crisis on a surer foundation." All the same an indirect compulsion was henceforth exercised by means of preferential supplies to the Co-operatives. In 1925 we hear from the mouth of the then president of the Central Council of the Trades Unions that the Government, when issuing subsidies and loans, took account of a person's membership in a manner that came very near to compulsion. And ten years afterwards the urban Co-operatives, which had long suffered gravely under State interference, were abolished at a stroke in 654 cities.

What has been said will suffice to show how the Soviet régime continually oscillated in practice between immediate radical centralization and provisional tolerance of relatively decentralized areas, but never, even to the slightest degree, made the trend towards the goal of Socialism as formulated by Marx, namely, "the sloughing off of the political husk," the maxim of its conduct. One might amplify this by mentioning the changing attitude it adopted during the Five Year Plan of 1926 to 1931 to the collectivization of the peasantry. I shall content myself with listing a few characteristic proclamations and procedures in chronological sequence.

Towards the end of 1927, Molotov drew attention to the backwardness of agriculture and in order to overcome it demanded that the village Collectives—valuable despite their defects—should develop in conjunction with the general plan of industrialization. In June, 1928, Stalin declared it necessary to expand the existing Collectives as intensively as possible and establish new ones. In April, 1929, the slogan was given out at the Party Congress for the creation, still within the framework of the Five Year Plan, of a socialized area of production as a counterbalance to individual economy. The process of collectivization soon took on more or less obvious forms of compulsion and seemed so successful at first that Stalin stated at the end of the same year: "If collectivization goes on at this rate the contrast between town and village will be wiped out in accelerated tempo." At the beginning of 1930 the Central Committee of the Party estimated that the tempo envisaged in the Plan had been outstripped, and emphatically stressed the need for a concerted campaign against all attempts to slow the movement down. In three years' time complete collectivization would have been achieved with the techniques of persuasion, "aided by certain levers." The Executive Committees of the various districts vied with one another in the thoroughness of their administrative measures; a district was not infrequently declared an "area of complete collectivization" and where persuasion did not help threats were used. But it soon proved that the impression of smashing success, an impression fostered by the marked increase in the number of collective farm-economies, was a delusion. The peasants reacted in their own way, by anything from the slaughtering of cattle to actual uprisings, and the measures taken to liquidate the kulaks did little to remedy the evil; the small peasants often joined forces and the Red Army itself with its peasant sons reflected the prevailing dissatisfaction. Then Stalin, in his famous article "Dizzy with Success," performed the volte face that seemed necessary. The policy of collectivization, he declared, rested according to Lenin's doctrine on voluntary action. "You cannot create collective economies by force. That would be stupid and reactionary." Lenin had also taught, he said, that "it would be the greatest folly to try to introduce collective cultivation of the land by decree." The voluntary principle had suffered injury, the tempo of action had not corresponded to that of development, important intermediate stages on the way to the complete Village Commune had been by-passed. The Central Committee was therefore arranging, he said, for an end to be made of compulsory methods. In July the Party Congress proclaimed that collective economies could only be based on the principle of voluntary admission, all attempts to apply force or administrative coercion were "an offence against the Party line and an abuse of power." In the autumn the Commissar for Agriculture once more criticized "the crude and ultra-administrative methods which have been employed in respect of the collective economies and their members." But less than five months later, after a considerable number of peasants, as a result of the greater measure of freedom but in spite of the privileges newly offered, had left the Collectives, the same Commissar said in his Report to the Congress of the Soviets regarding the small and middling peasants who had not joined the Collective Movement: "Who are they for, for the kulaks or for the Collectives? . . . Is it possible to remain neutral to-day?" In other words: he who is not for collectivization is against the Soviet régime. The Congress confirmed this view. During the next few years renewed measures of severity followed the alleviations necessitated by the famine crisis, until in 1936 nearly 90 per cent of the peasants had been collectivized, of which the Full Communes comprised only a diminishing fraction.

The old rustic Russia, as Maynard has rightly said, lasted up to 1929. That it was bundled out of the world with its traditional system of land-cultivation can, from the point of view of economic efficiency, only be approved. But, from the point of view of social structure, the question must be put very differently. From this angle there should be no talk of an Either-Or; the specific task was so to transform the existing structural units that they should be equal to the new conditions and demands, and at the same time retain their structural character and nature as self-activating cells. This task has not been fulfilled. It has been said, rightly enough, that Marxist thinking, geared as it is to the rationalized big-business form of farming, the industrialization and mechanization of agriculture, has been grafted onto the old Russian Village Community which had accustomed the peasants to the communal management of land. But the politically inspired tendency to turn agriculture into a department of industry and the peasants into the hired workers of this industry; the tendency to an all-embracing and all-regulating State economy; a tendency which regards the Agricultural Co-operative only as a stepping-stone to the Full Commune and this in its turn only as a stepping-stone to the local branch of the Agricultural Department of the Universal State Factory—such a tendency destroyed and was bound to destroy the whole structural value of the Village Community. One cannot treat either an individual or a social organism as a means to an end absolutely, without robbing it of its life-substance. "From the stand-point of Leninism," said Stalin in 1933, "the collective economies, and the Soviets as well, are, taken as a form of organization, a weapon and nothing but a weapon." One cannot in the nature of things expect a little tree that has been turned into a club to put forth leaves.

Far longer than with any other people the "medieval" tendency to associate in little bands for the purpose of common work has been preserved among the Russians. Of the most singular social formation to have sprung from this tendency, the *Artel,* Kropotkin could say some forty years ago that it constituted the proper substance of Russian peasant life—a loose, shifting association of fishermen and hunters, manual workers and traders, hauliers and returned Siberian convicts, peasants who travelled to the city to work as weavers or carpenters, and peasants who went in for communal corn-growing or cattle-raising in the village, with, however, divisions as between communal and individual property.

Here an incomparable building element lay ready to hand for a great re-structural idea. The Bolshevist Revolution never used it. It had no use for independent small communities. Among the various types of "Kolkhoz" it favoured "for the present," as Stalin said, the agricultural *Artel* for economic reasons, but naturally the revolution saw in it nothing but a stepping-stone. One of Russia's best theoreticians of economics has defined the aim. Land cultivation, he said, would only be regarded as socialized when all the agricultural *Artels* had been replaced by State Collectives, when land, means of production and livestock belonged to the State. Then the peasants would live in community-houses as hired labourers of the State, in huge agrarian cities, themselves the nodes of areas blessed with more and more electrification. The fantastic picture to which this conception belongs is in very truth the picture of a society finally and utterly de-structured and destroyed. It is more—it is the picture of a State that has devoured society altogether.

The Soviet régime has achieved great things in the technology of economics and still greater things in the technology of war. Its citizens seem in the main to approve of it, for a variety of reasons, negative and positive, fictitious and real. In their attitude vague resignation appears mixed with practical confidence. It can be said in general that the individual submits to this régime, which grants him so little freedom of thought and action, perhaps because there is no going back and as regards technical achievements there is at least a going forward. Things look very different, at least to the impartial eye, when it comes to what has actually been achieved in the matter of Socialism: a mass of socialistic expostulations, no Socialist form at all. "What," asked the great sociologist Max Weber in 1918, "will that 'association' look like of which the Communist Manifesto speaks? What germ-cells of that kind of organization has Socialism in particular to offer if ever it gets a real chance to seize power and rule as it wills?" In the country where Socialism did get this chance there still existed such germ-cells, which no other country in our epoch could rival; but they were not brought to fruition. Nevertheless, there is still breathing-space for change and transformation—by which is meant not a change of tactics such as Lenin and his fellow-workers often effected, but a change of fundamentals. The change cannot go backwards, only forwards—but in a new direction. Whether forces as yet unnamed are stirring in the depths and will suddenly burst forth to bring about this change, on this question tremendous things depend.

Pierre Leroux, the man who appears to have used the word "Socialism" for the first time, knew what he was saying when he addressed the

National Assembly in 1848 with these words: "If you have no will for human association I tell you that you are exposing civilization to the fate of dying in fearful agony."

Notes

Society and the State

1. This does not mean that in that epoch there was no further development of Althusius' ideas, particularly in the doctrine of Leibniz.

The Demand of the Spirit and Historical Reality

1. Lorenz von Stein, *System der Staatswissenschaft* (1856), II, 384.

The Validity and Limitation of the Political Principle

1. Buchsel in Kittel's *Theologisches Wörterbuch zum Neuen Testament*, II, 170.